# TREMOR DOSE

WRITTEN BY
## MICHAEL W. CONRAD

ART BY
## NOAH BAILEY

DARK HORSE BOOKS

"IF A LITTLE DREAMING IS DANGEROUS, THE
CURE FOR IT IS NOT TO DREAM LESS, BUT TO
DREAM MORE, TO DREAM ALL THE TIME."
--PROUST

# PART I

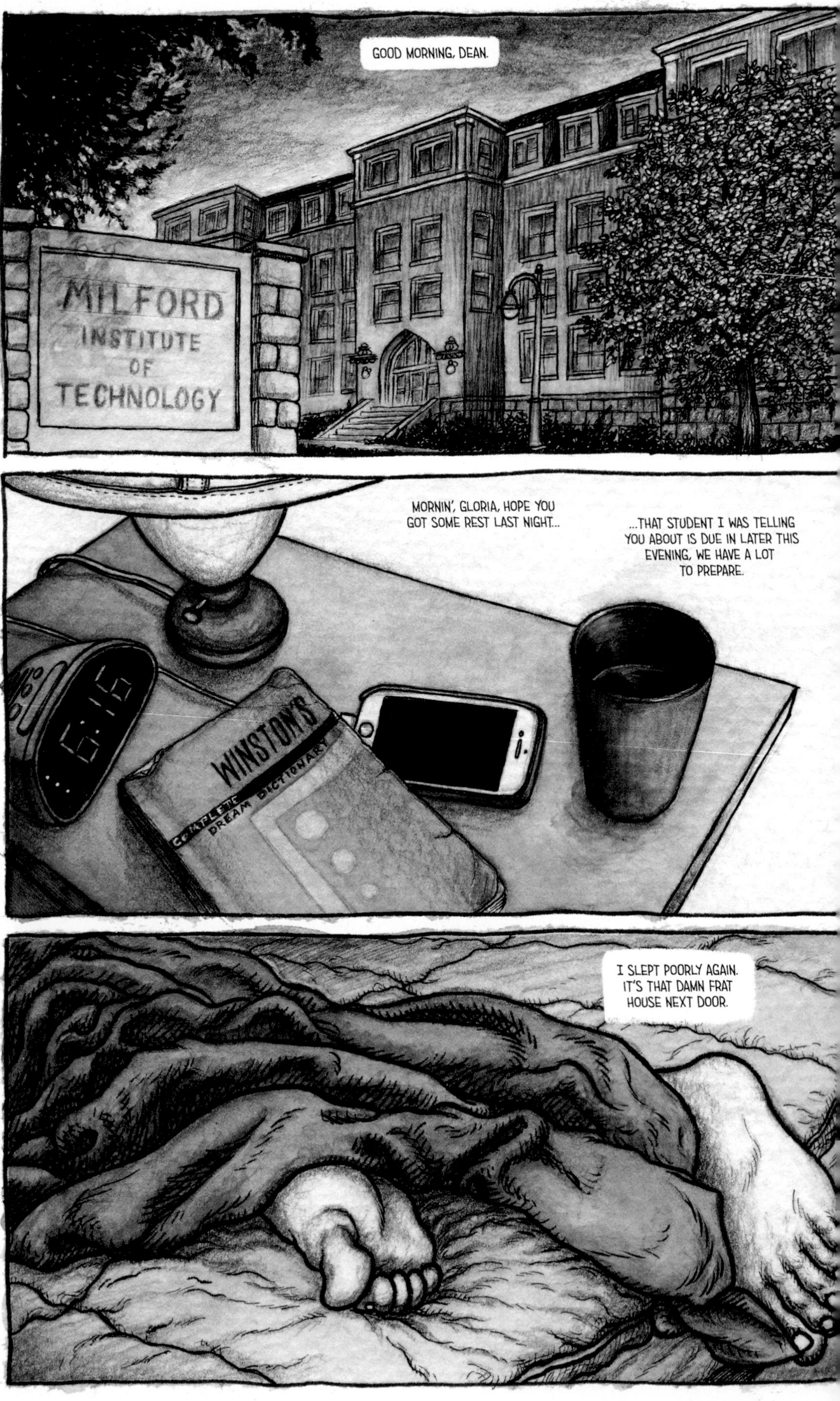
GOOD MORNING, DEAN.
MILFORD INSTITUTE OF TECHNOLOGY
MORNIN', GLORIA, HOPE YOU GOT SOME REST LAST NIGHT...
...THAT STUDENT I WAS TELLING YOU ABOUT IS DUE IN LATER THIS EVENING, WE HAVE A LOT TO PREPARE.
WINSTON'S
COMPLETE DREAM DICTIONARY
I SLEPT POORLY AGAIN. IT'S THAT DAMN FRAT HOUSE NEXT DOOR.

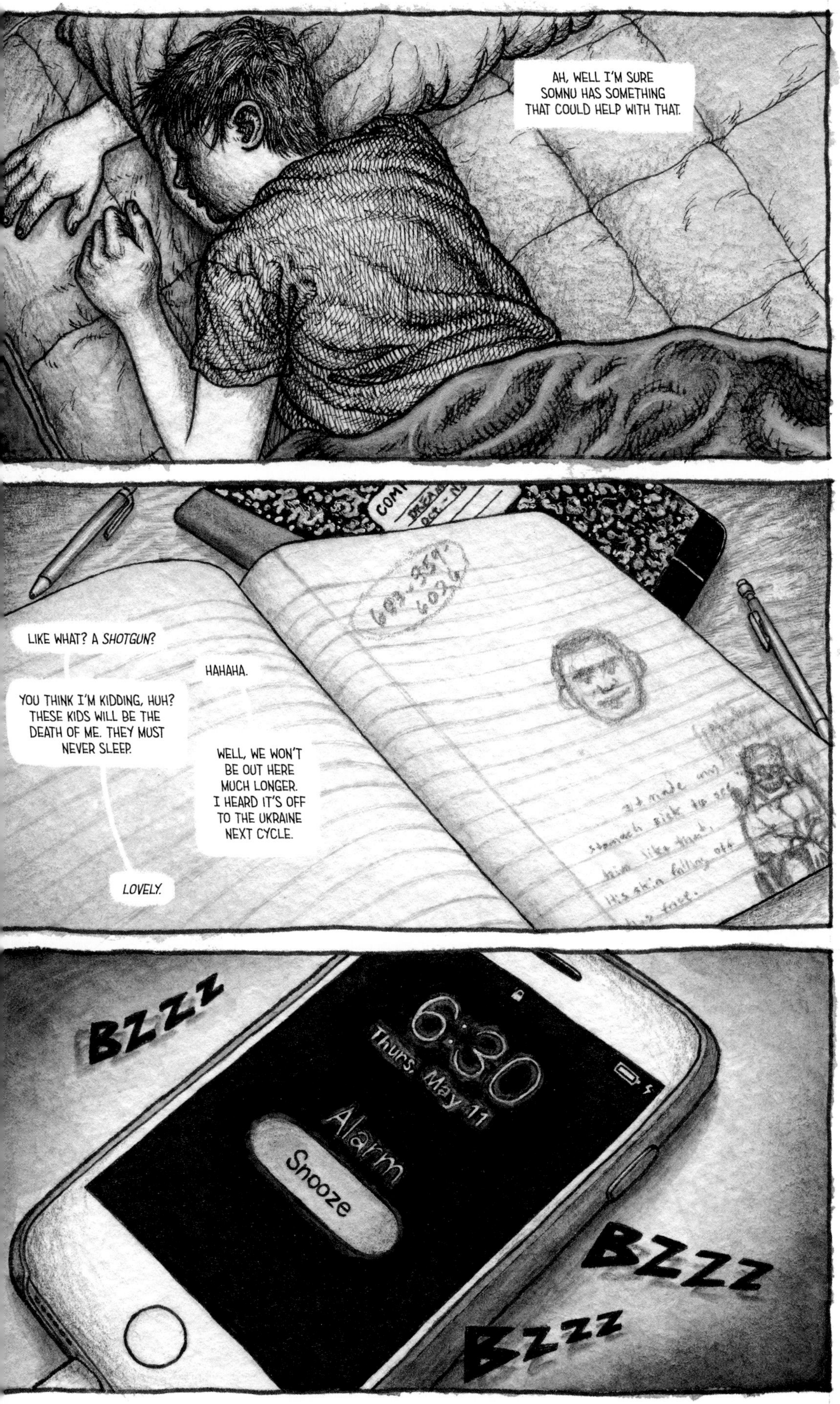
AH, WELL I'M SURE SOMNU HAS SOMETHING THAT COULD HELP WITH THAT.
LIKE WHAT? A *SHOTGUN*?
HAHAHA.
YOU THINK I'M KIDDING, HUH? THESE KIDS WILL BE THE DEATH OF ME. THEY MUST NEVER SLEEP.
WELL, WE WON'T BE OUT HERE MUCH LONGER. I HEARD IT'S OFF TO THE UKRAINE NEXT CYCLE.
*LOVELY.*
BZZZ
6:30
Thurs, May 11
Alarm
Snooze
BZZZ
BZZZ

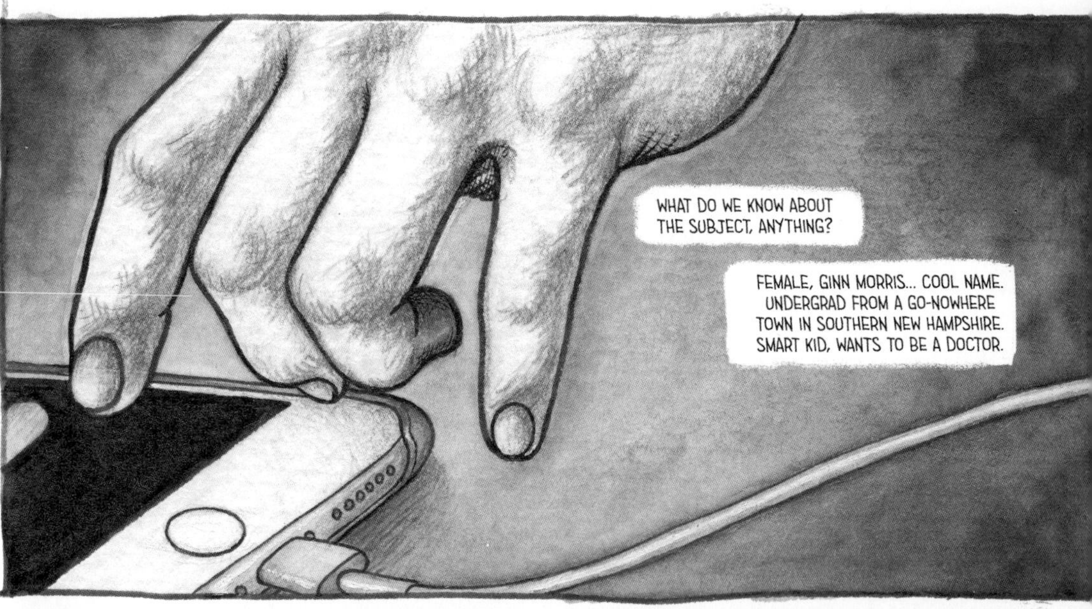
WHAT DO WE KNOW ABOUT THE SUBJECT, ANYTHING?
FEMALE, GINN MORRIS... COOL NAME. UNDERGRAD FROM A GO-NOWHERE TOWN IN SOUTHERN NEW HAMPSHIRE. SMART KID, WANTS TO BE A DOCTOR.

# TREMOR DOSE

MICHAEL W. CONRAD NOAH BAILEY

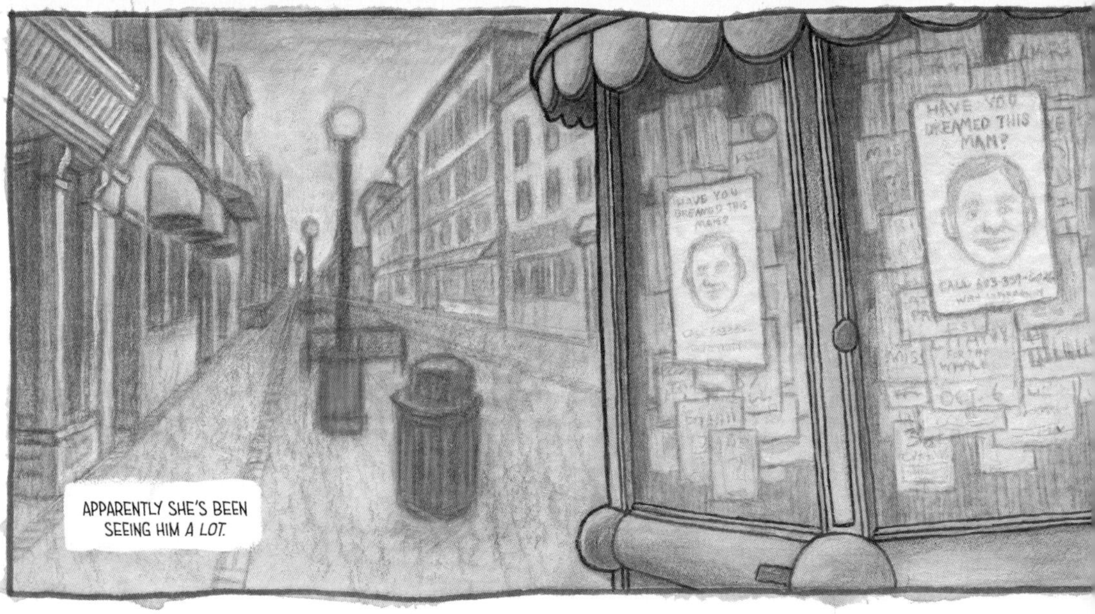
HAVE YOU DREAMED THIS MAN?
APPARENTLY SHE'S BEEN SEEING HIM *A LOT.*

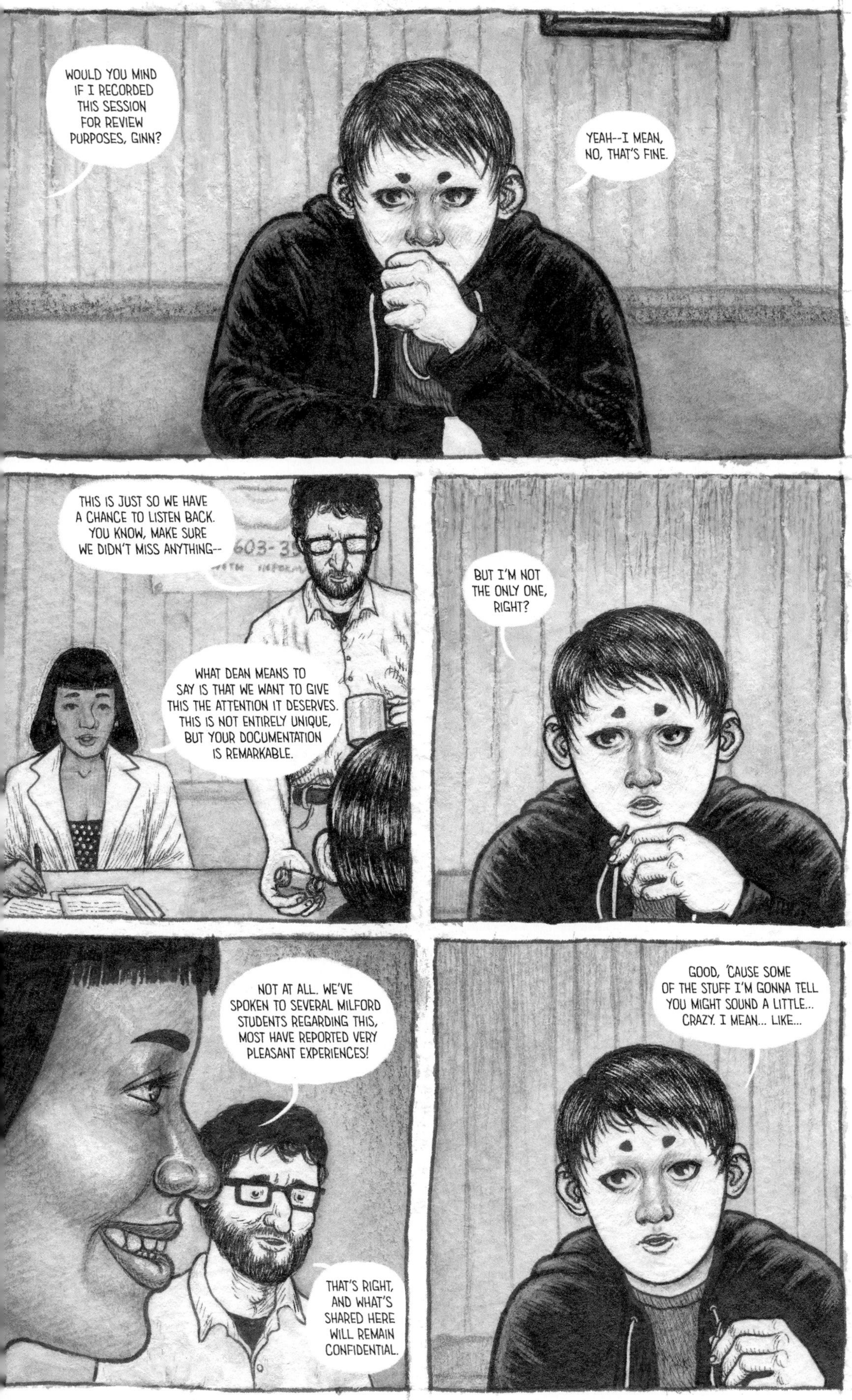

WOULD YOU MIND IF I RECORDED THIS SESSION FOR REVIEW PURPOSES, GINN?
YEAH--I MEAN, NO, THAT'S FINE.
THIS IS JUST SO WE HAVE A CHANCE TO LISTEN BACK. YOU KNOW, MAKE SURE WE DIDN'T MISS ANYTHING--
WHAT DEAN MEANS TO SAY IS THAT WE WANT TO GIVE THIS THE ATTENTION IT DESERVES. THIS IS NOT ENTIRELY UNIQUE, BUT YOUR DOCUMENTATION IS REMARKABLE.
BUT I'M NOT THE ONLY ONE, RIGHT?
NOT AT ALL. WE'VE SPOKEN TO SEVERAL MILFORD STUDENTS REGARDING THIS, MOST HAVE REPORTED VERY PLEASANT EXPERIENCES!
THAT'S RIGHT, AND WHAT'S SHARED HERE WILL REMAIN CONFIDENTIAL.
GOOD, 'CAUSE SOME OF THE STUFF I'M GONNA TELL YOU MIGHT SOUND A LITTLE... CRAZY. I MEAN... LIKE...

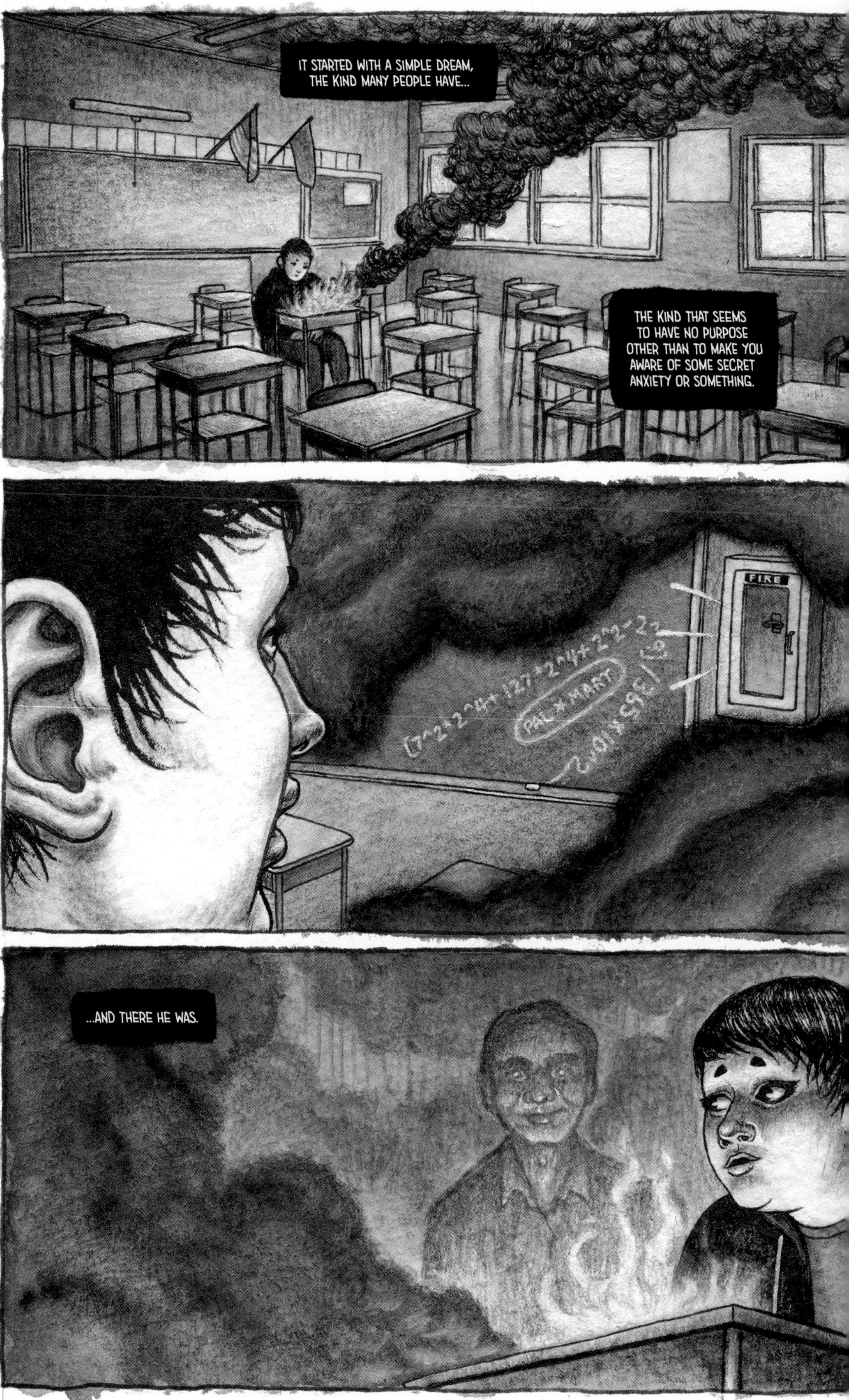
IT STARTED WITH A SIMPLE DREAM, THE KIND MANY PEOPLE HAVE...
THE KIND THAT SEEMS TO HAVE NO PURPOSE OTHER THAN TO MAKE YOU AWARE OF SOME SECRET ANXIETY OR SOMETHING.
FIRE
PAL*MART
...AND THERE HE WAS.

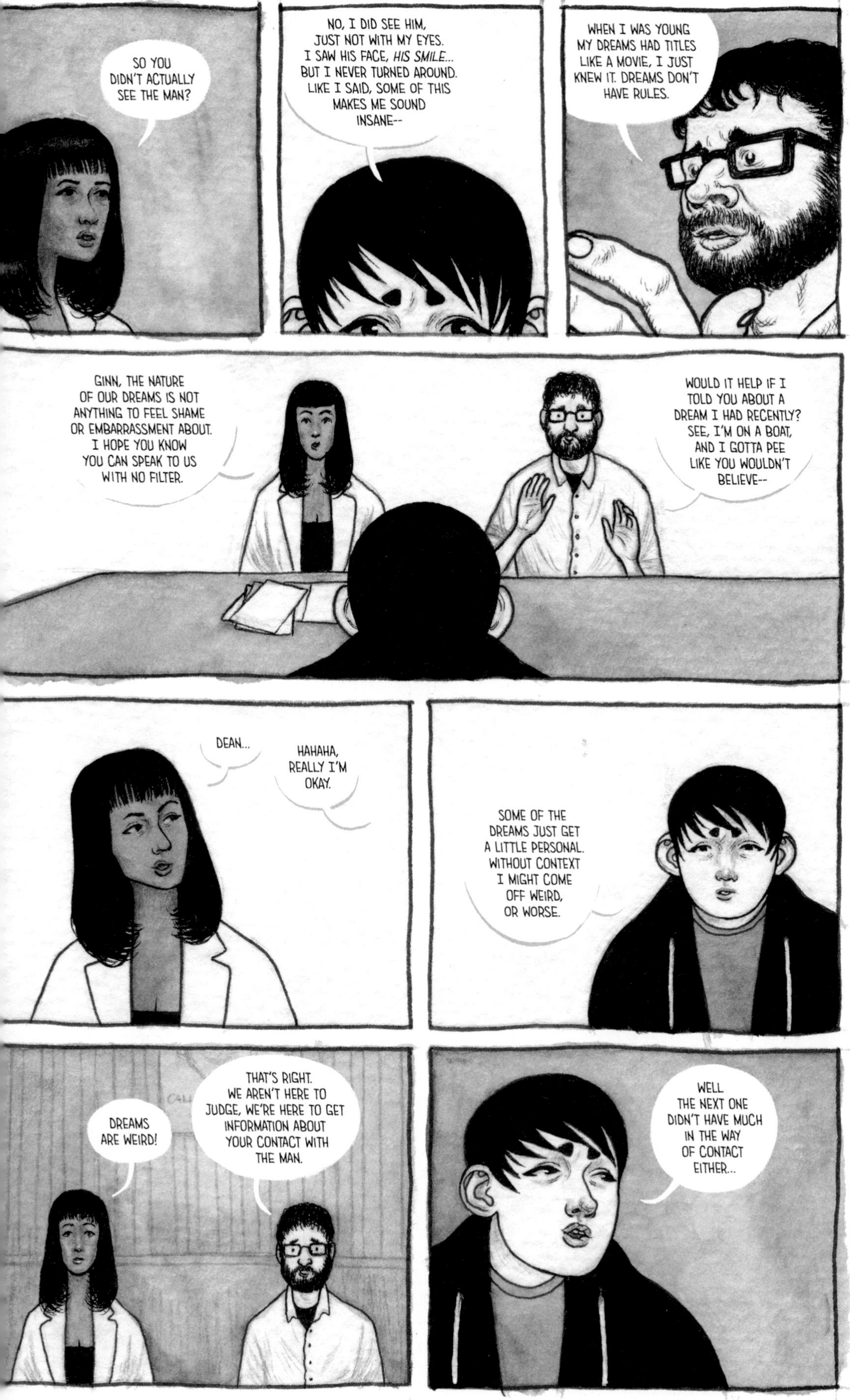

SO YOU DIDN'T ACTUALLY SEE THE MAN?
NO, I DID SEE HIM, JUST NOT WITH MY EYES. I SAW HIS FACE, *HIS SMILE*... BUT I NEVER TURNED AROUND. LIKE I SAID, SOME OF THIS MAKES ME SOUND INSANE--
WHEN I WAS YOUNG MY DREAMS HAD TITLES LIKE A MOVIE, I JUST KNEW IT. DREAMS DON'T HAVE RULES.
GINN, THE NATURE OF OUR DREAMS IS NOT ANYTHING TO FEEL SHAME OR EMBARRASSMENT ABOUT. I HOPE YOU KNOW YOU CAN SPEAK TO US WITH NO FILTER.
WOULD IT HELP IF I TOLD YOU ABOUT A DREAM I HAD RECENTLY? SEE, I'M ON A BOAT, AND I GOTTA PEE LIKE YOU WOULDN'T BELIEVE--
DEAN...
HAHAHA, REALLY I'M OKAY.
SOME OF THE DREAMS JUST GET A LITTLE PERSONAL. WITHOUT CONTEXT I MIGHT COME OFF WEIRD, OR WORSE.
DREAMS ARE WEIRD!
THAT'S RIGHT. WE AREN'T HERE TO JUDGE, WE'RE HERE TO GET INFORMATION ABOUT YOUR CONTACT WITH THE MAN.
WELL THE NEXT ONE DIDN'T HAVE MUCH IN THE WAY OF CONTACT EITHER...

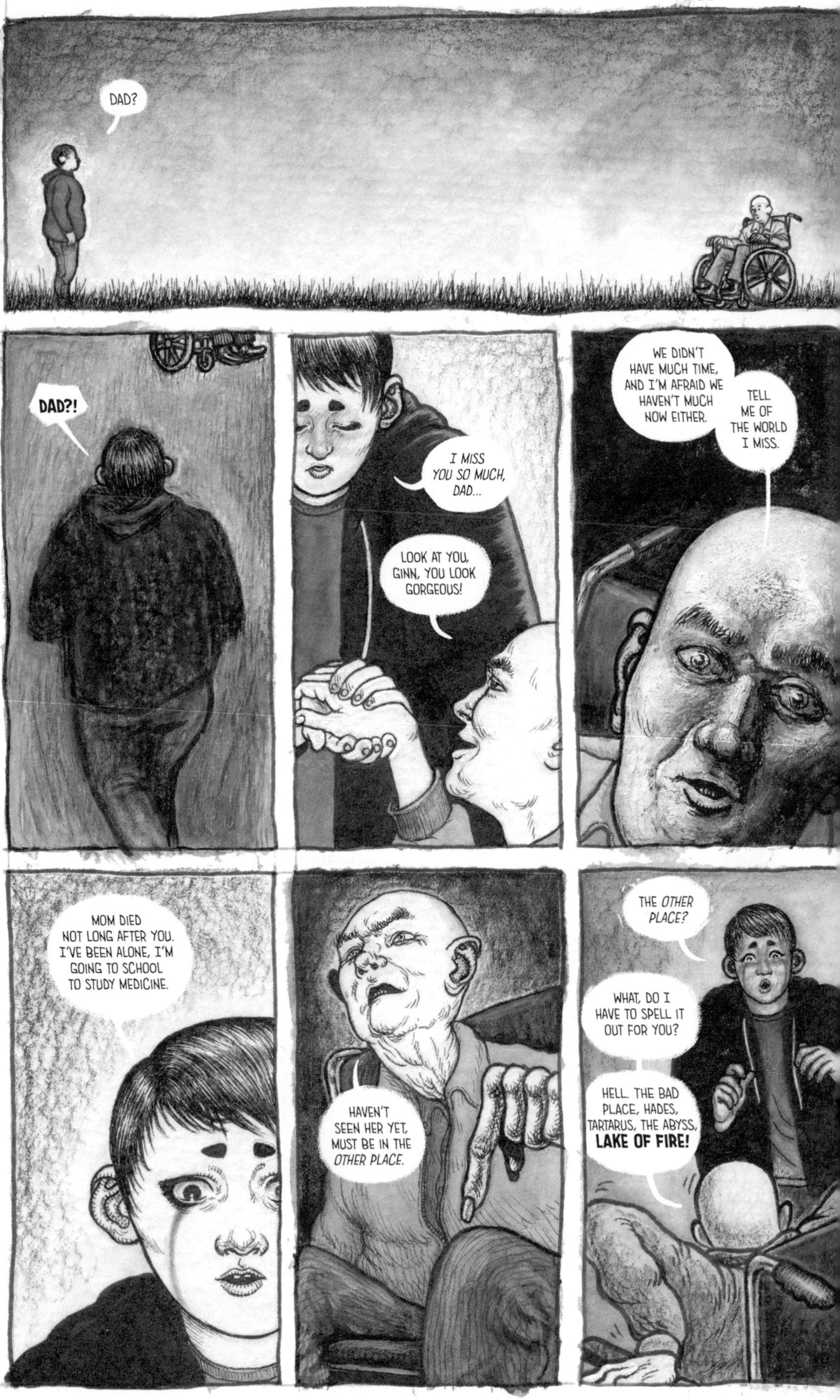
DAD?
DAD?!
I MISS YOU SO MUCH, DAD...
LOOK AT YOU, GINN, YOU LOOK GORGEOUS!
WE DIDN'T HAVE MUCH TIME, AND I'M AFRAID WE HAVEN'T MUCH NOW EITHER.
TELL ME OF THE WORLD I MISS.
MOM DIED NOT LONG AFTER YOU. I'VE BEEN ALONE, I'M GOING TO SCHOOL TO STUDY MEDICINE.
HAVEN'T SEEN HER YET, MUST BE IN THE *OTHER PLACE.*
THE *OTHER PLACE?*
WHAT, DO I HAVE TO SPELL IT OUT FOR YOU?
HELL. THE BAD PLACE, HADES, TARTARUS, THE ABYSS, **LAKE OF FIRE!**

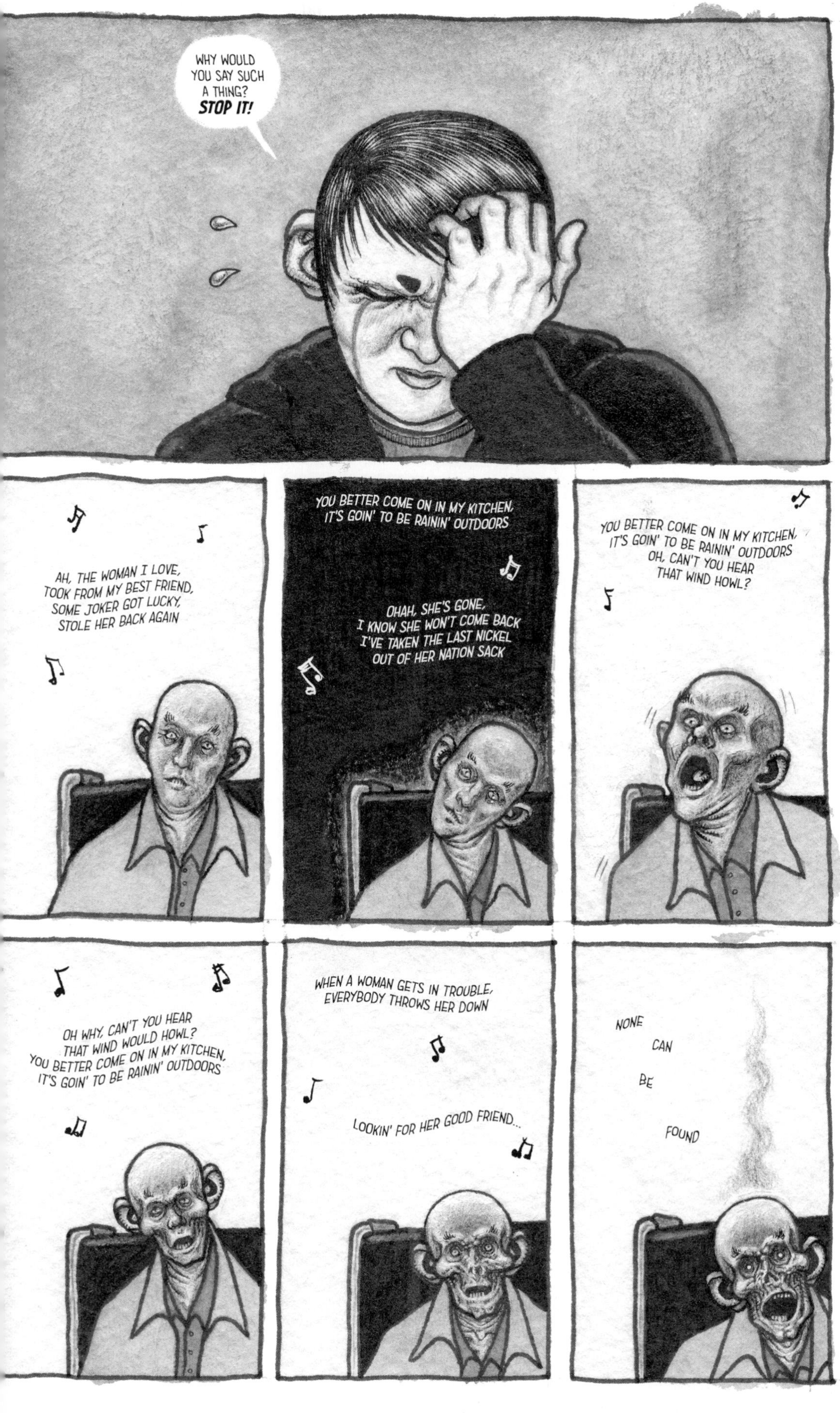
WHY WOULD YOU SAY SUCH A THING? **STOP IT!**
AH, THE WOMAN I LOVE, TOOK FROM MY BEST FRIEND, SOME JOKER GOT LUCKY, STOLE HER BACK AGAIN
YOU BETTER COME ON IN MY KITCHEN, IT'S GOIN' TO BE RAININ' OUTDOORS
OHAH, SHE'S GONE, I KNOW SHE WON'T COME BACK I'VE TAKEN THE LAST NICKEL OUT OF HER NATION SACK
YOU BETTER COME ON IN MY KITCHEN, IT'S GOIN' TO BE RAININ' OUTDOORS OH, CAN'T YOU HEAR THAT WIND HOWL?
OH WHY, CAN'T YOU HEAR THAT WIND WOULD HOWL? YOU BETTER COME ON IN MY KITCHEN, IT'S GOIN' TO BE RAININ' OUTDOORS
WHEN A WOMAN GETS IN TROUBLE, EVERYBODY THROWS HER DOWN
LOOKIN' FOR HER GOOD FRIEND...
NONE
CAN
BE
FOUND

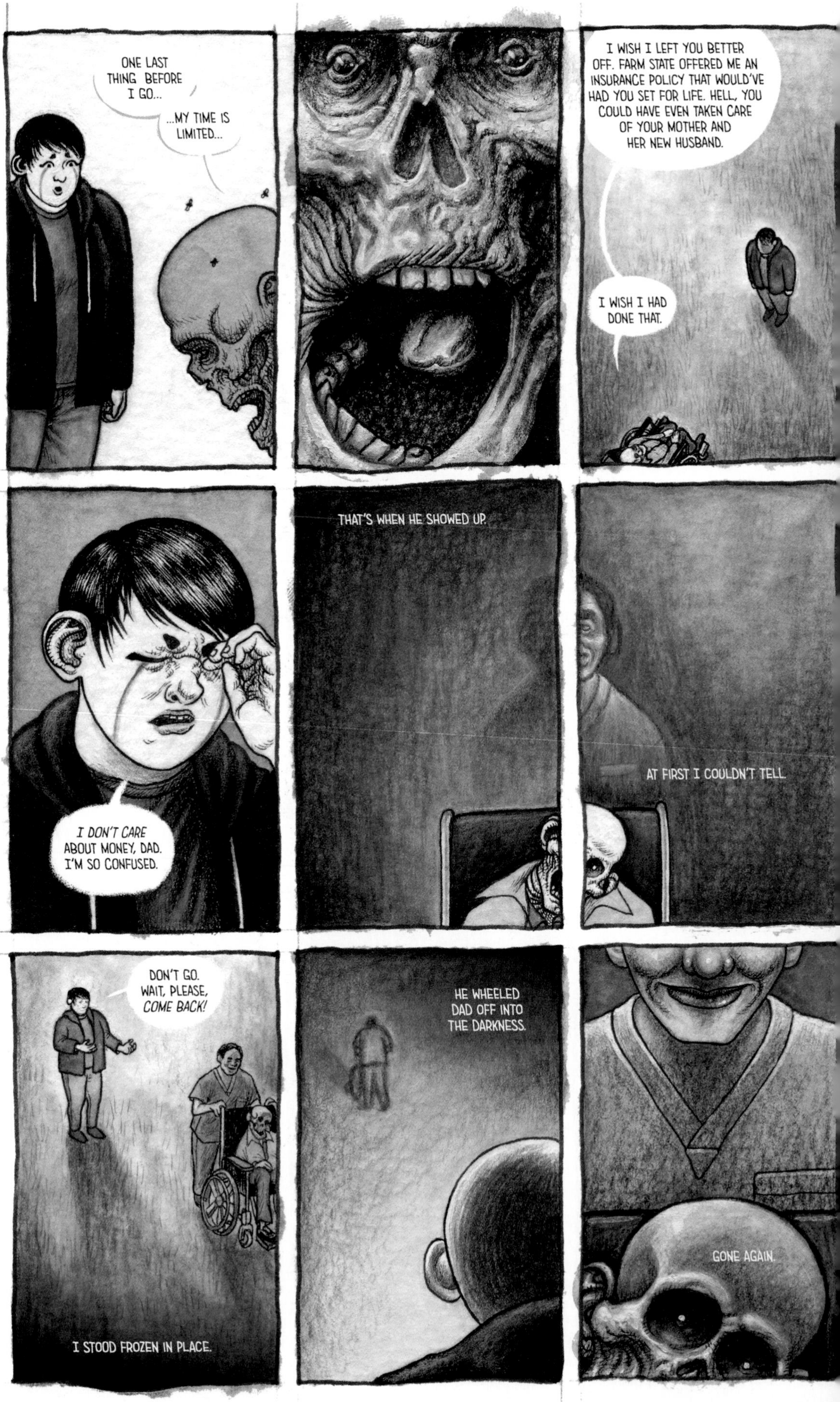
ONE LAST THING BEFORE I GO...
...MY TIME IS LIMITED...
I WISH I LEFT YOU BETTER OFF. FARM STATE OFFERED ME AN INSURANCE POLICY THAT WOULD'VE HAD YOU SET FOR LIFE. HELL, YOU COULD HAVE EVEN TAKEN CARE OF YOUR MOTHER AND HER NEW HUSBAND.
I WISH I HAD DONE THAT.
I DON'T CARE ABOUT MONEY, DAD. I'M SO CONFUSED.
THAT'S WHEN HE SHOWED UP.
AT FIRST I COULDN'T TELL.
DON'T GO. WAIT, PLEASE, COME BACK!
I STOOD FROZEN IN PLACE.
HE WHEELED DAD OFF INTO THE DARKNESS.
GONE AGAIN.

IT WAS ONE OF THOSE DREAMS THAT STICK WITH YOU, NOT SO MUCH WHAT I SAW, BUT THE FEELING.

LIKE, I WOKE UP THINKING MY DAD WAS ALIVE FOR A SECOND, LIKE I NEEDED TO CALL HIM.

CAN I GET YOU A WATER? SOME COFFEE?

COFFEE WOULD BE GREAT, THANKS.

HOW DID YOU FEEL WHEN YOU SAW THE DREAM MAN? THE DREAM ITSELF SOUNDS VERY TROUBLING, BUT WHAT WAS IT LIKE SEEING *HIM* AGAIN?

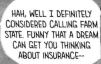

I WASN'T SCARED. I DON'T EVEN KNOW IF I WAS FULLY AWARE THAT I RECOGNIZED HIM UNTIL I WOKE UP.

HAH, WELL I DEFINITELY CONSIDERED CALLING FARM STATE. FUNNY THAT A DREAM CAN GET YOU THINKING ABOUT INSURANCE--

THAT'S PRETTY NORMAL. MOST OF THE PEOPLE WE'VE INTERVIEWED FIND HIM TO KIND OF BLEND IN AT FIRST, OR TO BRING A SENSE OF FAMILIARITY. DID ANYTHING ELSE STAND OUT IN THIS DREAM?

--ONE HOT COFFEE FOR THE LADY!

THANK YOU.

ANYWAY...

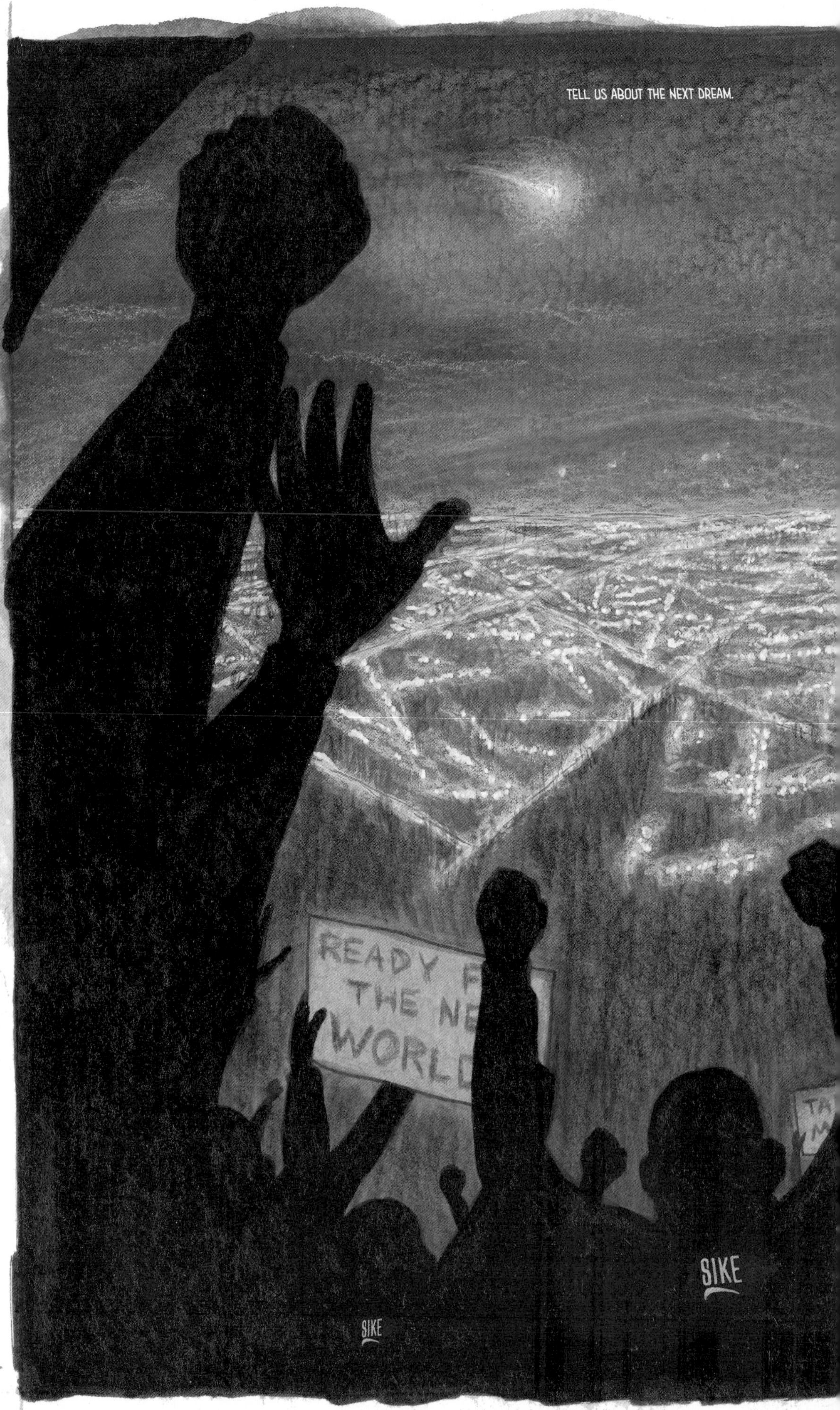
TELL US ABOUT THE NEXT DREAM.
READY F
THE NE
WORL
SIKE
SIKE

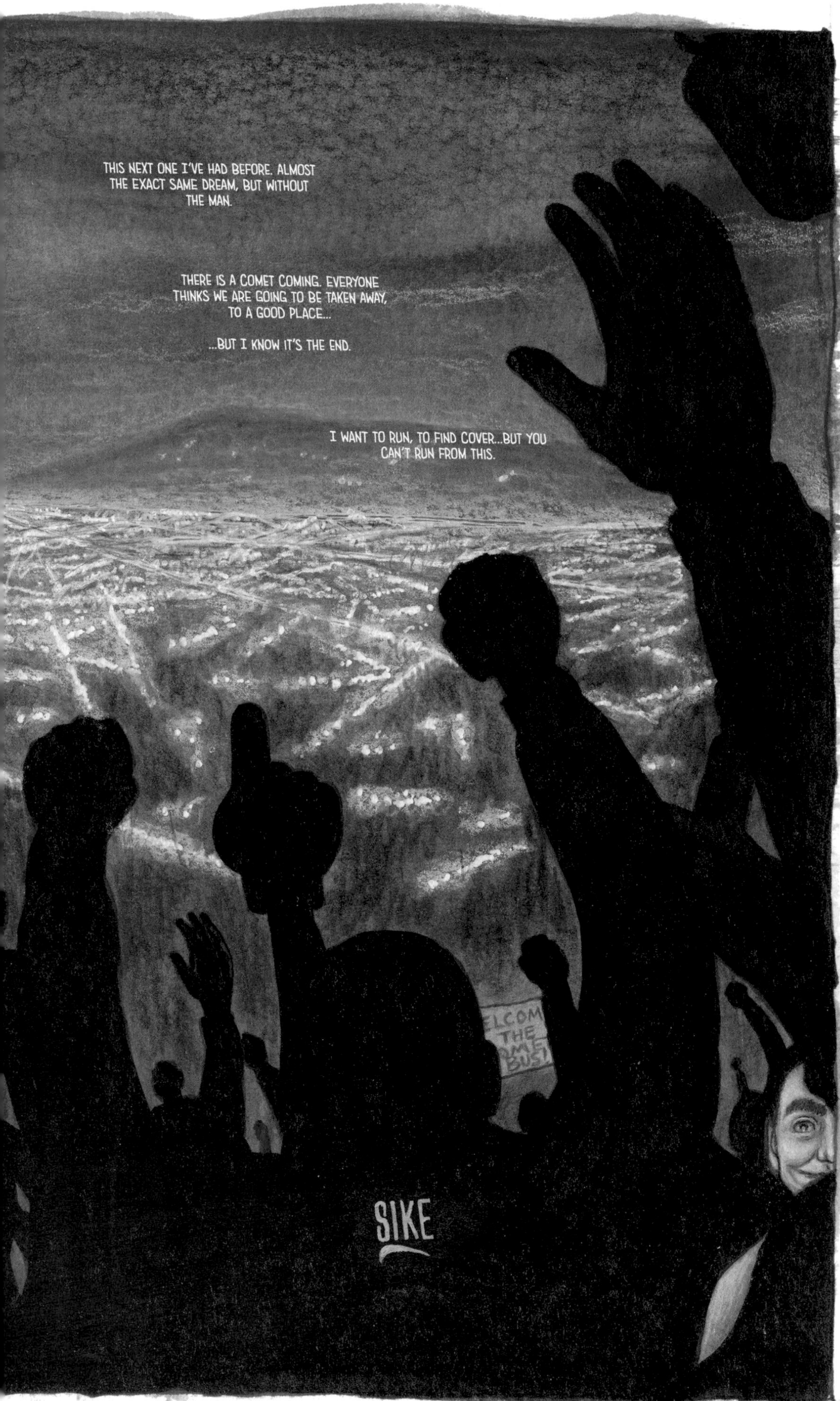
THIS NEXT ONE I'VE HAD BEFORE. ALMOST THE EXACT SAME DREAM, BUT WITHOUT THE MAN.
THERE IS A COMET COMING. EVERYONE THINKS WE ARE GOING TO BE TAKEN AWAY, TO A GOOD PLACE...
...BUT I KNOW IT'S THE END.
I WANT TO RUN, TO FIND COVER...BUT YOU CAN'T RUN FROM THIS.
SIKE

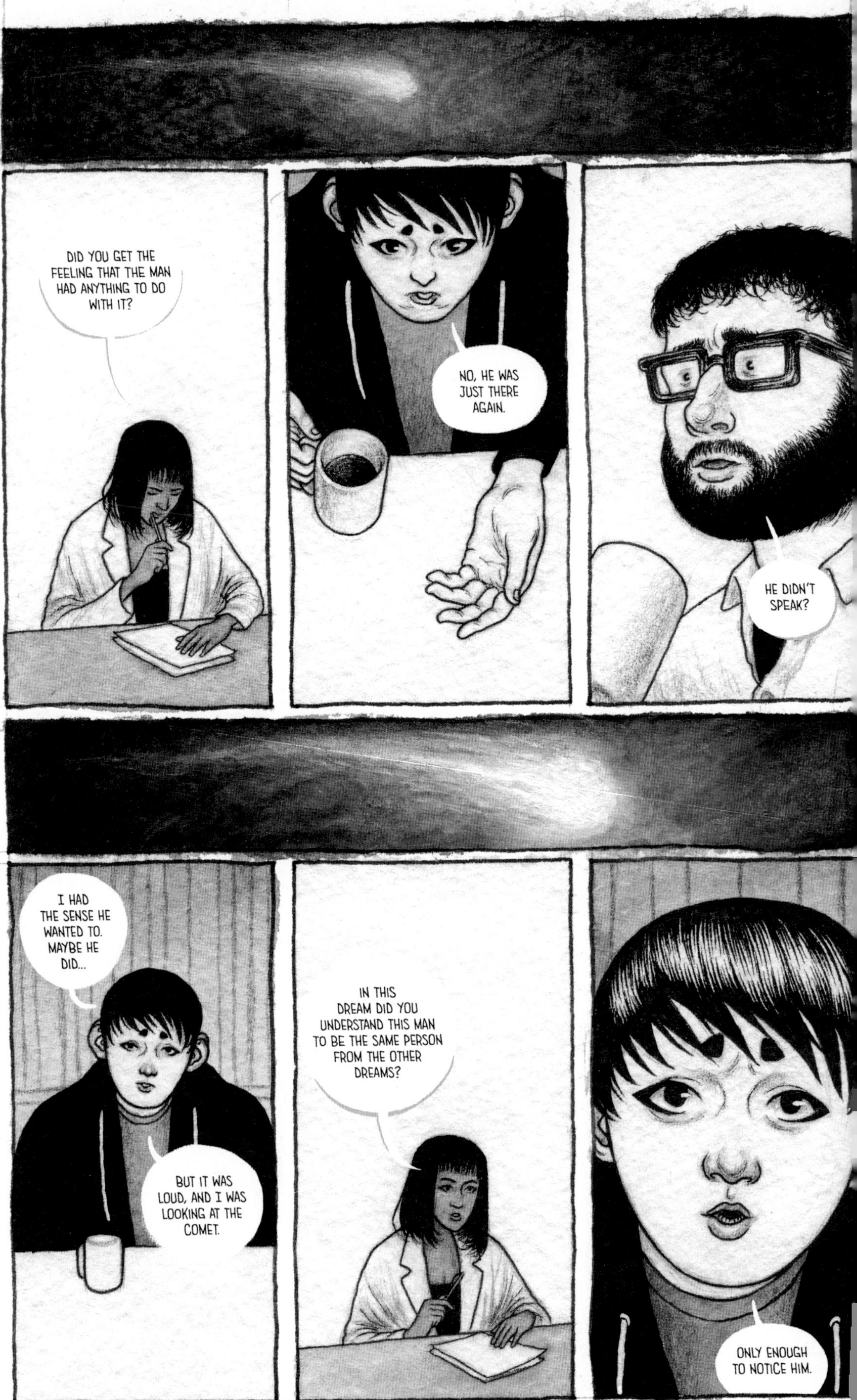
DID YOU GET THE FEELING THAT THE MAN HAD ANYTHING TO DO WITH IT?
NO, HE WAS JUST THERE AGAIN.
HE DIDN'T SPEAK?
I HAD THE SENSE HE WANTED TO. MAYBE HE DID...
BUT IT WAS LOUD, AND I WAS LOOKING AT THE COMET.
IN THIS DREAM DID YOU UNDERSTAND THIS MAN TO BE THE SAME PERSON FROM THE OTHER DREAMS?
ONLY ENOUGH TO NOTICE HIM.

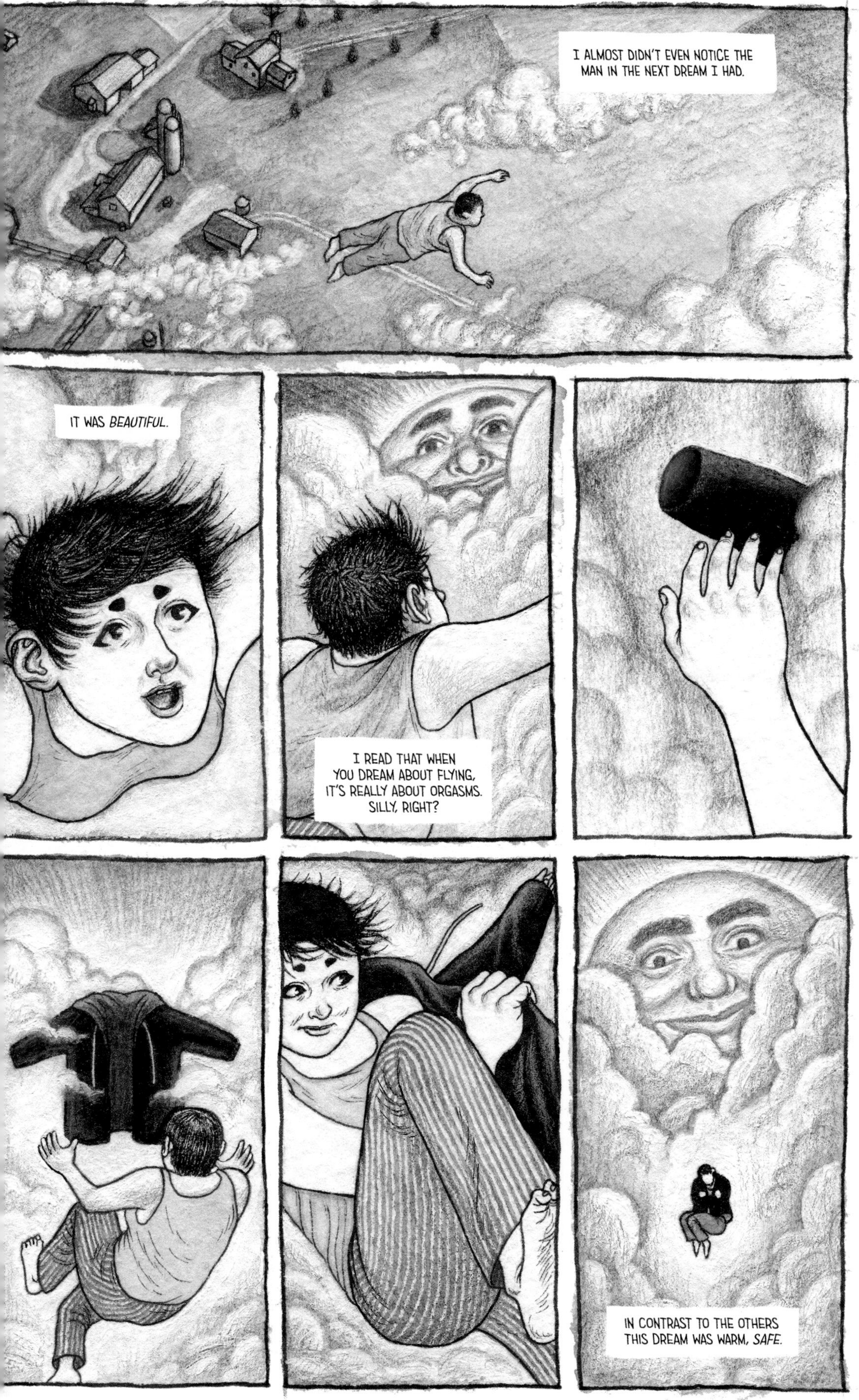
I ALMOST DIDN'T EVEN NOTICE THE MAN IN THE NEXT DREAM I HAD.
IT WAS *BEAUTIFUL*.
I READ THAT WHEN YOU DREAM ABOUT FLYING, IT'S REALLY ABOUT ORGASMS. SILLY, RIGHT?
IN CONTRAST TO THE OTHERS THIS DREAM WAS WARM, *SAFE*.

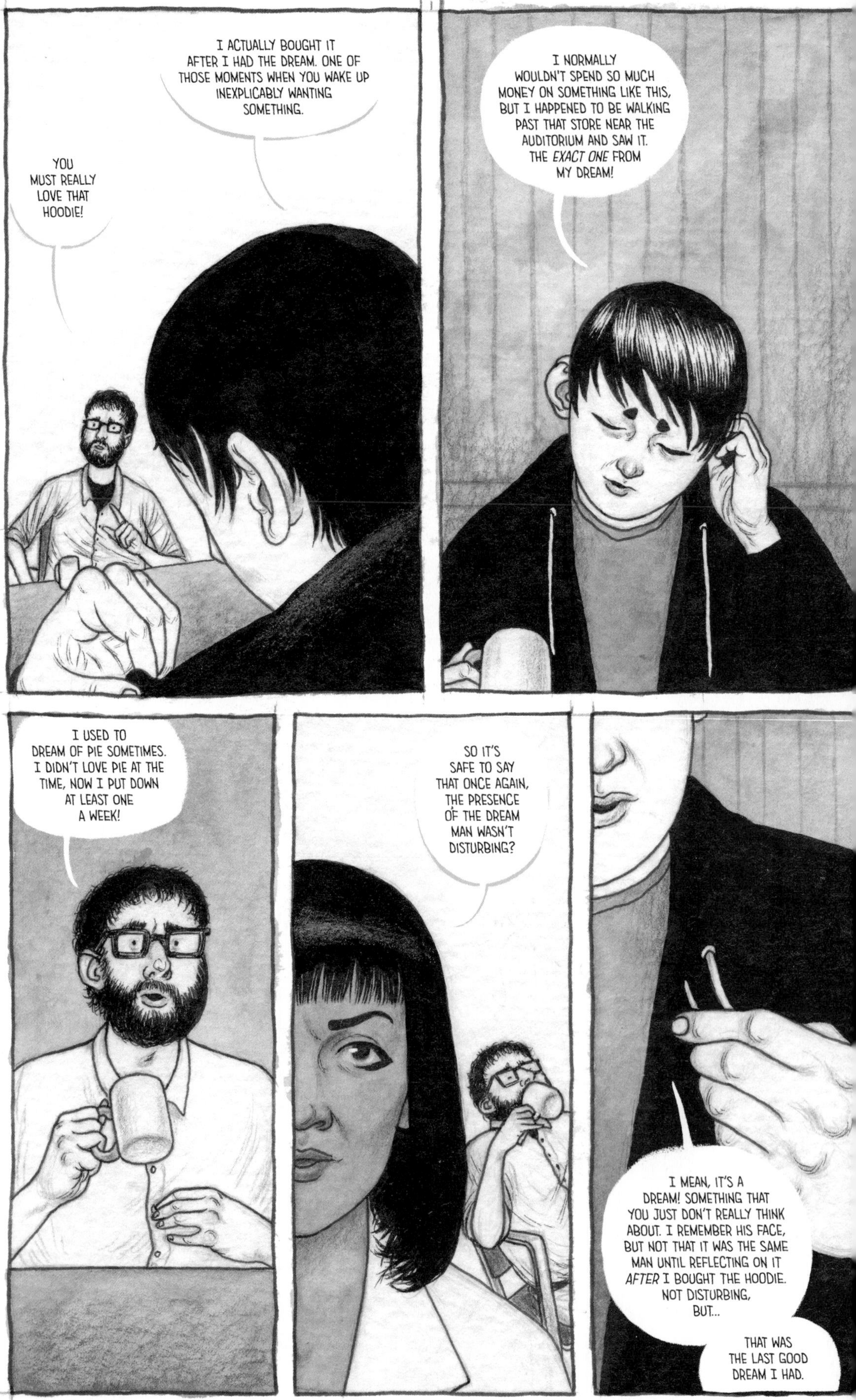
YOU MUST REALLY LOVE THAT HOODIE!
I ACTUALLY BOUGHT IT AFTER I HAD THE DREAM. ONE OF THOSE MOMENTS WHEN YOU WAKE UP INEXPLICABLY WANTING SOMETHING.
I NORMALLY WOULDN'T SPEND SO MUCH MONEY ON SOMETHING LIKE THIS, BUT I HAPPENED TO BE WALKING PAST THAT STORE NEAR THE AUDITORIUM AND SAW IT. THE *EXACT ONE* FROM MY DREAM!
I USED TO DREAM OF PIE SOMETIMES. I DIDN'T LOVE PIE AT THE TIME, NOW I PUT DOWN AT LEAST ONE A WEEK!
SO IT'S SAFE TO SAY THAT ONCE AGAIN, THE PRESENCE OF THE DREAM MAN WASN'T DISTURBING?
I MEAN, IT'S A DREAM! SOMETHING THAT YOU JUST DON'T REALLY THINK ABOUT. I REMEMBER HIS FACE, BUT NOT THAT IT WAS THE SAME MAN UNTIL REFLECTING ON IT *AFTER* I BOUGHT THE HOODIE. NOT DISTURBING, BUT...
THAT WAS THE LAST GOOD DREAM I HAD.

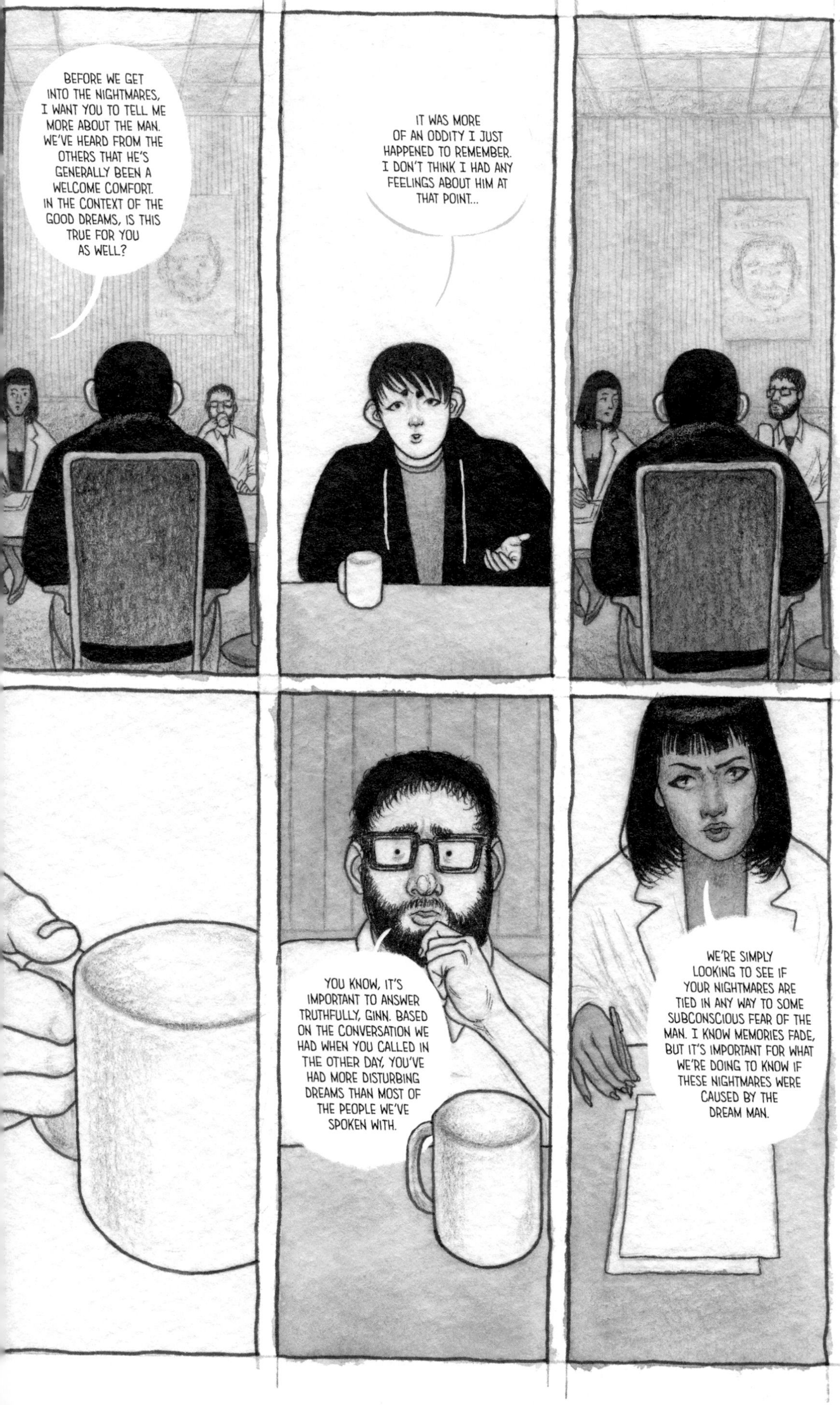
BEFORE WE GET INTO THE NIGHTMARES, I WANT YOU TO TELL ME MORE ABOUT THE MAN. WE'VE HEARD FROM THE OTHERS THAT HE'S GENERALLY BEEN A WELCOME COMFORT. IN THE CONTEXT OF THE GOOD DREAMS, IS THIS TRUE FOR YOU AS WELL?
IT WAS MORE OF AN ODDITY I JUST HAPPENED TO REMEMBER. I DON'T THINK I HAD ANY FEELINGS ABOUT HIM AT THAT POINT...
YOU KNOW, IT'S IMPORTANT TO ANSWER TRUTHFULLY, GINN. BASED ON THE CONVERSATION WE HAD WHEN YOU CALLED IN THE OTHER DAY, YOU'VE HAD MORE DISTURBING DREAMS THAN MOST OF THE PEOPLE WE'VE SPOKEN WITH.
WE'RE SIMPLY LOOKING TO SEE IF YOUR NIGHTMARES ARE TIED IN ANY WAY TO SOME SUBCONSCIOUS FEAR OF THE MAN. I KNOW MEMORIES FADE, BUT IT'S IMPORTANT FOR WHAT WE'RE DOING TO KNOW IF THESE NIGHTMARES WERE CAUSED BY THE DREAM MAN.

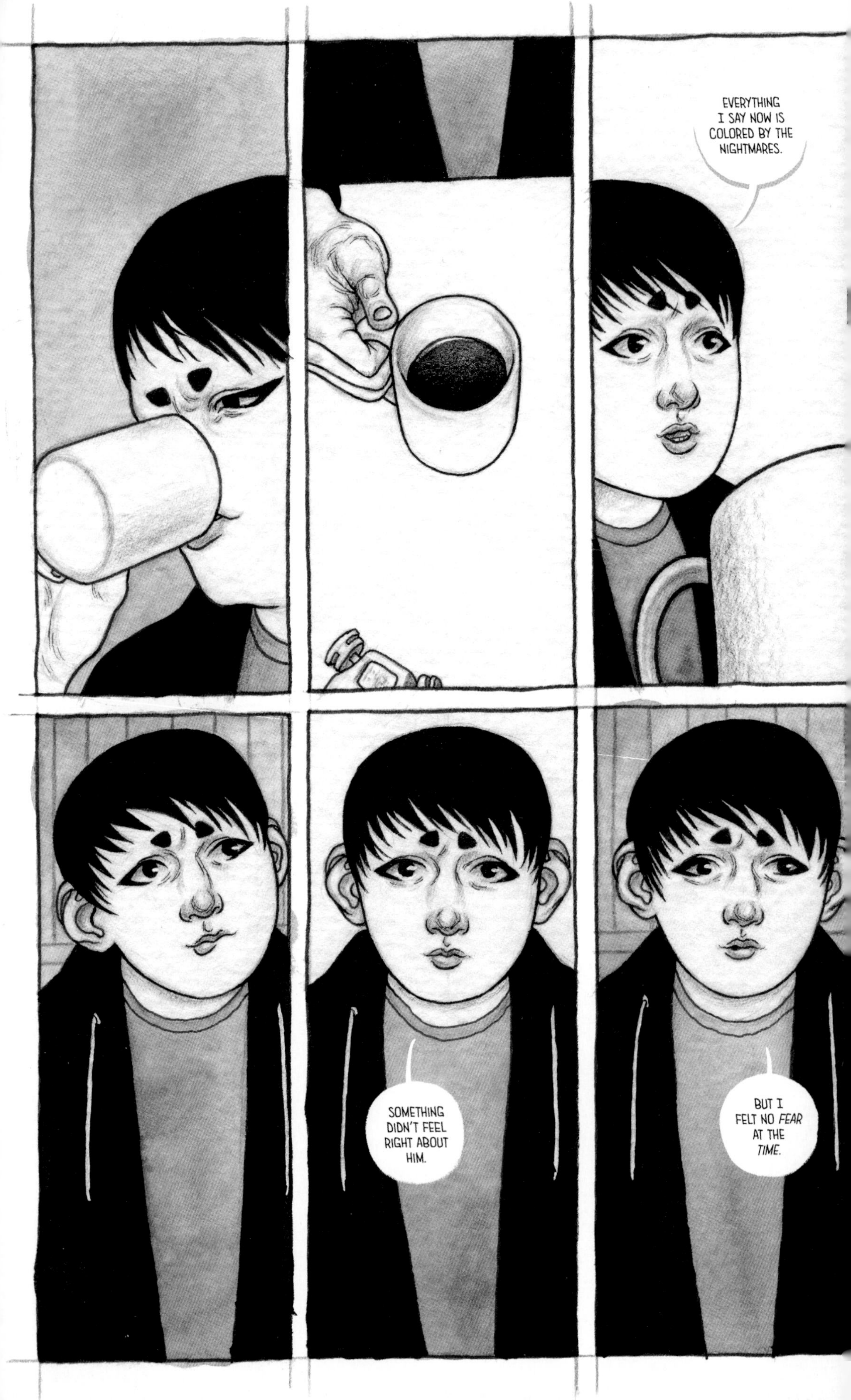
EVERYTHING I SAY NOW IS COLORED BY THE NIGHTMARES.
SOMETHING DIDN'T FEEL RIGHT ABOUT HIM.
BUT I FELT NO *FEAR* AT THE *TIME*.

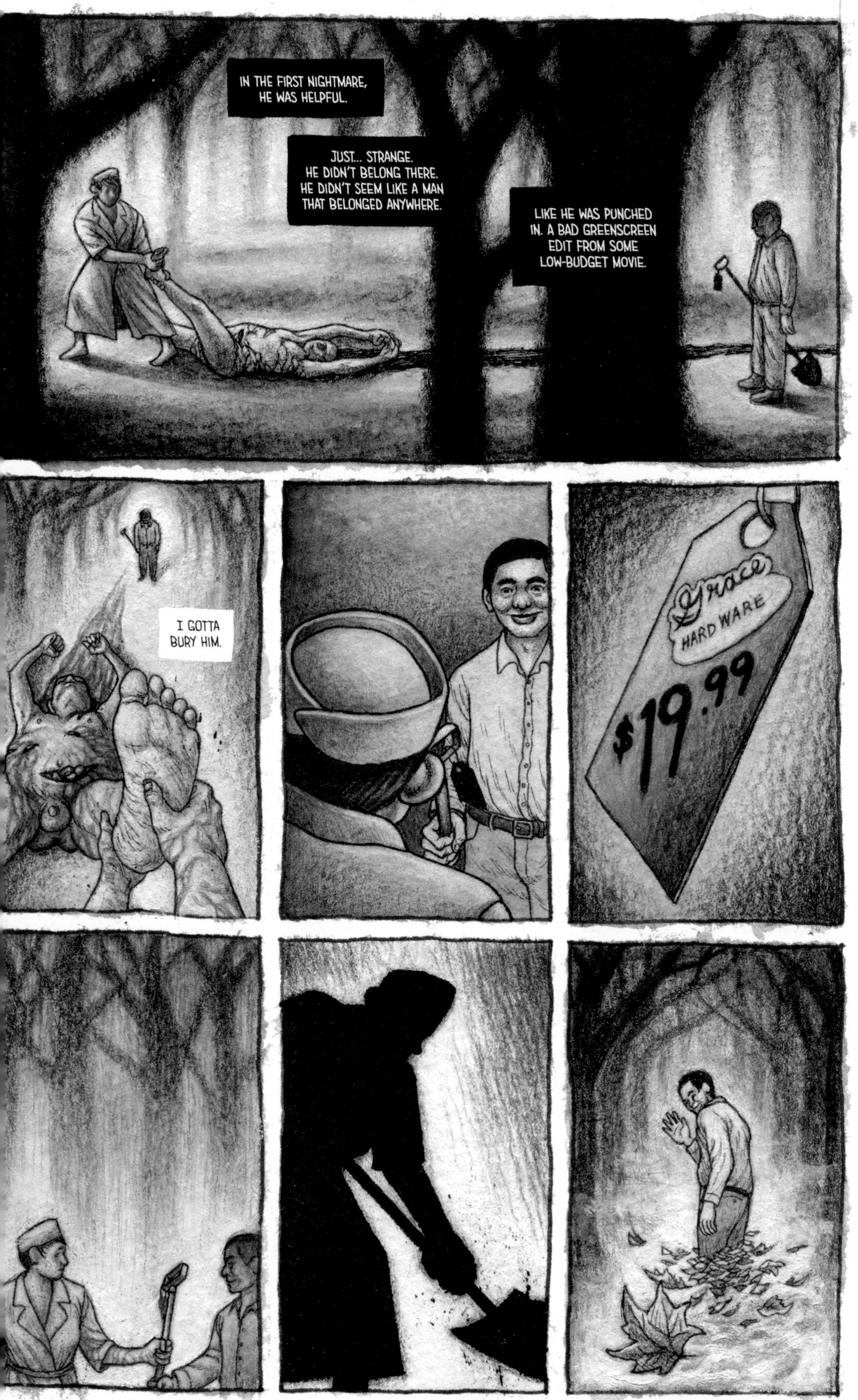

IN THE FIRST NIGHTMARE, HE WAS HELPFUL.
JUST... STRANGE. HE DIDN'T BELONG THERE. HE DIDN'T SEEM LIKE A MAN THAT BELONGED ANYWHERE.
LIKE HE WAS PUNCHED IN. A BAD GREENSCREEN EDIT FROM SOME LOW-BUDGET MOVIE.
I GOTTA BURY HIM.
Grace HARDWARE
$19.99

WOW, SO... THAT'S PRETTY SPOOKY STUFF, HUH?

IT WAS *HORRIBLE*, AND VERY REAL. I WOKE UP FEELING GUILTY, LIKE IT ACTUALLY HAPPENED.

THE MAN WASN'T THE CREEPY BIT. HE WAS TRYING TO HELP, I APPRECIATED THAT.

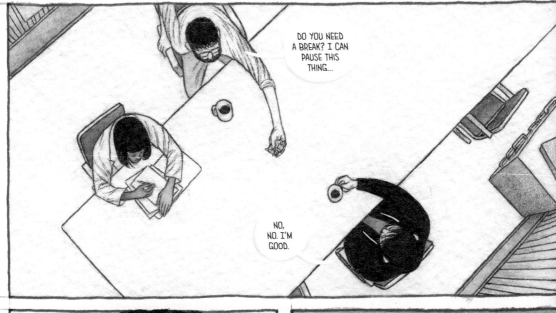

DO YOU NEED A BREAK? I CAN PAUSE THIS THING...

NO, NO. I'M GOOD.

THANK YOU.

GREAT. I THINK WE'RE GETTING SOMEWHERE. AGAIN, WE APPRECIATE YOU DOING THIS.

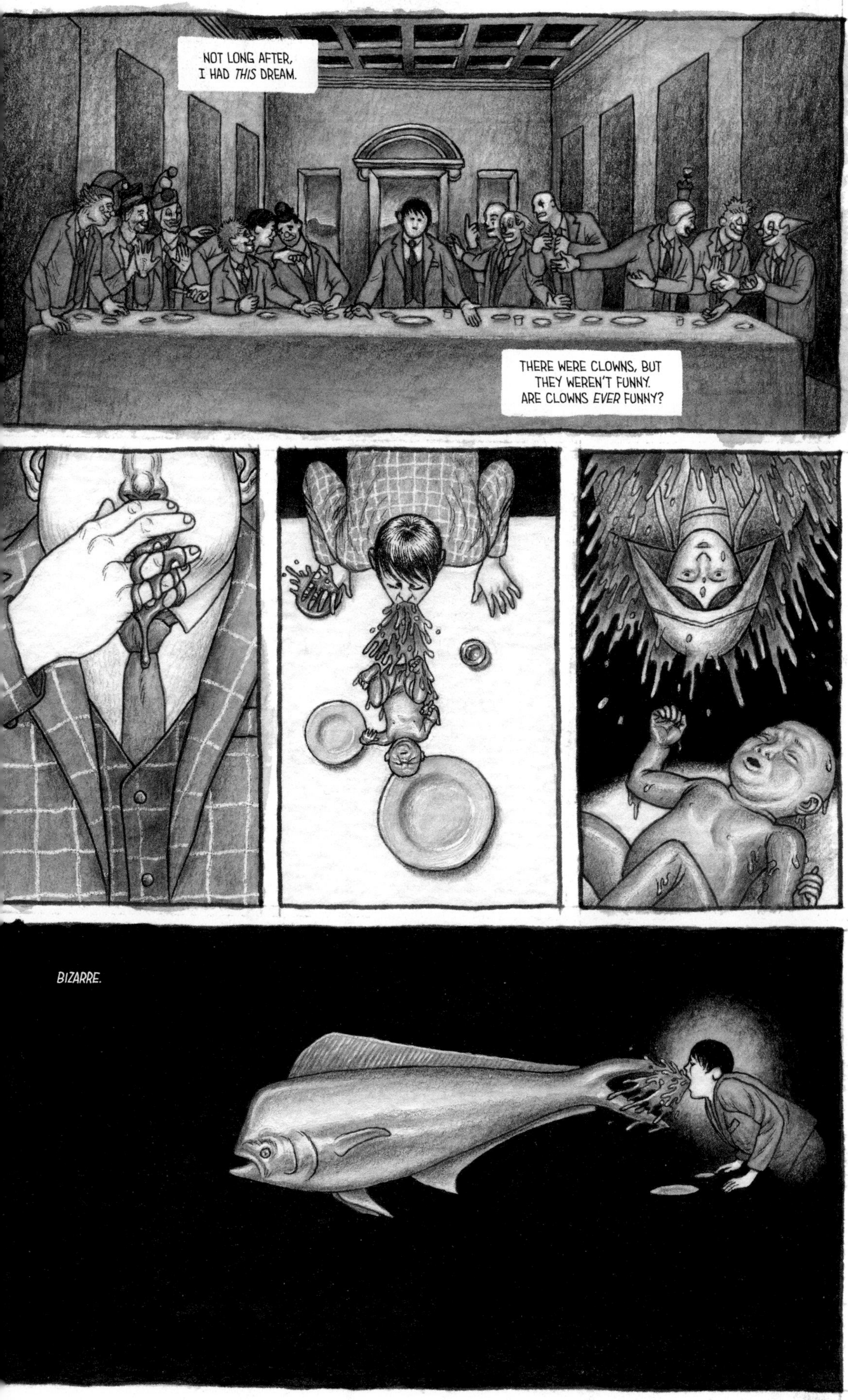
NOT LONG AFTER,
I HAD *THIS* DREAM.
THERE WERE CLOWNS, BUT
THEY WEREN'T FUNNY.
ARE CLOWNS *EVER* FUNNY?
*BIZARRE.*

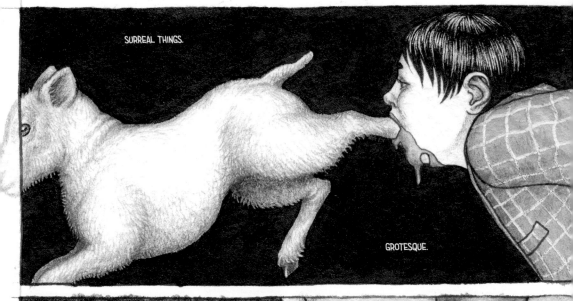

SURREAL THINGS.

GROTESQUE.

PROFANE AND REPUGNANT.

SICKLY IDEAS, LIKE A
SWEET CANDY GONE FOUL,
MOCKED AND NEGLECTED.

DESPERATE.
I WAS DESPERATE TO ESCAPE,
TO WAKE UP.

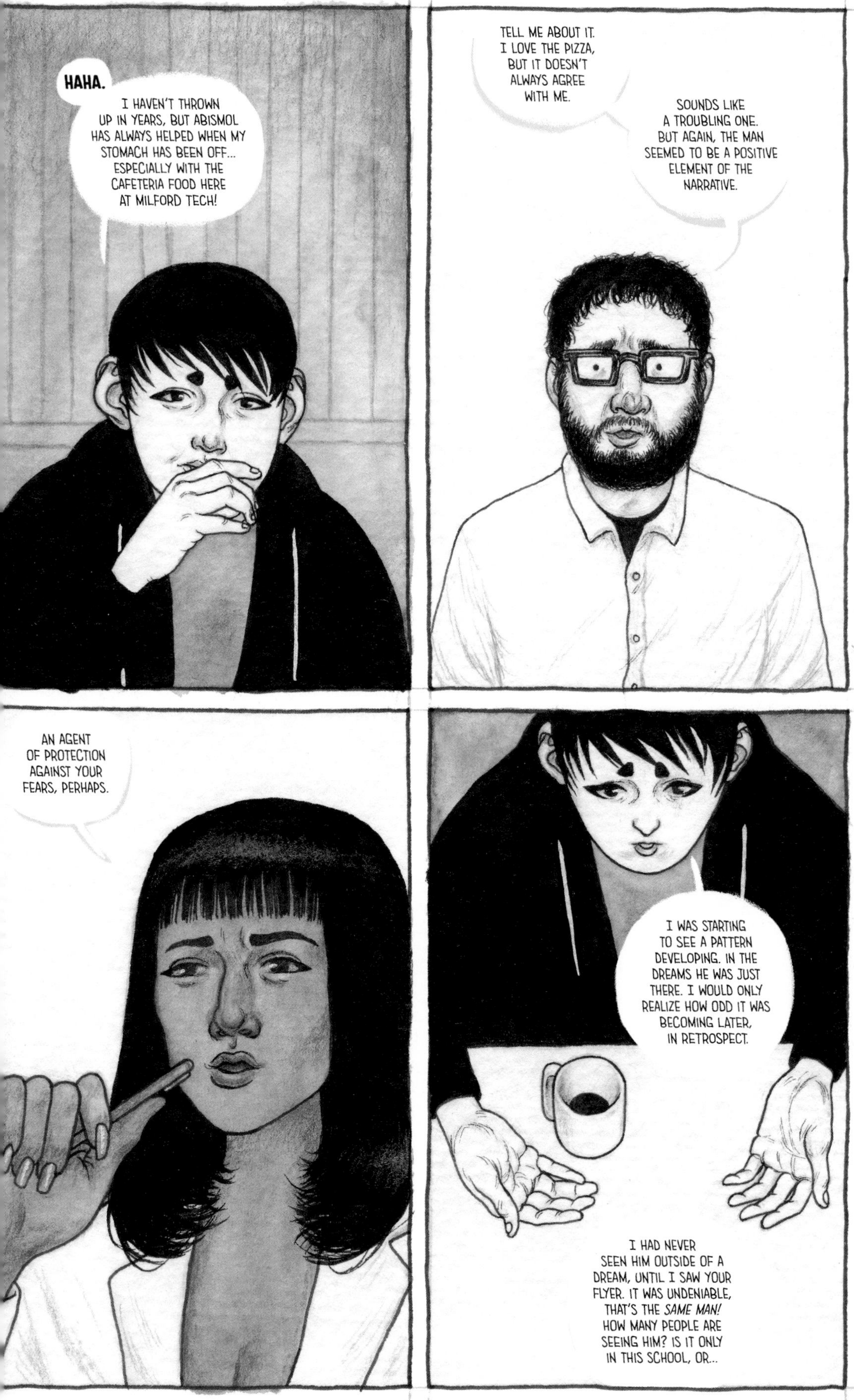
HAHA.
I HAVEN'T THROWN UP IN YEARS, BUT ABISMOL HAS ALWAYS HELPED WHEN MY STOMACH HAS BEEN OFF... ESPECIALLY WITH THE CAFETERIA FOOD HERE AT MILFORD TECH!
TELL ME ABOUT IT. I LOVE THE PIZZA, BUT IT DOESN'T ALWAYS AGREE WITH ME.
SOUNDS LIKE A TROUBLING ONE. BUT AGAIN, THE MAN SEEMED TO BE A POSITIVE ELEMENT OF THE NARRATIVE.
AN AGENT OF PROTECTION AGAINST YOUR FEARS, PERHAPS.
I WAS STARTING TO SEE A PATTERN DEVELOPING. IN THE DREAMS HE WAS JUST THERE. I WOULD ONLY REALIZE HOW ODD IT WAS BECOMING LATER, IN RETROSPECT.
I HAD NEVER SEEN HIM OUTSIDE OF A DREAM, UNTIL I SAW YOUR FLYER. IT WAS UNDENIABLE, THAT'S THE *SAME MAN!* HOW MANY PEOPLE ARE SEEING HIM? IS IT ONLY IN THIS SCHOOL, OR...

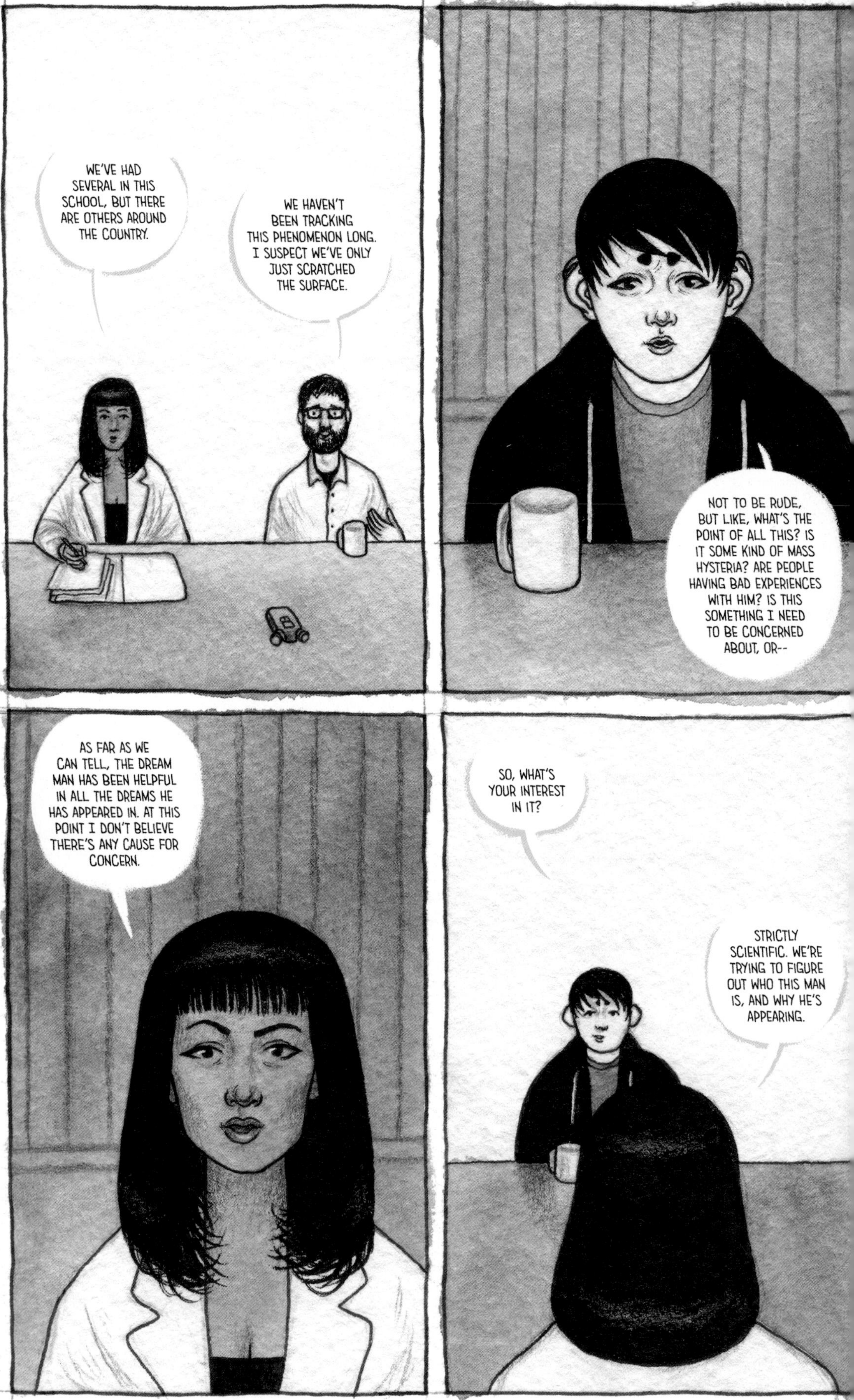
WE'VE HAD SEVERAL IN THIS SCHOOL, BUT THERE ARE OTHERS AROUND THE COUNTRY.
WE HAVEN'T BEEN TRACKING THIS PHENOMENON LONG. I SUSPECT WE'VE ONLY JUST SCRATCHED THE SURFACE.
NOT TO BE RUDE, BUT LIKE, WHAT'S THE POINT OF ALL THIS? IS IT SOME KIND OF MASS HYSTERIA? ARE PEOPLE HAVING BAD EXPERIENCES WITH HIM? IS THIS SOMETHING I NEED TO BE CONCERNED ABOUT, OR--
AS FAR AS WE CAN TELL, THE DREAM MAN HAS BEEN HELPFUL IN ALL THE DREAMS HE HAS APPEARED IN. AT THIS POINT I DON'T BELIEVE THERE'S ANY CAUSE FOR CONCERN.
SO, WHAT'S YOUR INTEREST IN IT?
STRICTLY SCIENTIFIC. WE'RE TRYING TO FIGURE OUT WHO THIS MAN IS, AND WHY HE'S APPEARING.

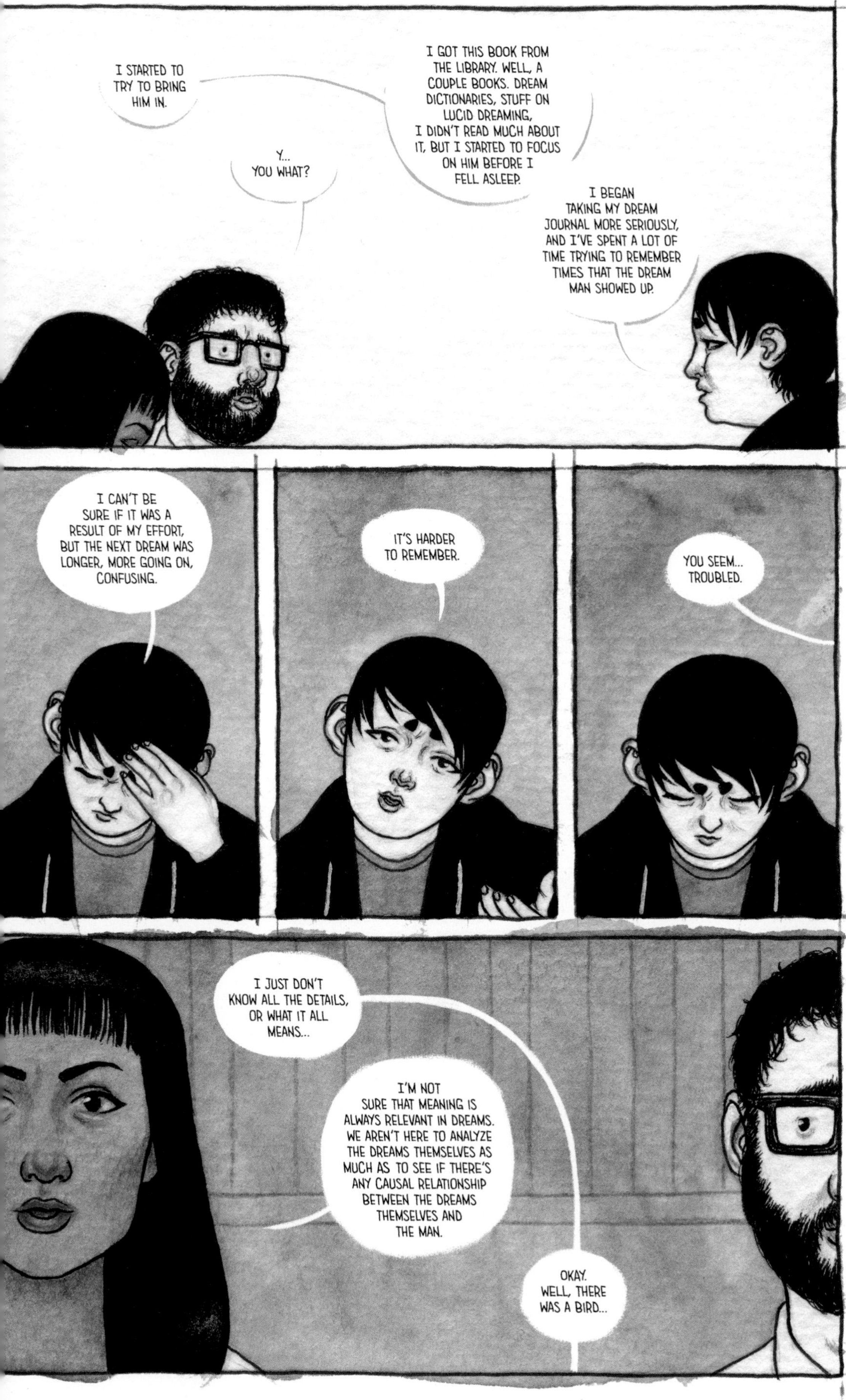
I STARTED TO TRY TO BRING HIM IN.
Y... YOU WHAT?
I GOT THIS BOOK FROM THE LIBRARY. WELL, A COUPLE BOOKS. DREAM DICTIONARIES, STUFF ON LUCID DREAMING, I DIDN'T READ MUCH ABOUT IT, BUT I STARTED TO FOCUS ON HIM BEFORE I FELL ASLEEP.
I BEGAN TAKING MY DREAM JOURNAL MORE SERIOUSLY, AND I'VE SPENT A LOT OF TIME TRYING TO REMEMBER TIMES THAT THE DREAM MAN SHOWED UP.
I CAN'T BE SURE IF IT WAS A RESULT OF MY EFFORT, BUT THE NEXT DREAM WAS LONGER, MORE GOING ON, CONFUSING.
IT'S HARDER TO REMEMBER.
YOU SEEM... TROUBLED.
I JUST DON'T KNOW ALL THE DETAILS, OR WHAT IT ALL MEANS...
I'M NOT SURE THAT MEANING IS ALWAYS RELEVANT IN DREAMS. WE AREN'T HERE TO ANALYZE THE DREAMS THEMSELVES AS MUCH AS TO SEE IF THERE'S ANY CAUSAL RELATIONSHIP BETWEEN THE DREAMS THEMSELVES AND THE MAN.
OKAY. WELL, THERE WAS A BIRD...

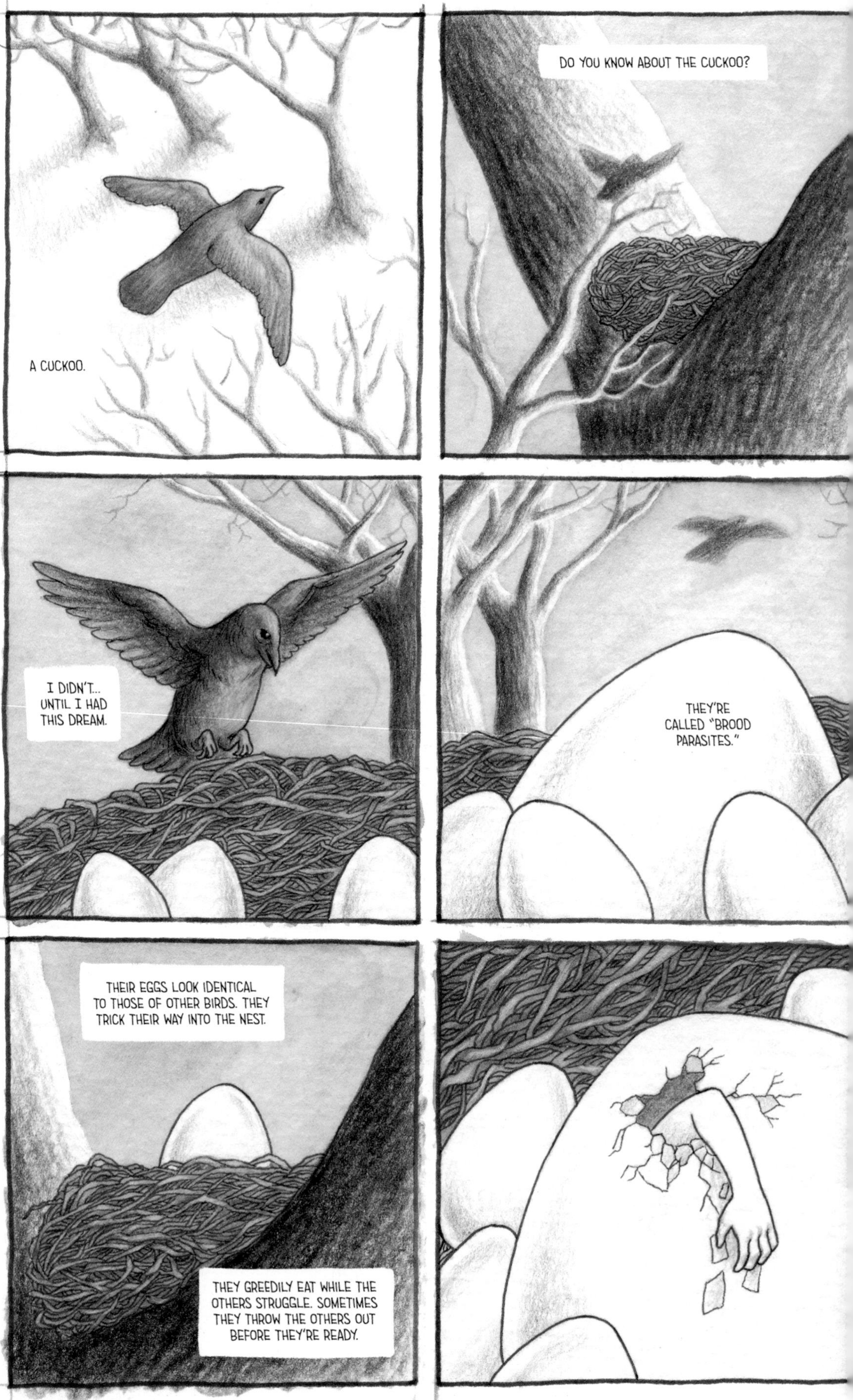
A CUCKOO.
DO YOU KNOW ABOUT THE CUCKOO?
I DIDN'T... UNTIL I HAD THIS DREAM.
THEY'RE CALLED "BROOD PARASITES."
THEIR EGGS LOOK IDENTICAL TO THOSE OF OTHER BIRDS. THEY TRICK THEIR WAY INTO THE NEST.
THEY GREEDILY EAT WHILE THE OTHERS STRUGGLE. SOMETIMES THEY THROW THE OTHERS OUT BEFORE THEY'RE READY.

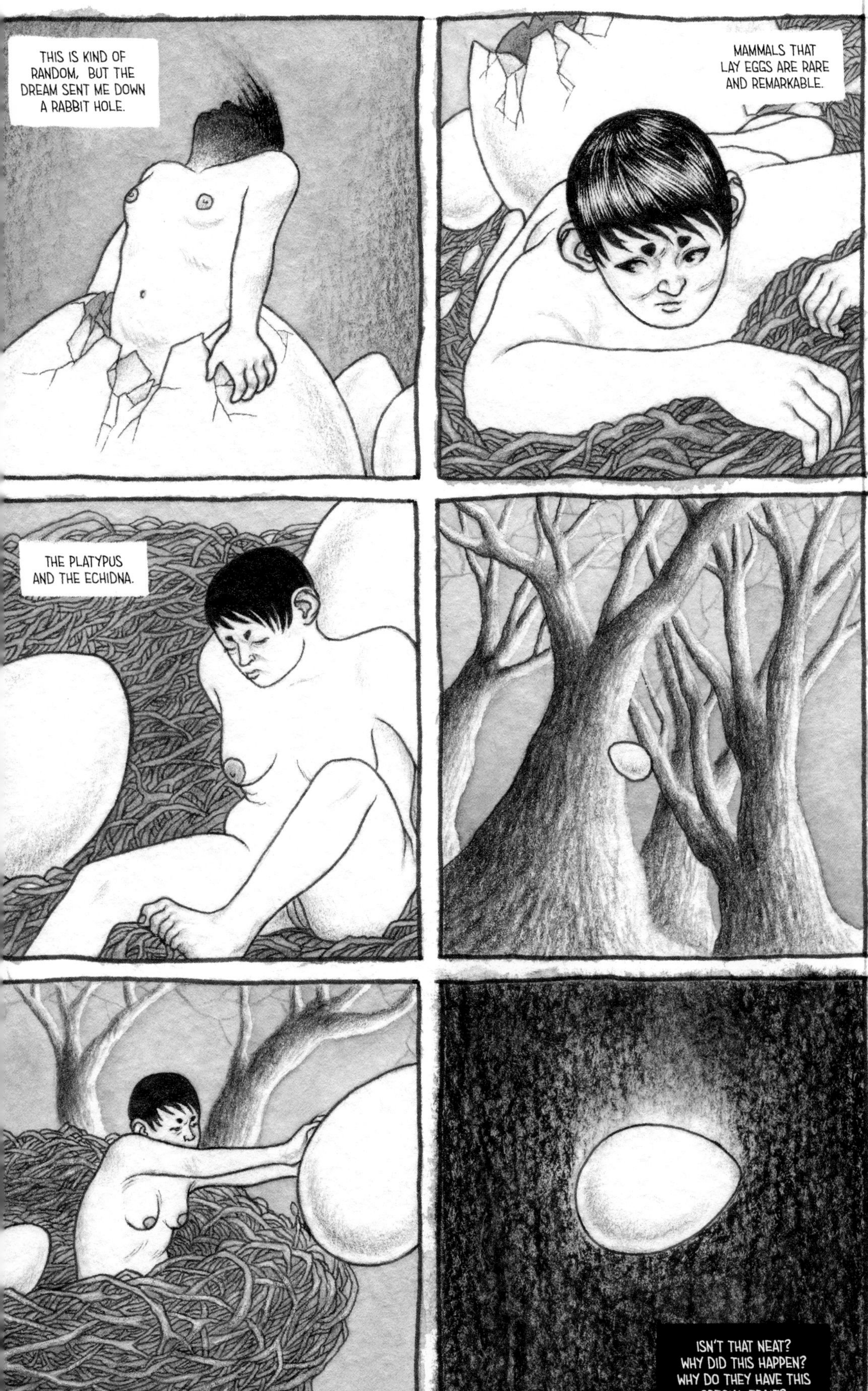
THIS IS KIND OF RANDOM, BUT THE DREAM SENT ME DOWN A RABBIT HOLE.
MAMMALS THAT LAY EGGS ARE RARE AND REMARKABLE.
THE PLATYPUS AND THE ECHIDNA.
ISN'T THAT NEAT? WHY DID THIS HAPPEN? WHY DO THEY HAVE THIS SPECIAL TRAIT?

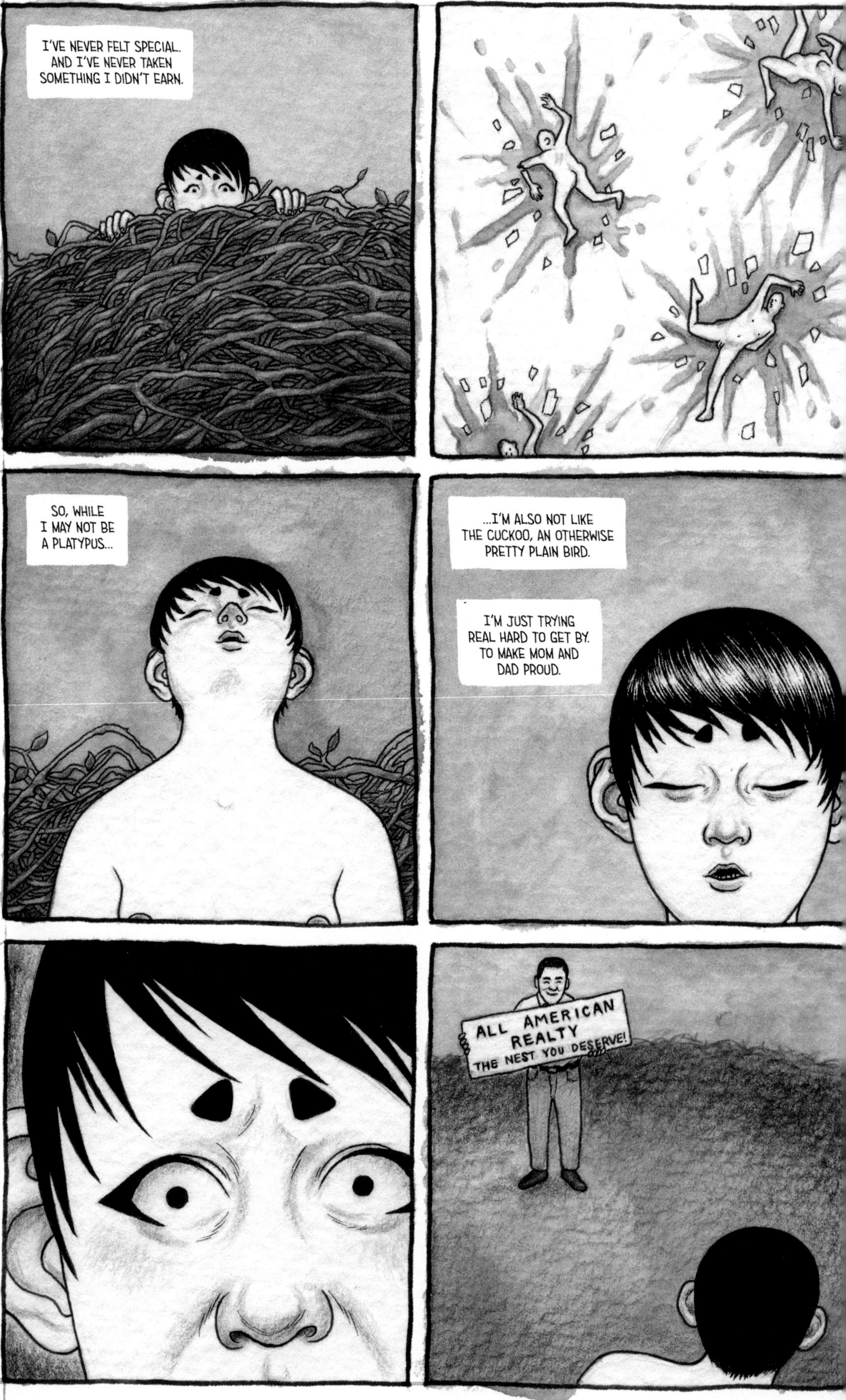
I'VE NEVER FELT SPECIAL. AND I'VE NEVER TAKEN SOMETHING I DIDN'T EARN.
SO, WHILE I MAY NOT BE A PLATYPUS...
...I'M ALSO NOT LIKE THE CUCKOO, AN OTHERWISE PRETTY PLAIN BIRD.
I'M JUST TRYING REAL HARD TO GET BY. TO MAKE MOM AND DAD PROUD.
ALL AMERICAN REALTY
THE NEST YOU DESERVE!

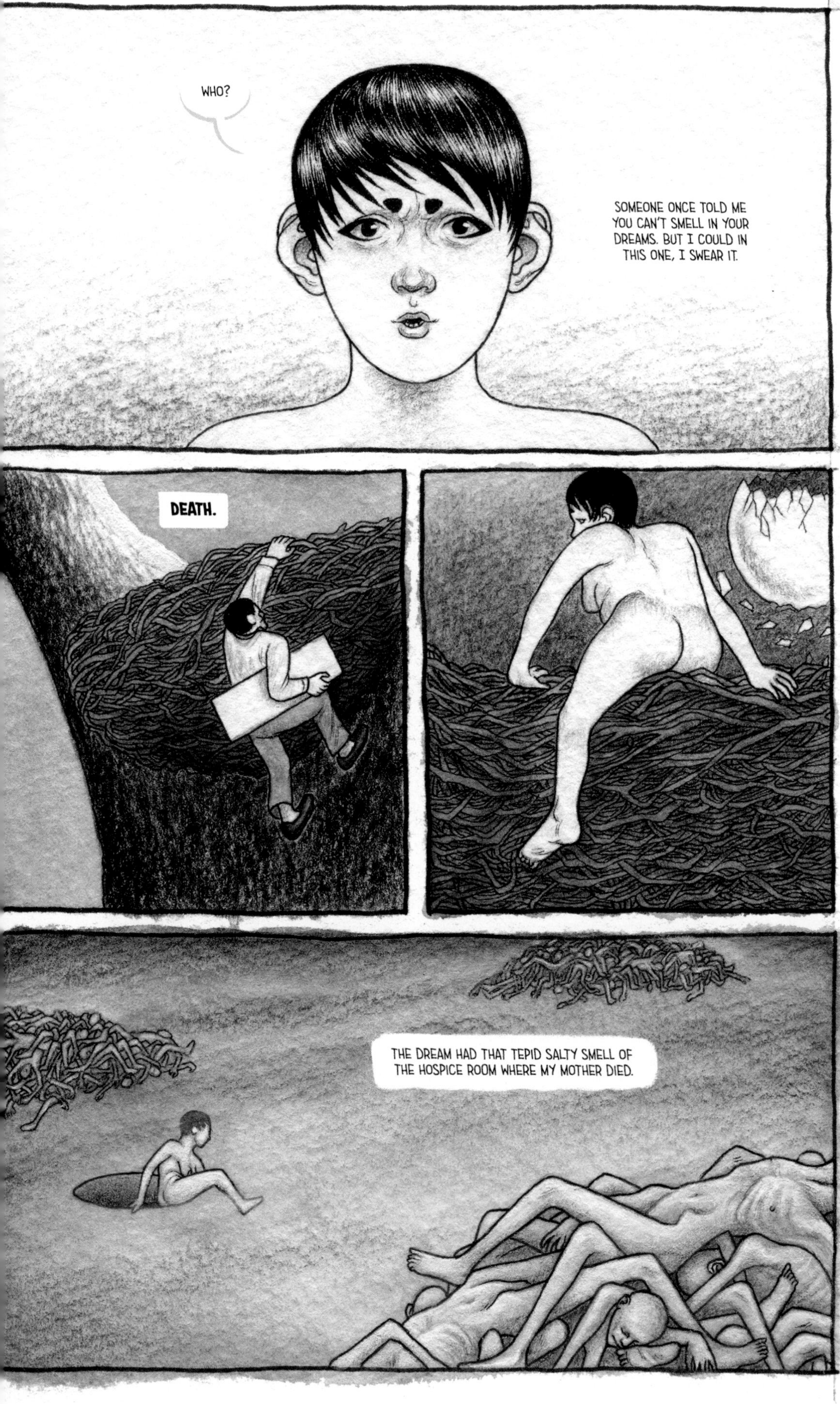
WHO?
SOMEONE ONCE TOLD ME YOU CAN'T SMELL IN YOUR DREAMS. BUT I COULD IN THIS ONE, I SWEAR IT.
DEATH.
THE DREAM HAD THAT TEPID SALTY SMELL OF THE HOSPICE ROOM WHERE MY MOTHER DIED.

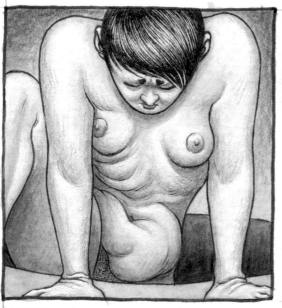

THERE WASN'T MUCH TIME TO PREPARE. WE HADN'T SPOKEN MUCH SINCE SHE LEFT DAD. I WASN'T READY TO LOSE HER.

WHEN SHE DIED I FELT HELPLESS.

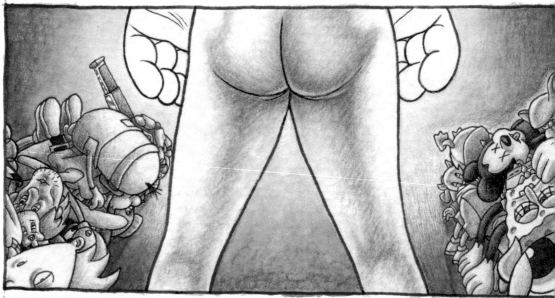

I HAD TO FACE MYSELF I DIDN'T LIKE WHAT I FOUND.

McMoon's
OVER 666
BILLION SERVED

SELFISH, ALWAYS THE VICTIM. BLAME MOM, BLAME DAD, HIDE. ALWAYS RUNNING.

THIS WAS THE LAST DREAM I HAD WITH THE MAN.

WOW! I MEAN, THAT'S A LOT, HUH? FUNNY WHAT THE MIND DOES WHEN WE AREN'T AT THE WHEEL!

WHEN YOU TRIED TO TALK TO HIM, WAS THAT LUCID STUFF? OR WAS THAT THE DREAM?

I HAVE NO CLUE. THE DREAM DID FEEL DIFFERENT THOUGH, EVEN WITH THE WACKY STUFF. IT FELT MORE MY OWN OR SOMETHING.

I COULDN'T FIND ANYTHING HELPFUL IN THE BOOKS.

DREAM DICTIONARIES ARE TRASH ANYWAY. ONE WILL TELL YOU IT'S ABOUT DEATH, THE NEXT ABOUT MONEY, OR THAT YOUR ROOT CHAKRA'S BLOWN OUT.

I GAVE UP TRYING TO FIGURE OUT WHAT THEY MEAN. I JUST DON'T KNOW WHERE SOME OF THIS STUFF IS COMING FROM. SHOULD I LIKE, CALL YOU GUYS IF I SEE THE MAN AGAIN?

THAT WOULD BE *PERFECT*.

THIS CARD HAS OUR OFFICE NUMBER ON IT, YOU CAN CALL ANY TIME. IF NO ONE IS HERE JUST LEAVE A MESSAGE. WE WANT TO REMAIN UP TO DATE ON ANY FURTHER DREAM ACTIVITY.

CAN I ASK ABOUT THE OTHER PEOPLE WHO ARE SEEING THE MAN? LIKE, WHAT ARE THEIR DREAMS LIKE? I'D *REALLY* LIKE TO TALK TO THEM--

I'M AFRAID THAT WOULD BE UNETHICAL. WE *ARE* PUTTING TOGETHER A GROUP THOUGH, I'LL BE SURE TO CONNECT YOU TO THAT WHEN IT STARTS.

THANK YOU SO MUCH, GINN. WE REALLY APPRECIATE YOU COMING IN AND SHARING. I'M SURE WE'LL HAVE A FEW MORE QUESTIONS FOR YOU AFTER WE REVIEW THE INTERVIEW.

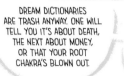

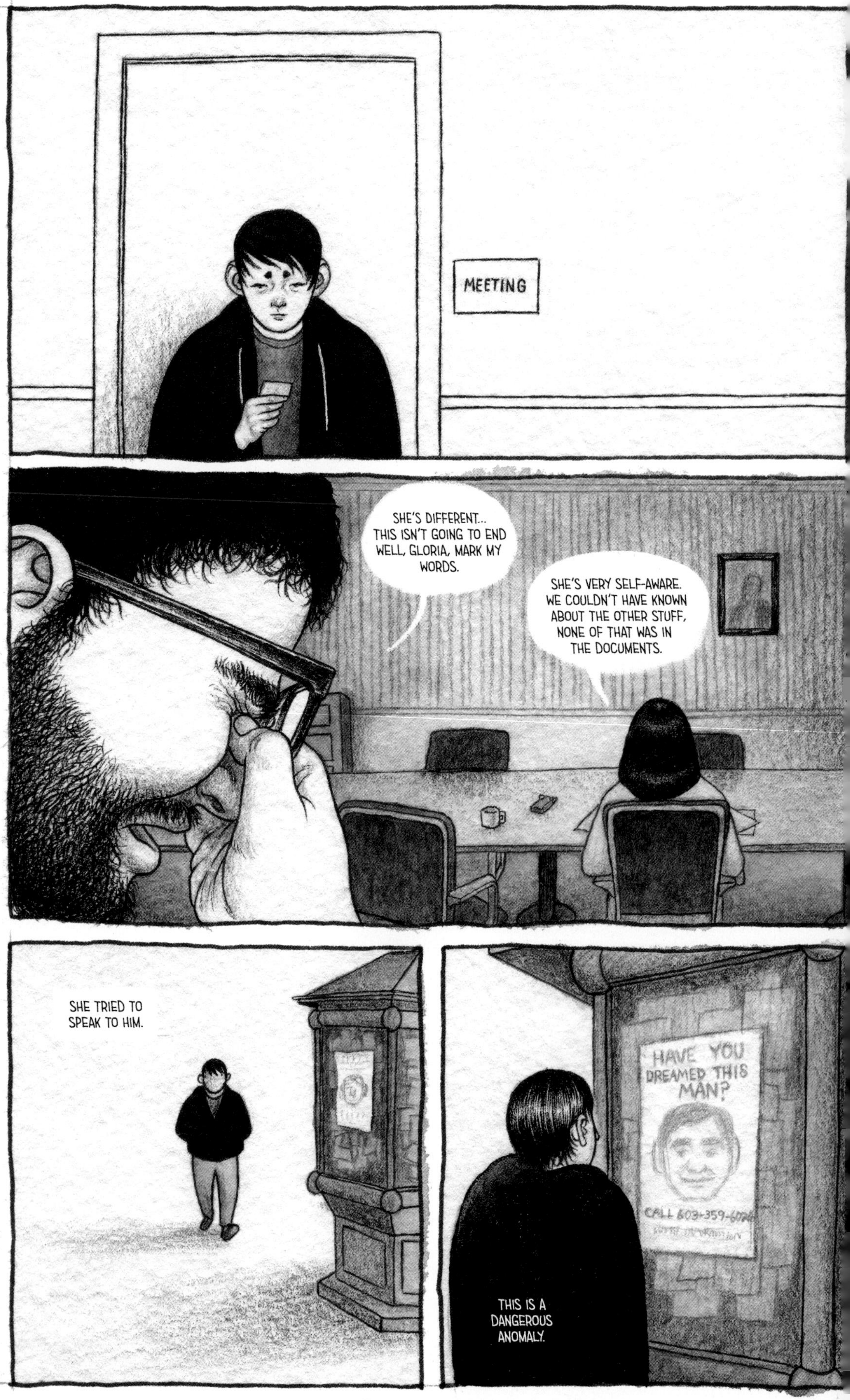
MEETING
SHE'S DIFFERENT... THIS ISN'T GOING TO END WELL, GLORIA, MARK MY WORDS.
SHE'S VERY SELF-AWARE. WE COULDN'T HAVE KNOWN ABOUT THE OTHER STUFF, NONE OF THAT WAS IN THE DOCUMENTS.
SHE TRIED TO SPEAK TO HIM.
HAVE YOU DREAMED THIS MAN?
CALL 603-359-6026
THIS IS A DANGEROUS ANOMALY.

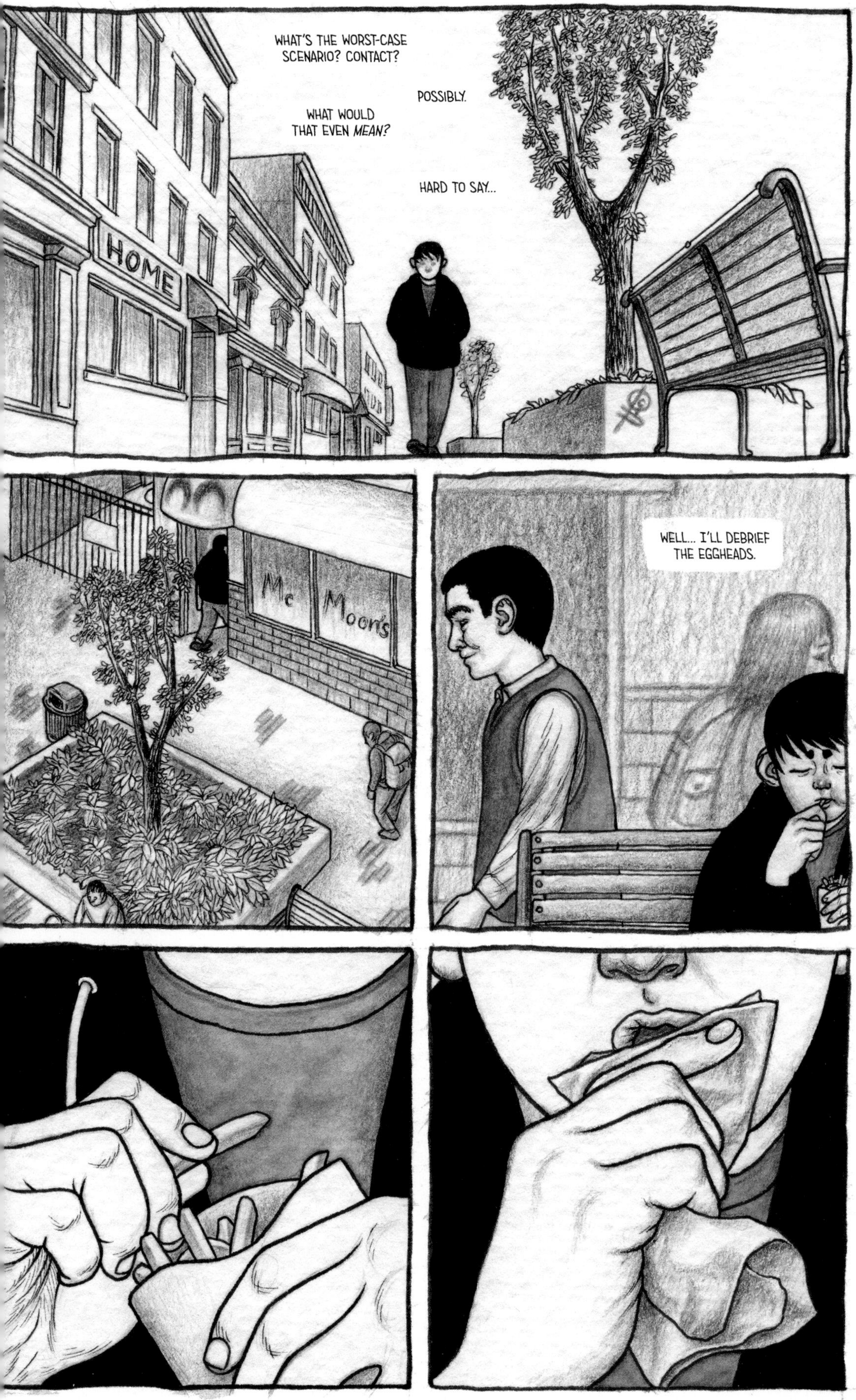
WHAT'S THE WORST-CASE SCENARIO? CONTACT?
POSSIBLY.
WHAT WOULD THAT EVEN *MEAN?*
HARD TO SAY...
HOME
Mc Moon's
WELL... I'LL DEBRIEF THE EGGHEADS.

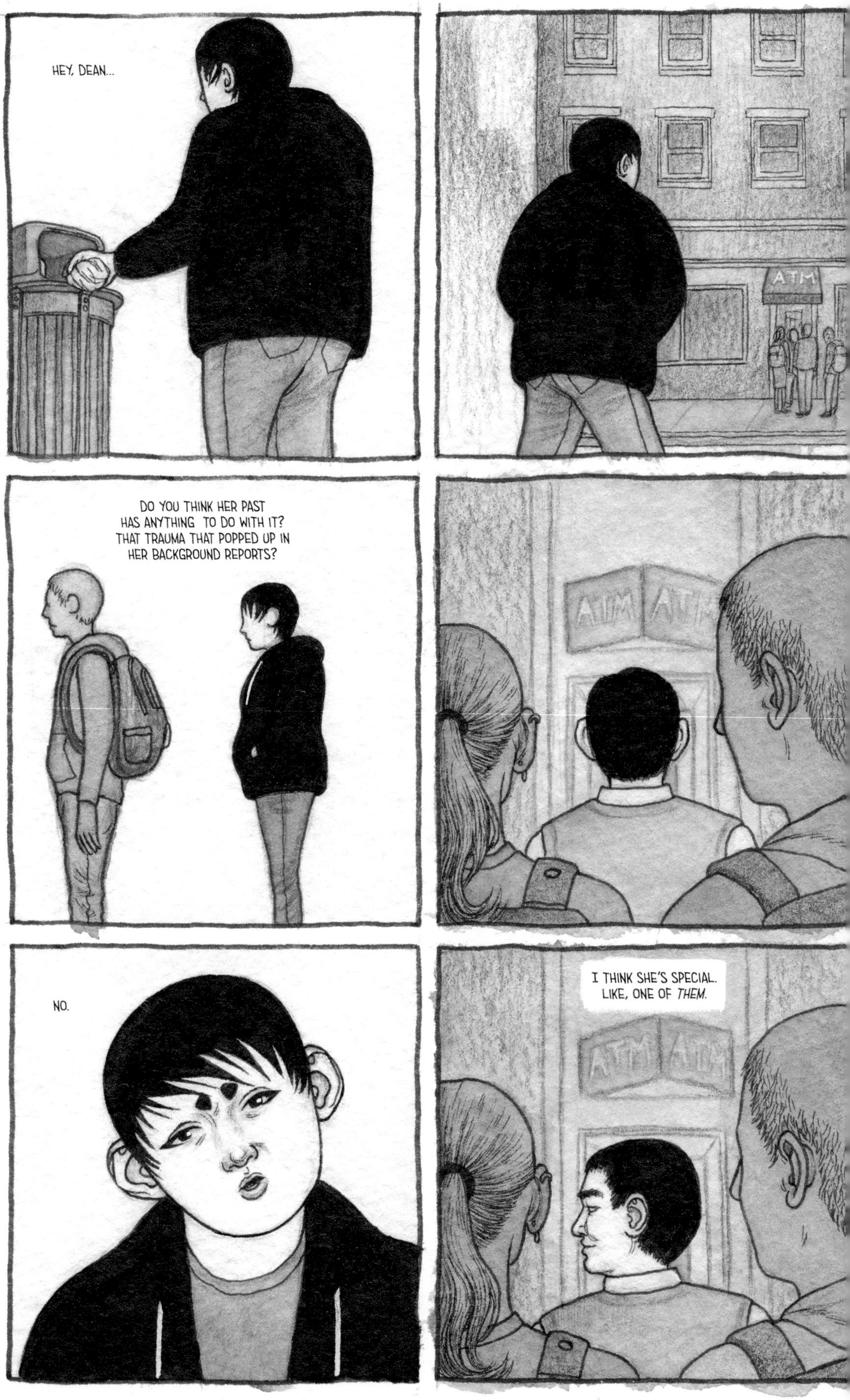
HEY, DEAN...
ATM
DO YOU THINK HER PAST HAS ANYTHING TO DO WITH IT? THAT TRAUMA THAT POPPED UP IN HER BACKGROUND REPORTS?
ATM ATM
NO.
I THINK SHE'S SPECIAL. LIKE, ONE OF *THEM*.
ATM ATM

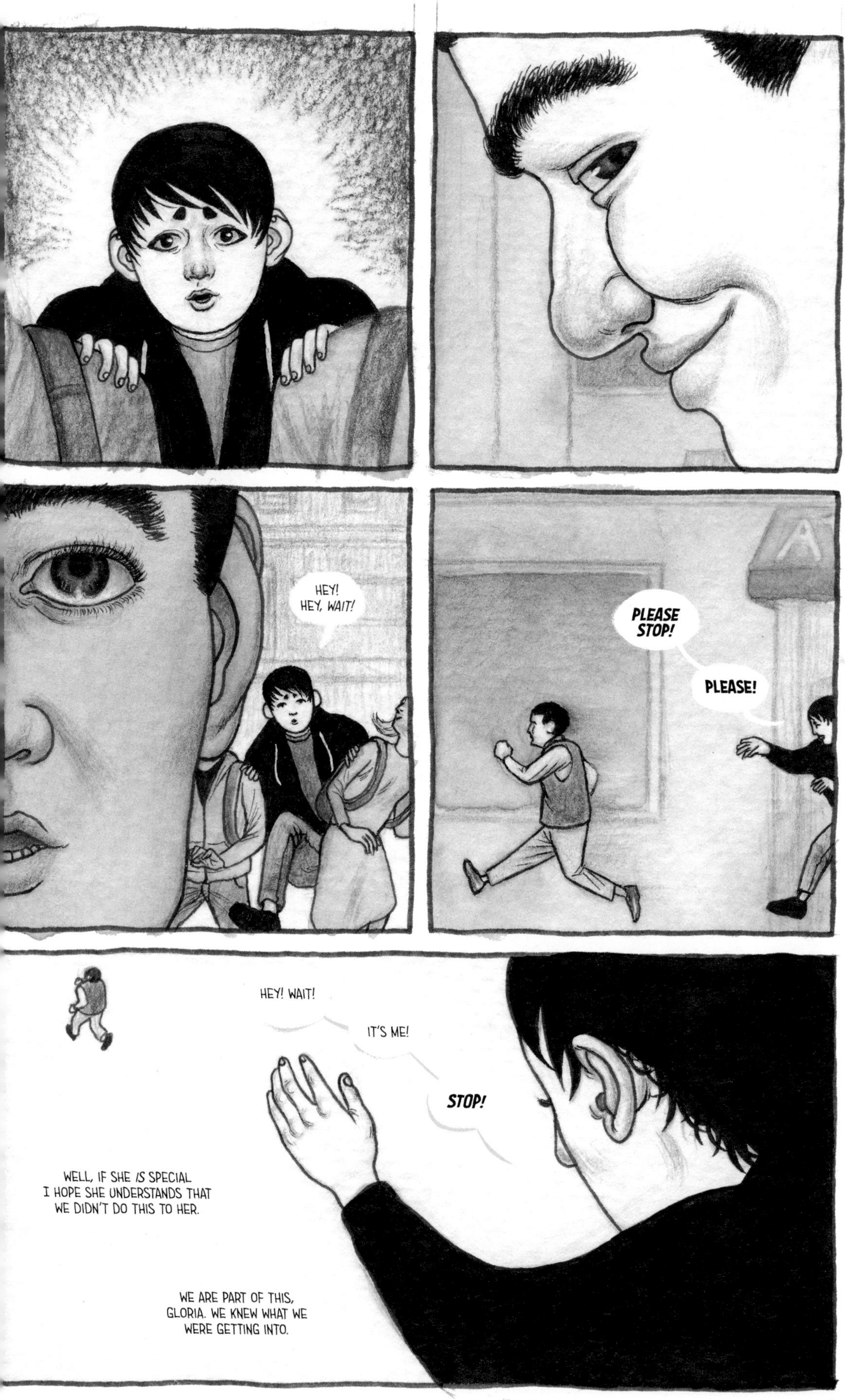
HEY!
HEY, WAIT!
PLEASE STOP!
PLEASE!
HEY! WAIT!
IT'S ME!
STOP!
WELL, IF SHE *IS* SPECIAL I HOPE SHE UNDERSTANDS THAT WE DIDN'T DO THIS TO HER.
WE ARE PART OF THIS, GLORIA. WE KNEW WHAT WE WERE GETTING INTO.

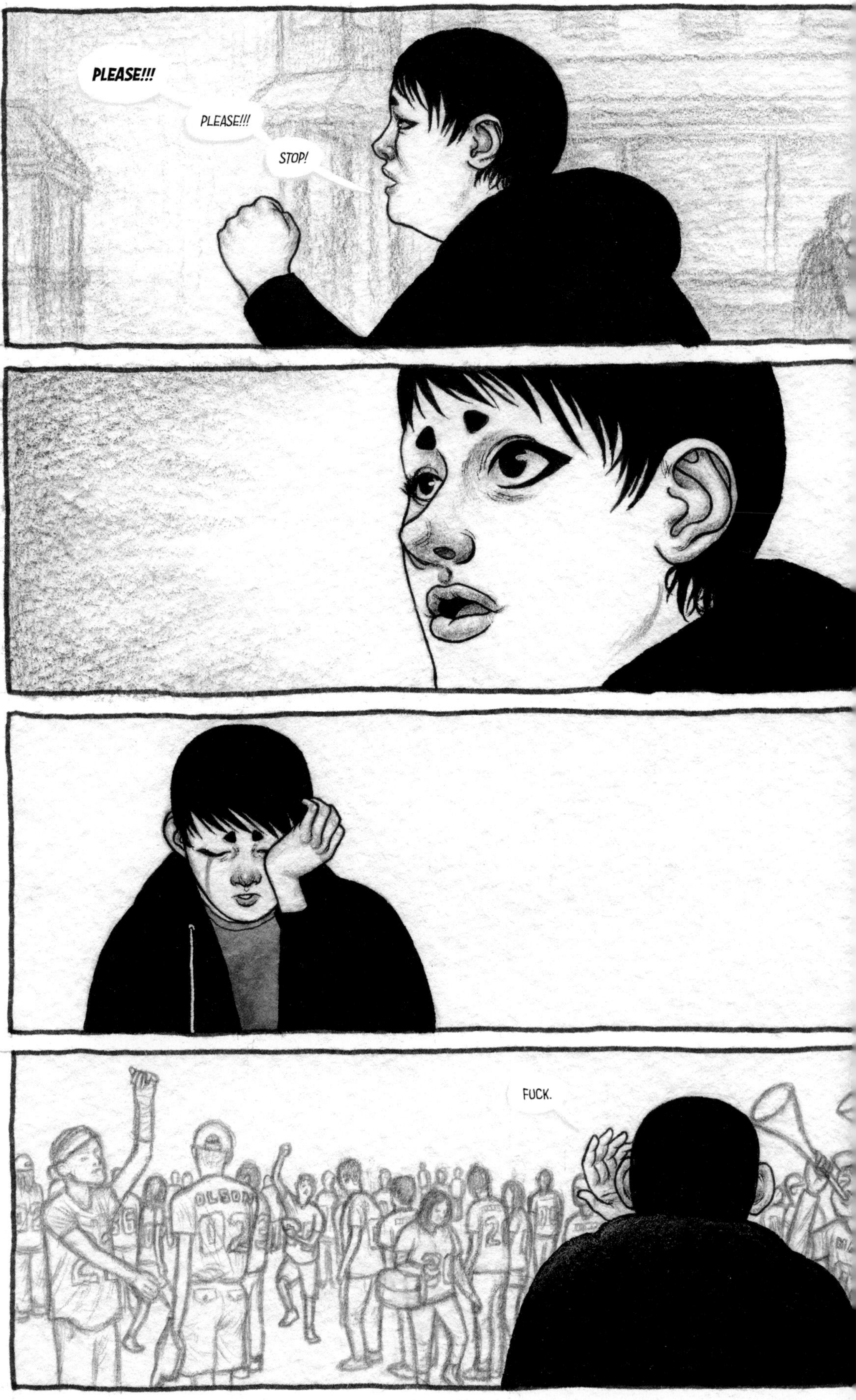
PLEASE!!!
PLEASE!!!
STOP!
FUCK.

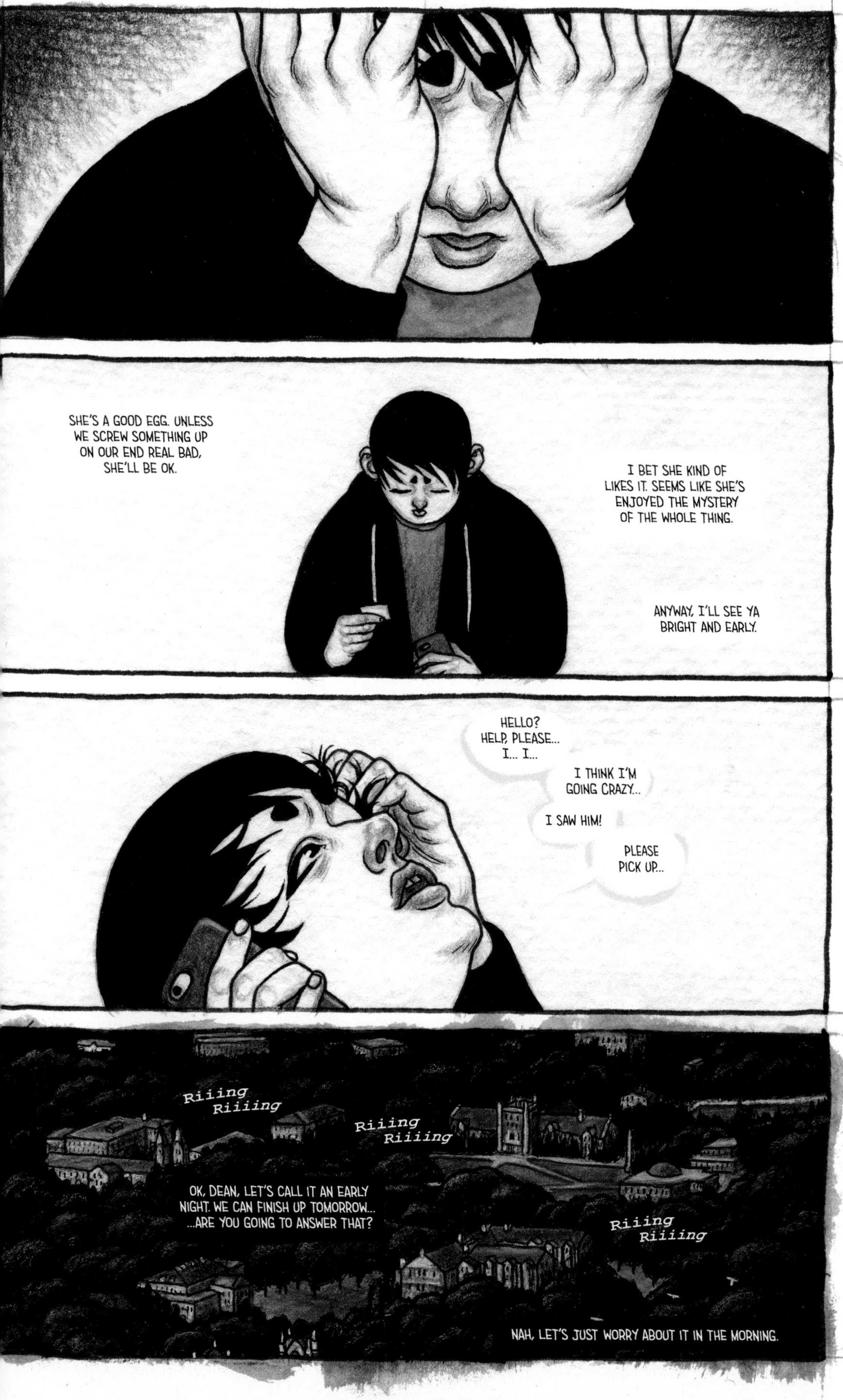
SHE'S A GOOD EGG. UNLESS WE SCREW SOMETHING UP ON OUR END REAL BAD, SHE'LL BE OK.
I BET SHE KIND OF LIKES IT. SEEMS LIKE SHE'S ENJOYED THE MYSTERY OF THE WHOLE THING.
ANYWAY, I'LL SEE YA BRIGHT AND EARLY.
HELLO? HELP, PLEASE... I... I...
I THINK I'M GOING CRAZY...
I SAW HIM!
PLEASE PICK UP...
Riiing Riiiing
Riiing Riiiing
OK, DEAN, LET'S CALL IT AN EARLY NIGHT. WE CAN FINISH UP TOMORROW... ...ARE YOU GOING TO ANSWER THAT?
Riiing Riiiing
NAH, LET'S JUST WORRY ABOUT IT IN THE MORNING.

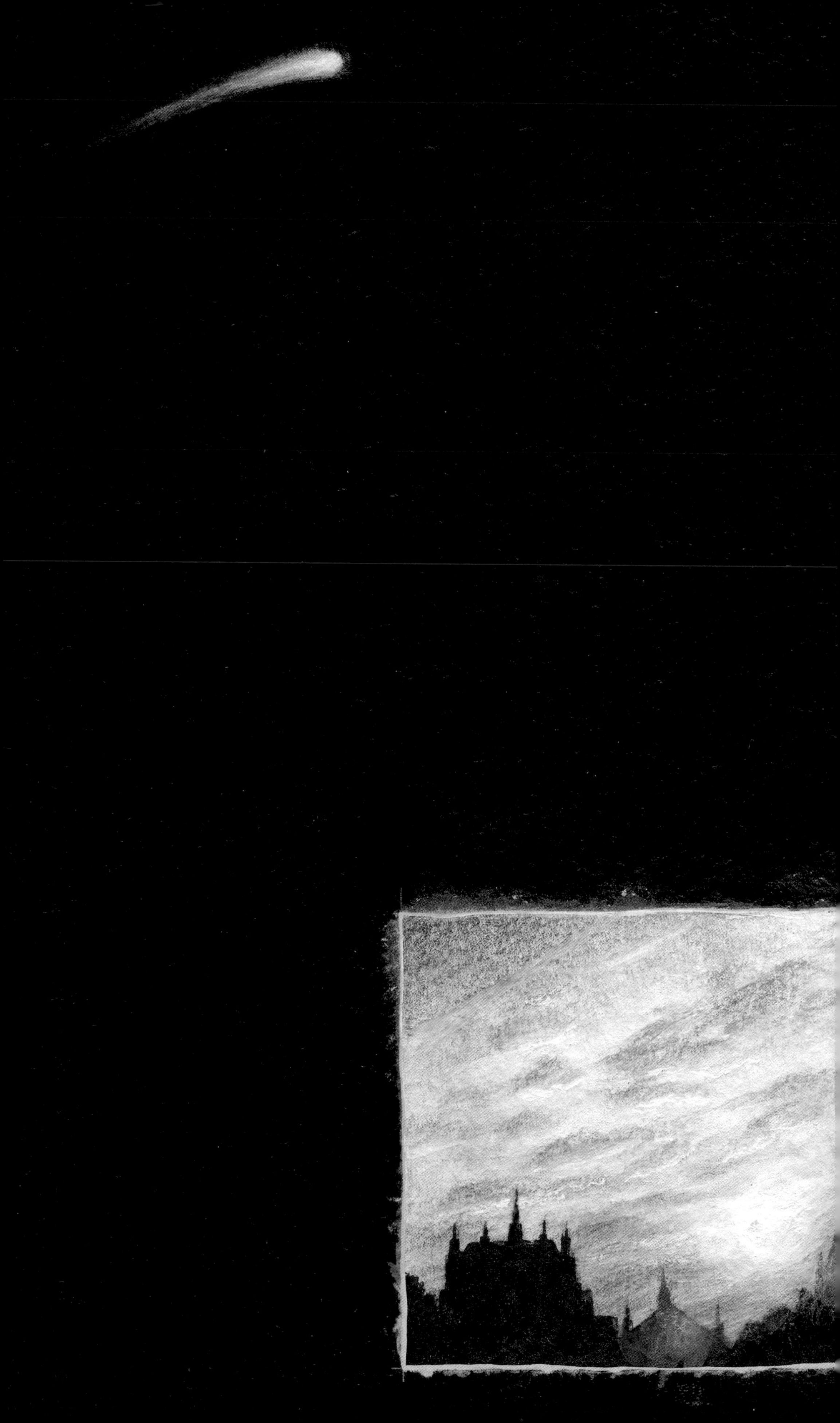

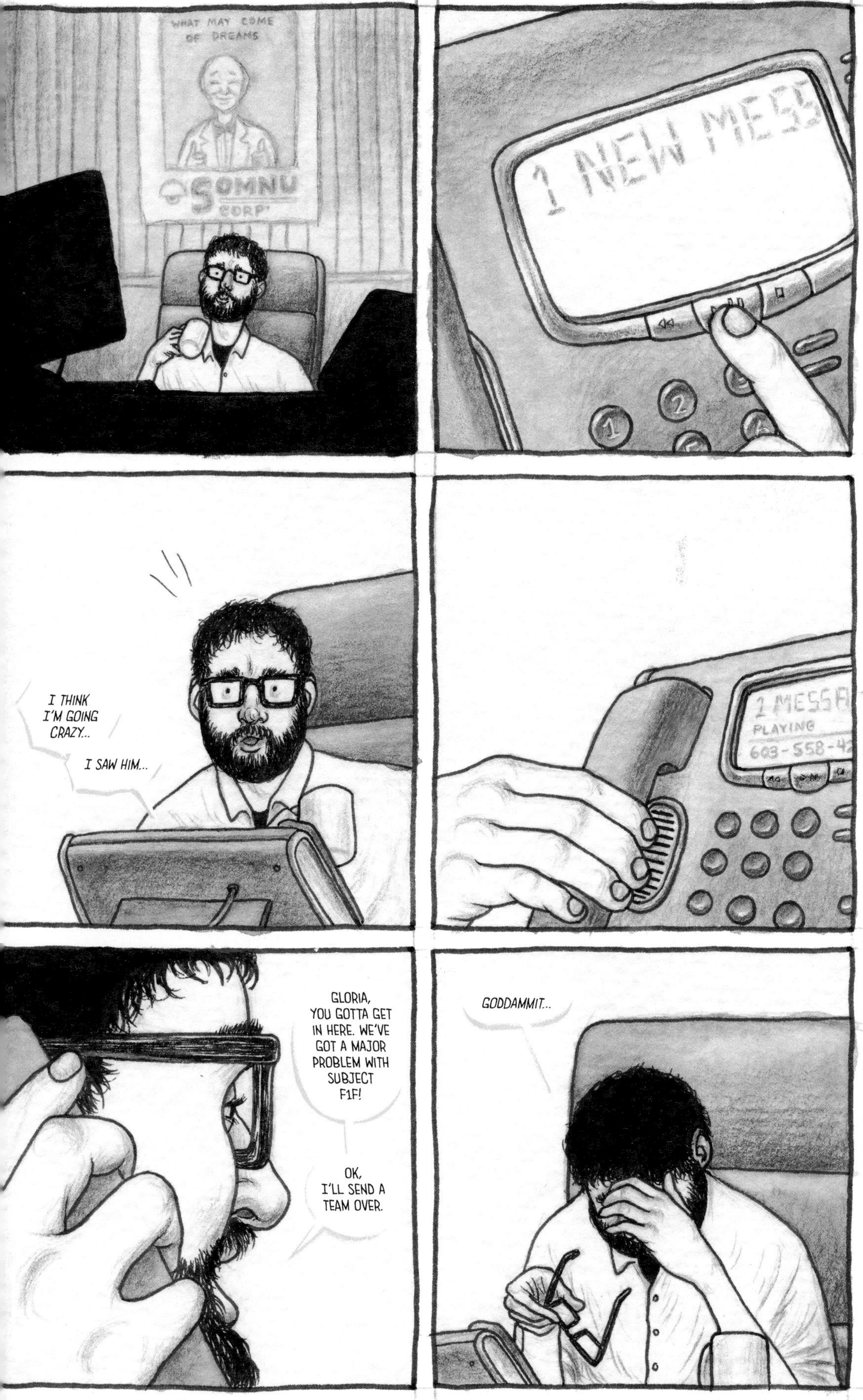
WHAT MAY COME OF DREAMS
SOMNU CORP
1 NEW MESS
I THINK I'M GOING CRAZY...
I SAW HIM...
1 MESSA
PLAYING
603-558-42
GLORIA, YOU GOTTA GET IN HERE. WE'VE GOT A MAJOR PROBLEM WITH SUBJECT F1F!
OK, I'LL SEND A TEAM OVER.
GODDAMMIT...

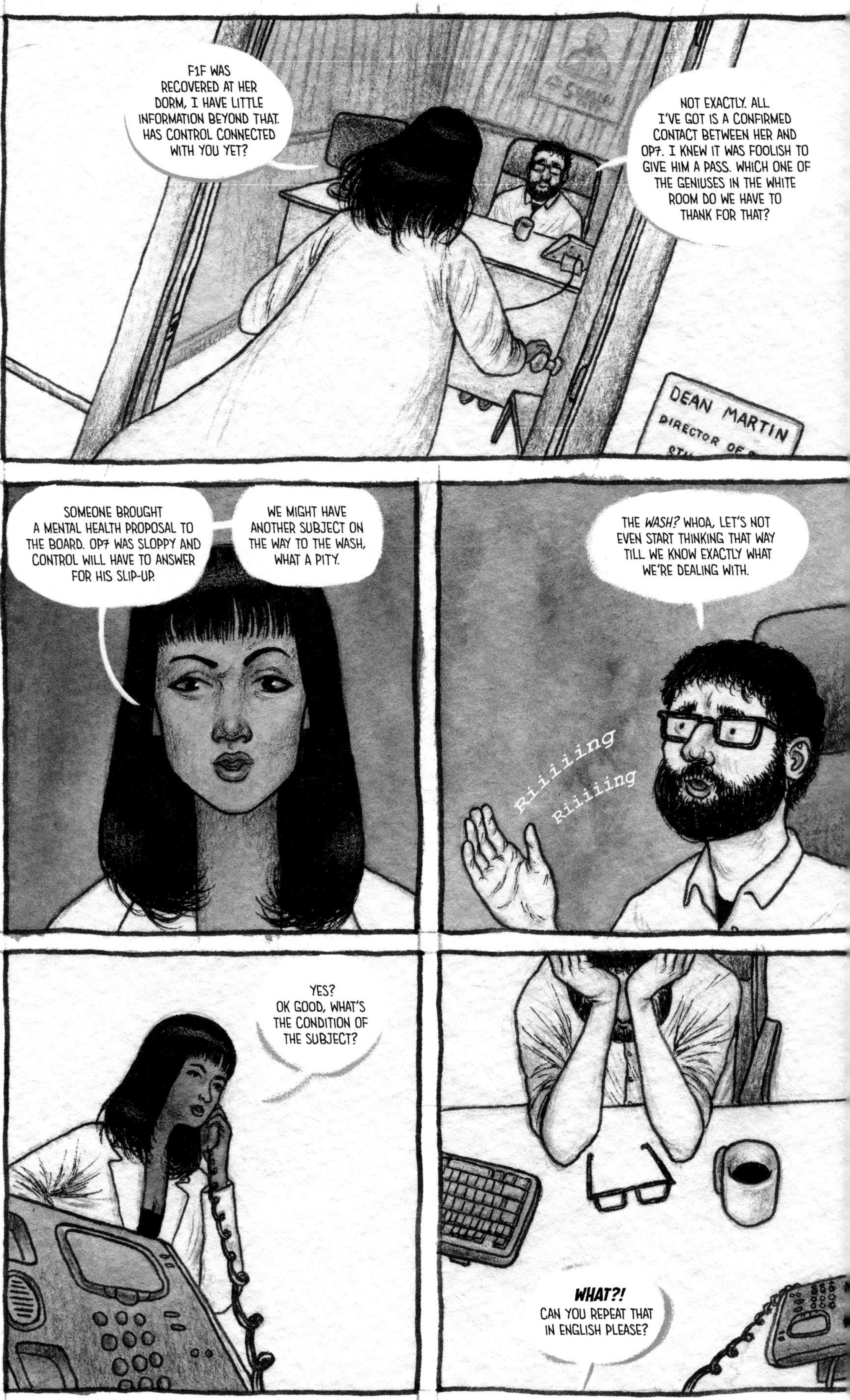
F1F WAS RECOVERED AT HER DORM, I HAVE LITTLE INFORMATION BEYOND THAT. HAS CONTROL CONNECTED WITH YOU YET?
NOT EXACTLY. ALL I'VE GOT IS A CONFIRMED CONTACT BETWEEN HER AND OP7. I KNEW IT WAS FOOLISH TO GIVE HIM A PASS. WHICH ONE OF THE GENIUSES IN THE WHITE ROOM DO WE HAVE TO THANK FOR THAT?
DEAN MARTIN
DIRECTOR OF
SOMEONE BROUGHT A MENTAL HEALTH PROPOSAL TO THE BOARD. OP7 WAS SLOPPY AND CONTROL WILL HAVE TO ANSWER FOR HIS SLIP-UP.
WE MIGHT HAVE ANOTHER SUBJECT ON THE WAY TO THE WASH, WHAT A PITY.
THE *WASH?* WHOA, LET'S NOT EVEN START THINKING THAT WAY TILL WE KNOW EXACTLY WHAT WE'RE DEALING WITH.
Riiiiing
Riiiiing
YES? OK GOOD, WHAT'S THE CONDITION OF THE SUBJECT?
**WHAT?!** CAN YOU REPEAT THAT IN ENGLISH PLEASE?

SHE'S CATATONIC. CONTROL RECOVERED HER IN HER ROOM-- NO, WE HAVE NO IDEA HOW SHE MADE IT BACK, OR WHAT CONDITION SHE WAS IN AFTER SHE LEFT THE MESSAGE.

WE DO HAVE RECORD OF A BRIEF DREAM SHE HAD AFTER THE ENCOUNTER, BUT WE HAVEN'T GOTTEN THE RESULTS BACK FROM THE TECHS YET.

CURRENTLY ALL WE HAVE IS A SIX-MINUTE REM DURATION. SOMETHING CUT IT SHORT. WE DON'T KNOW IF HER CONDITION NOW IS SOMEHOW RELATED TO THE DREAM.

WE AREN'T GOING TO RUSH THIS ONE TO THE WASH, WE HAVE HER IN OBSERVATION FOR NOW.

NO, OP7 HAS NOT BEEN MADE AWARE OF THE STATUS OF F1F. AS FAR AS HE KNOWS, HE JUST FUCKED UP BAD AND IS LOOKING TO MAKE THINGS RIGHT.

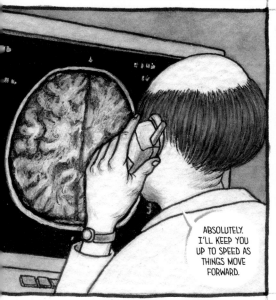

ABSOLUTELY. I'LL KEEP YOU UP TO SPEED AS THINGS MOVE FORWARD.

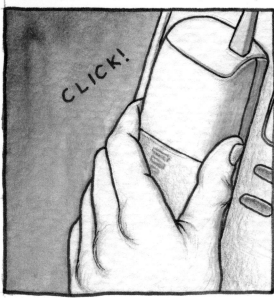

CLICK!

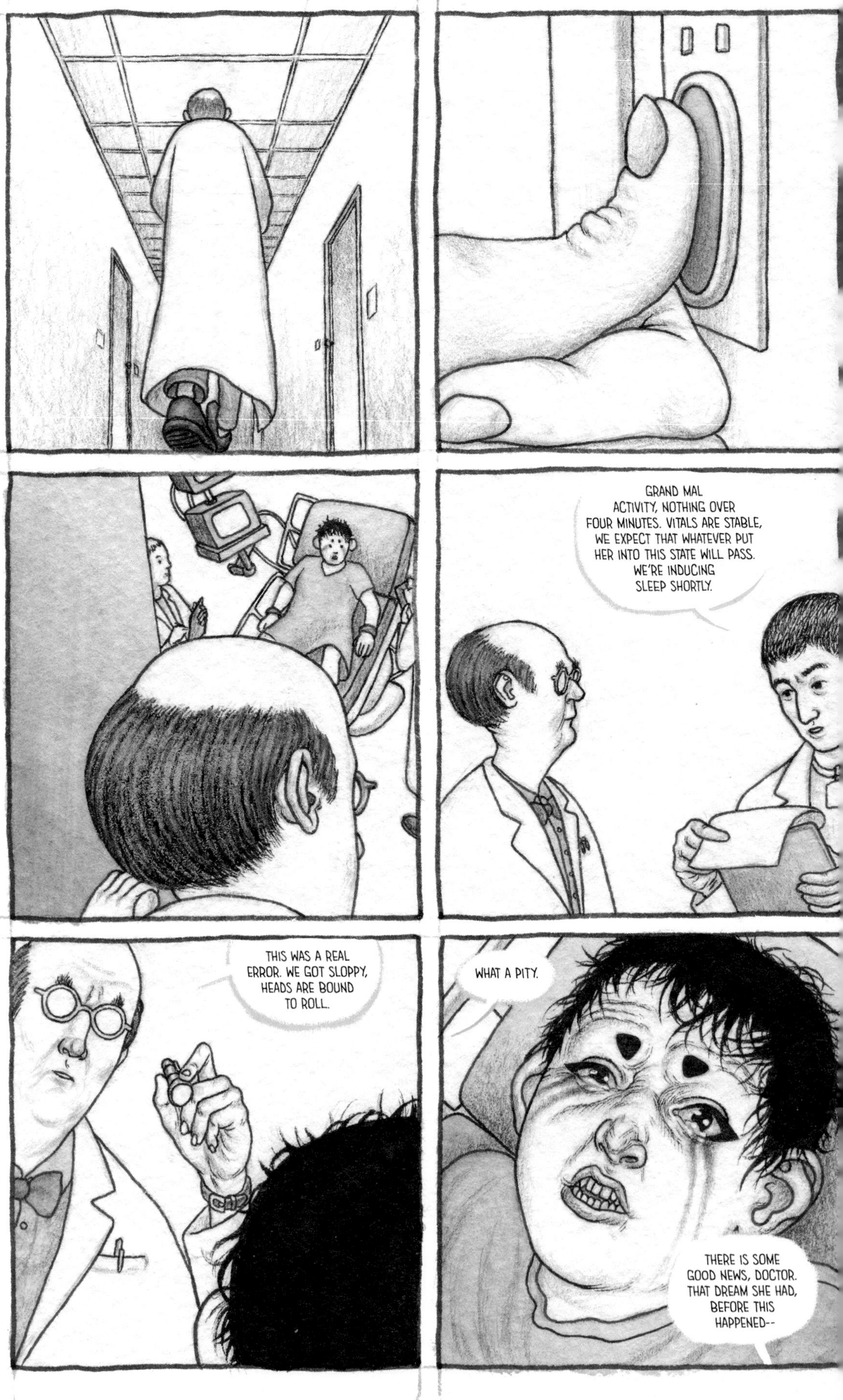
GRAND MAL ACTIVITY, NOTHING OVER FOUR MINUTES. VITALS ARE STABLE, WE EXPECT THAT WHATEVER PUT HER INTO THIS STATE WILL PASS. WE'RE INDUCING SLEEP SHORTLY.
THIS WAS A REAL ERROR. WE GOT SLOPPY, HEADS ARE BOUND TO ROLL.
WHAT A PITY.
THERE IS SOME GOOD NEWS, DOCTOR. THAT DREAM SHE HAD, BEFORE THIS HAPPENED--

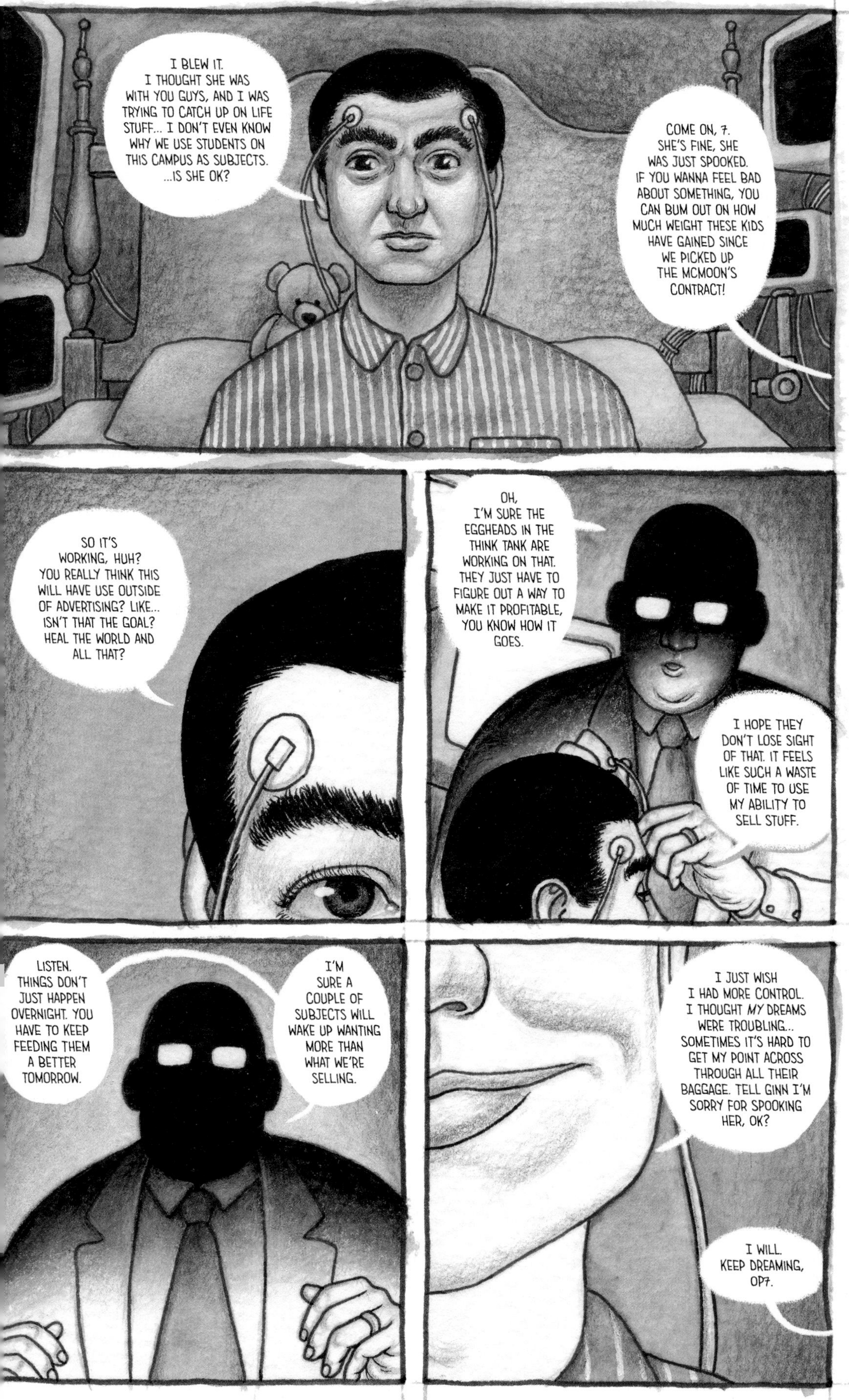
I BLEW IT. I THOUGHT SHE WAS WITH YOU GUYS, AND I WAS TRYING TO CATCH UP ON LIFE STUFF... I DON'T EVEN KNOW WHY WE USE STUDENTS ON THIS CAMPUS AS SUBJECTS. ...IS SHE OK?
COME ON, 7. SHE'S FINE, SHE WAS JUST SPOOKED. IF YOU WANNA FEEL BAD ABOUT SOMETHING, YOU CAN BUM OUT ON HOW MUCH WEIGHT THESE KIDS HAVE GAINED SINCE WE PICKED UP THE MCMOON'S CONTRACT!
SO IT'S WORKING, HUH? YOU REALLY THINK THIS WILL HAVE USE OUTSIDE OF ADVERTISING? LIKE... ISN'T THAT THE GOAL? HEAL THE WORLD AND ALL THAT?
OH, I'M SURE THE EGGHEADS IN THE THINK TANK ARE WORKING ON THAT. THEY JUST HAVE TO FIGURE OUT A WAY TO MAKE IT PROFITABLE, YOU KNOW HOW IT GOES.
I HOPE THEY DON'T LOSE SIGHT OF THAT. IT FEELS LIKE SUCH A WASTE OF TIME TO USE MY ABILITY TO SELL STUFF.
LISTEN. THINGS DON'T JUST HAPPEN OVERNIGHT. YOU HAVE TO KEEP FEEDING THEM A BETTER TOMORROW.
I'M SURE A COUPLE OF SUBJECTS WILL WAKE UP WANTING MORE THAN WHAT WE'RE SELLING.
I JUST WISH I HAD MORE CONTROL. I THOUGHT *MY* DREAMS WERE TROUBLING... SOMETIMES IT'S HARD TO GET MY POINT ACROSS THROUGH ALL THEIR BAGGAGE. TELL GINN I'M SORRY FOR SPOOKING HER, OK?
I WILL. KEEP DREAMING, OP7.

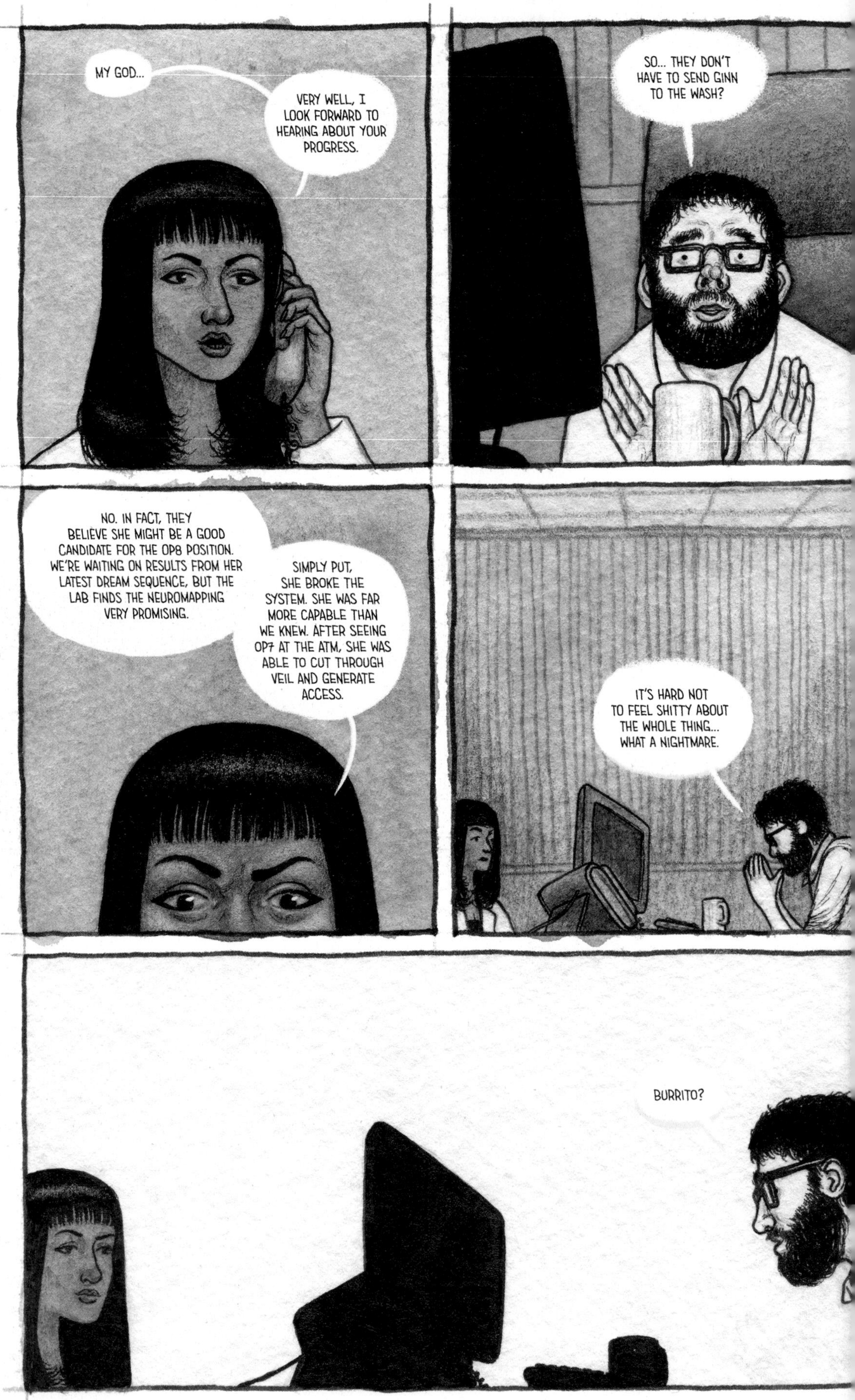
MY GOD...
VERY WELL, I LOOK FORWARD TO HEARING ABOUT YOUR PROGRESS.
SO... THEY DON'T HAVE TO SEND GINN TO THE WASH?
NO. IN FACT, THEY BELIEVE SHE MIGHT BE A GOOD CANDIDATE FOR THE OP8 POSITION. WE'RE WAITING ON RESULTS FROM HER LATEST DREAM SEQUENCE, BUT THE LAB FINDS THE NEUROMAPPING VERY PROMISING.
SIMPLY PUT, SHE BROKE THE SYSTEM. SHE WAS FAR MORE CAPABLE THAN WE KNEW. AFTER SEEING OP7 AT THE ATM, SHE WAS ABLE TO CUT THROUGH VEIL AND GENERATE ACCESS.
IT'S HARD NOT TO FEEL SHITTY ABOUT THE WHOLE THING... WHAT A NIGHTMARE.
BURRITO?

# PART II

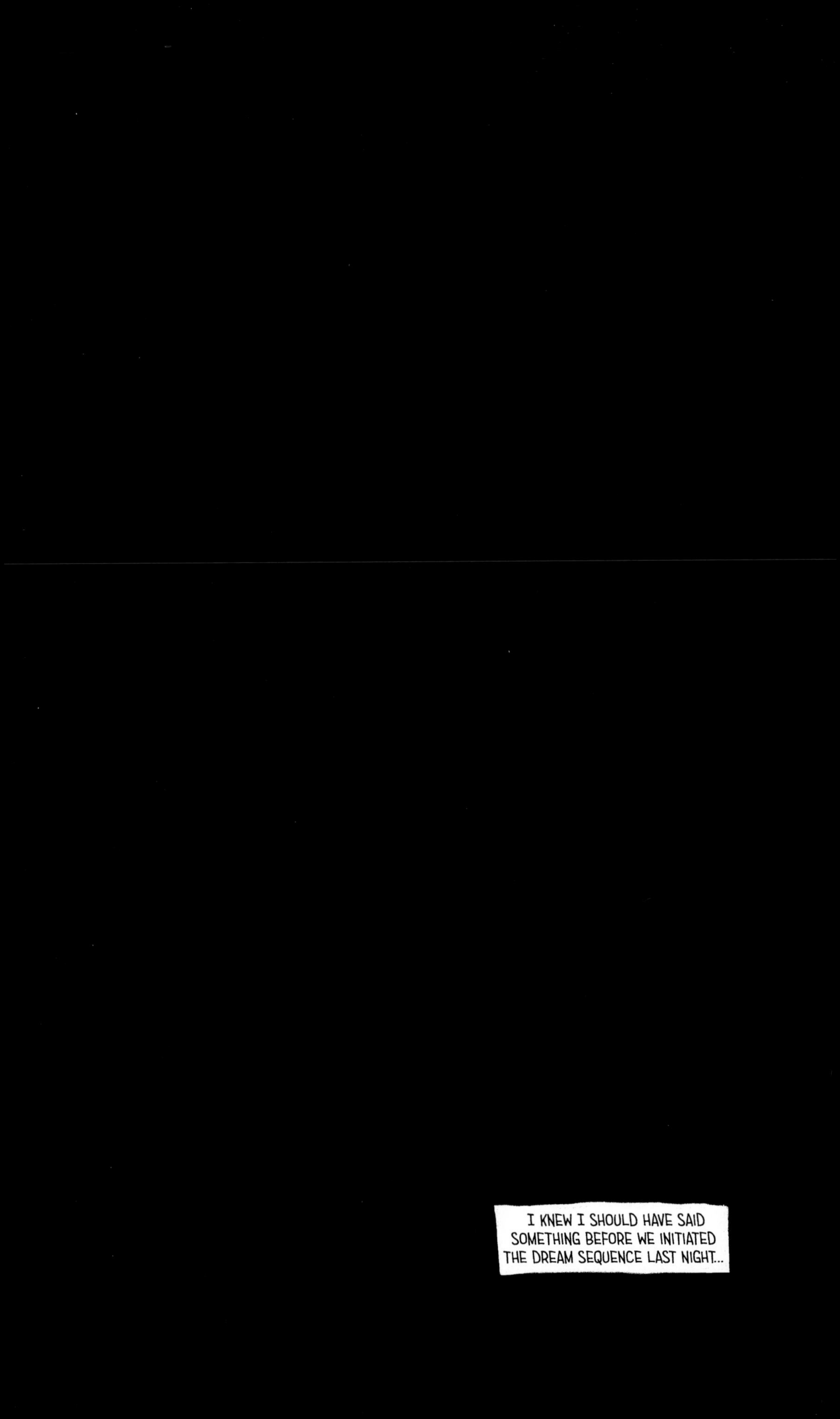
I KNEW I SHOULD HAVE SAID SOMETHING BEFORE WE INITIATED THE DREAM SEQUENCE LAST NIGHT...

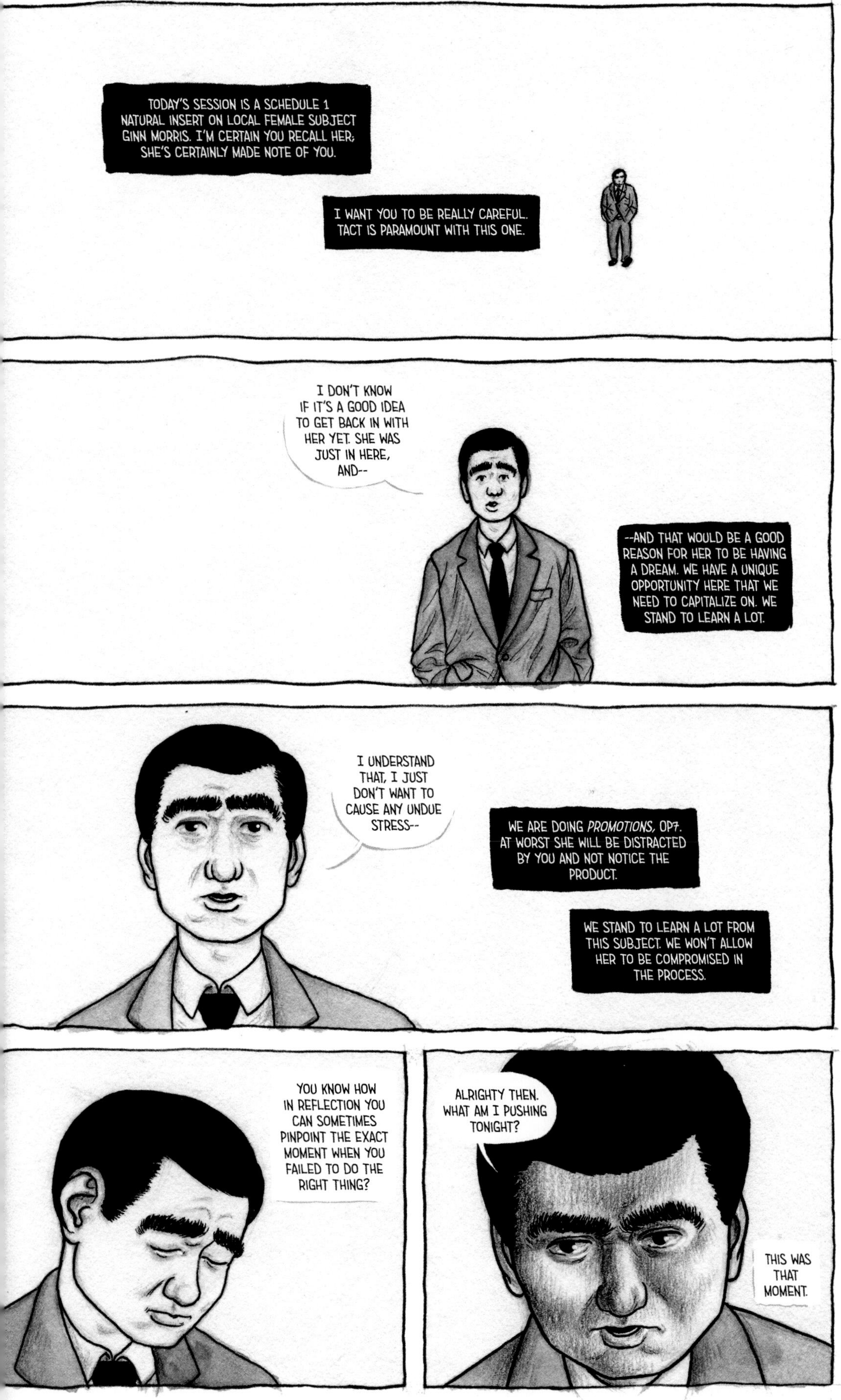
TODAY'S SESSION IS A SCHEDULE 1 NATURAL INSERT ON LOCAL FEMALE SUBJECT GINN MORRIS. I'M CERTAIN YOU RECALL HER; SHE'S CERTAINLY MADE NOTE OF YOU.
I WANT YOU TO BE REALLY CAREFUL. TACT IS PARAMOUNT WITH THIS ONE.
I DON'T KNOW IF IT'S A GOOD IDEA TO GET BACK IN WITH HER YET. SHE WAS JUST IN HERE, AND--
--AND THAT WOULD BE A GOOD REASON FOR HER TO BE HAVING A DREAM. WE HAVE A UNIQUE OPPORTUNITY HERE THAT WE NEED TO CAPITALIZE ON. WE STAND TO LEARN A LOT.
I UNDERSTAND THAT, I JUST DON'T WANT TO CAUSE ANY UNDUE STRESS--
WE ARE DOING *PROMOTIONS*, OP7. AT WORST SHE WILL BE DISTRACTED BY YOU AND NOT NOTICE THE PRODUCT.
WE STAND TO LEARN A LOT FROM THIS SUBJECT. WE WON'T ALLOW HER TO BE COMPROMISED IN THE PROCESS.
YOU KNOW HOW IN REFLECTION YOU CAN SOMETIMES PINPOINT THE EXACT MOMENT WHEN YOU FAILED TO DO THE RIGHT THING?
ALRIGHTY THEN. WHAT AM I PUSHING TONIGHT?
THIS WAS THAT MOMENT.

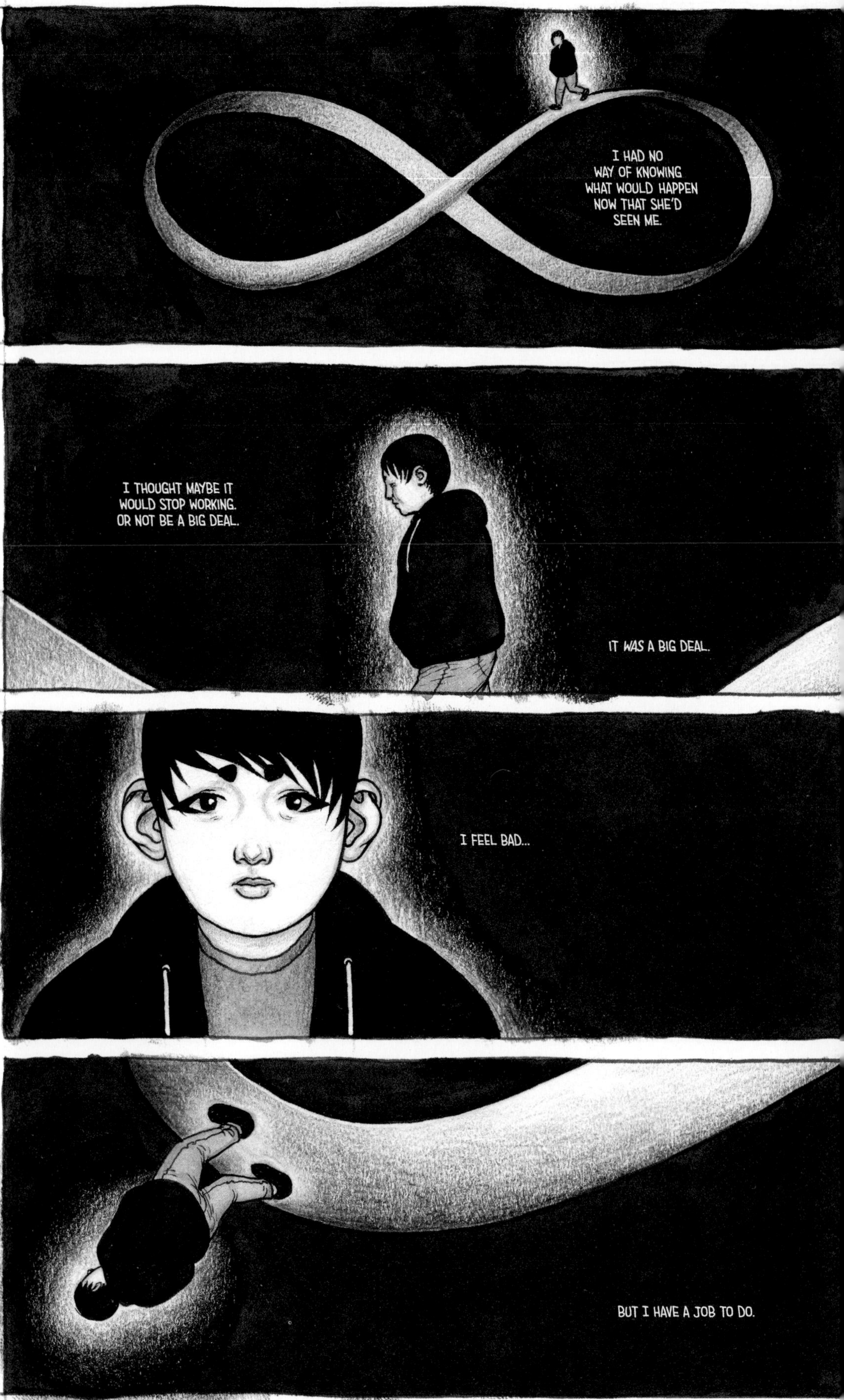
I HAD NO WAY OF KNOWING WHAT WOULD HAPPEN NOW THAT SHE'D SEEN ME.
I THOUGHT MAYBE IT WOULD STOP WORKING. OR NOT BE A BIG DEAL.
IT *WAS* A BIG DEAL.
I FEEL BAD...
BUT I HAVE A JOB TO DO.

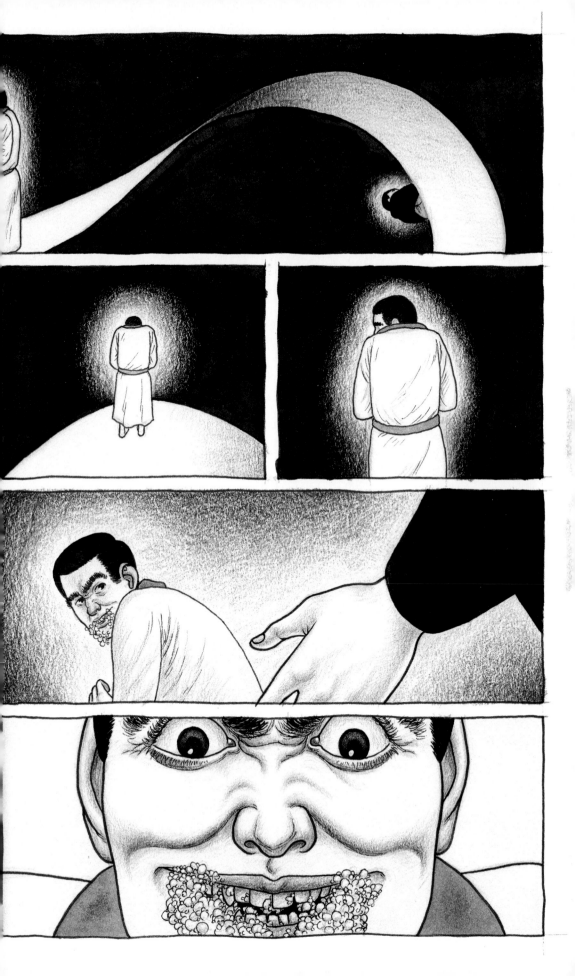

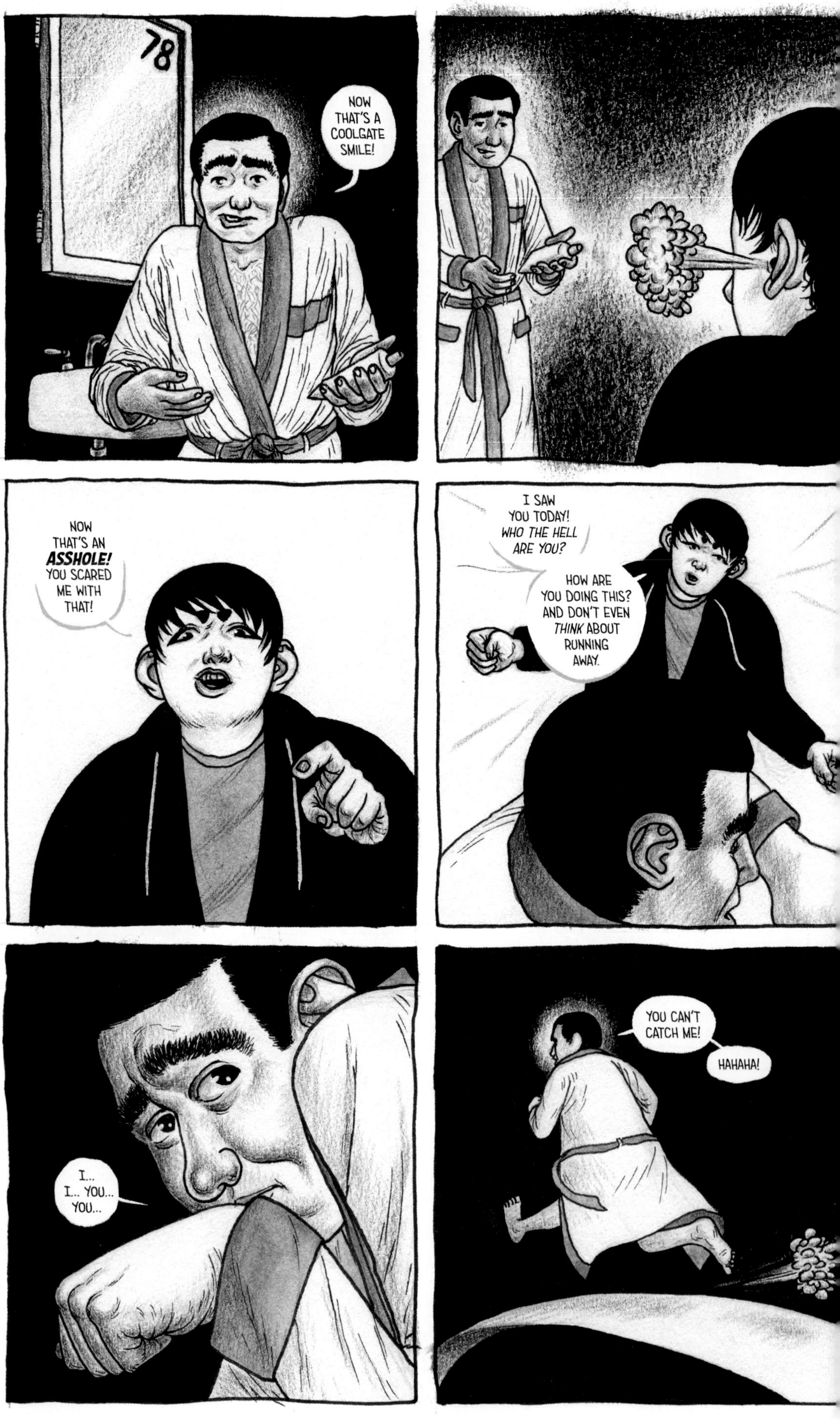
78
NOW THAT'S A COOLGATE SMILE!
NOW THAT'S AN ***ASSHOLE!*** YOU SCARED ME WITH THAT!
I SAW YOU TODAY! *WHO THE HELL ARE YOU?*
HOW ARE YOU DOING THIS? AND DON'T EVEN *THINK* ABOUT RUNNING AWAY.
I... I... YOU... YOU...
YOU CAN'T CATCH ME!
HAHAHA!

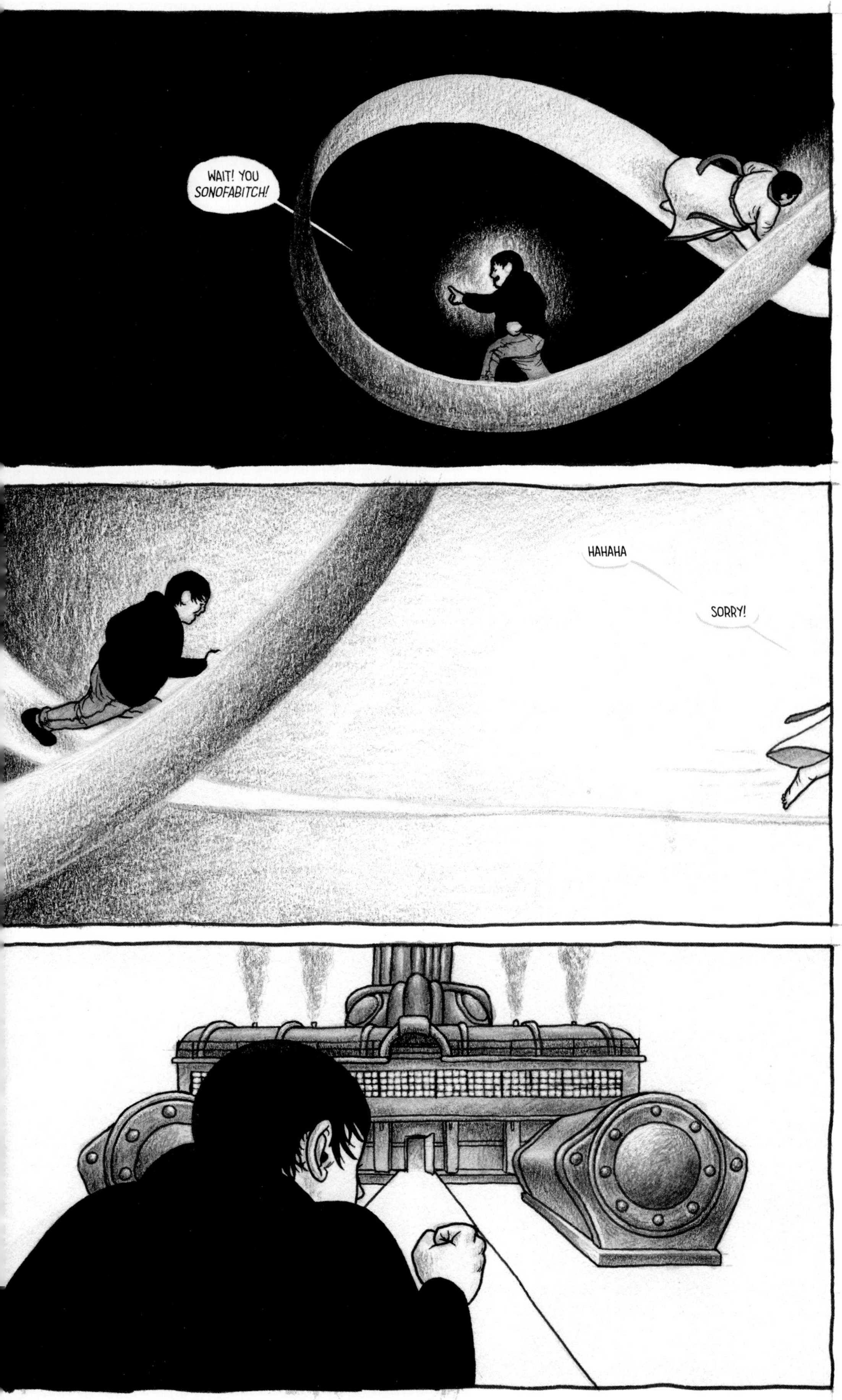
WAIT! YOU SONOFABITCH!
HAHAHA
SORRY!

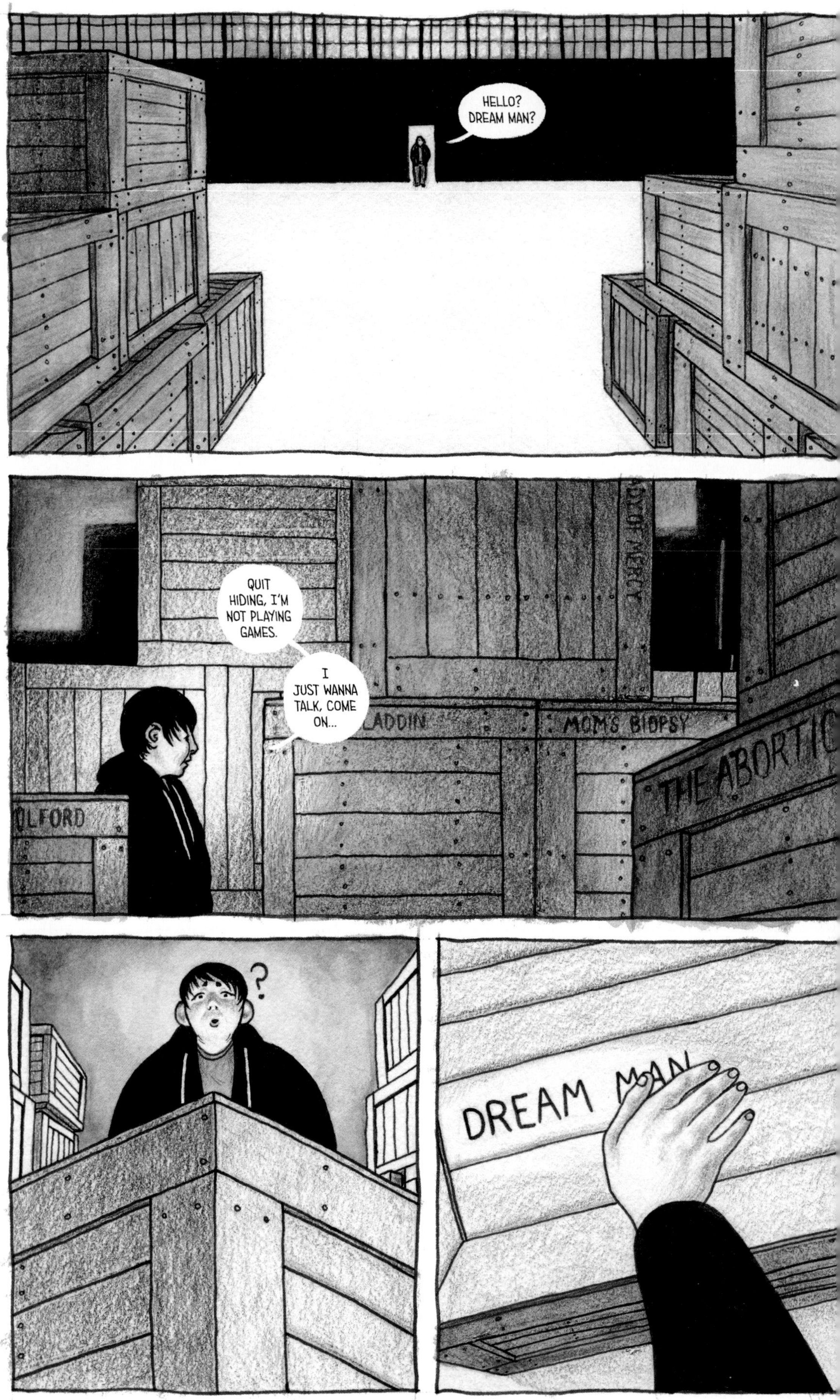
HELLO? DREAM MAN?
QUIT HIDING, I'M NOT PLAYING GAMES.
I JUST WANNA TALK, COME ON...
LADDIN
MOM'S BIOPSY
THE ABORTIO
LFORD
?
DREAM

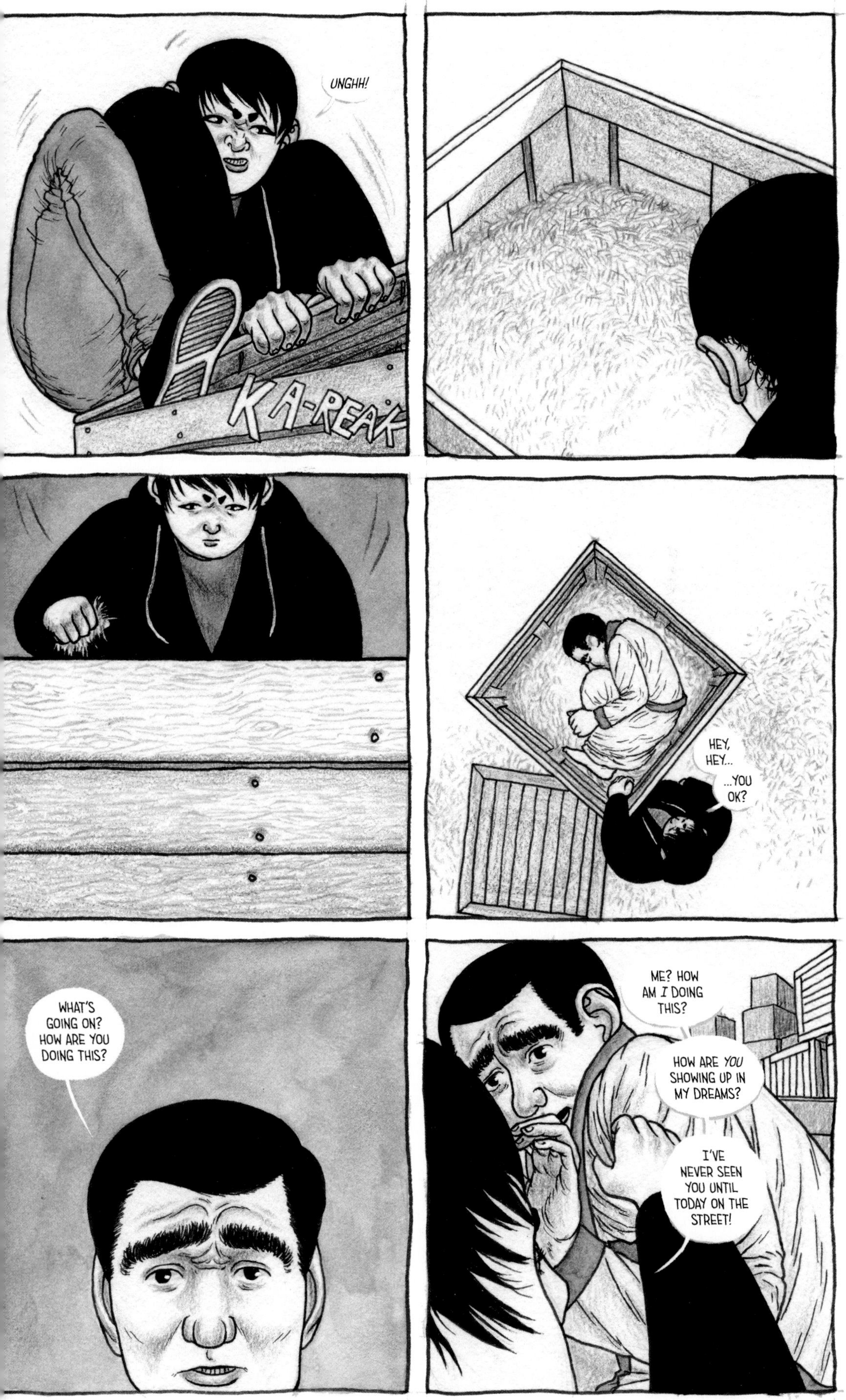
UNGHH!
KA-REAK
HEY, HEY...
...YOU OK?
WHAT'S GOING ON? HOW ARE YOU DOING THIS?
ME? HOW AM *I* DOING THIS?
HOW ARE *YOU* SHOWING UP IN MY DREAMS?
I'VE NEVER SEEN YOU UNTIL TODAY ON THE STREET!

YOU *MUST* HAVE SEEN ME BEFORE. IN THE QUAD, REMEMBER?

NO. THAT'S A LIE AND YOU KNOW IT!

I SWEAR IT. YOU'RE AS MAD AS A MARCH HARE!

OH, LET THE GASLIGHTING BEGIN! WHO *ARE* YOU?

I-I HARDLY KNOW, JUST AT PRESENT... I KNOW WHO I WAS WHEN I GOT UP THIS MORNING, BUT I THINK I MUST HAVE BEEN CHANGED SEVERAL TIMES SINCE THEN.

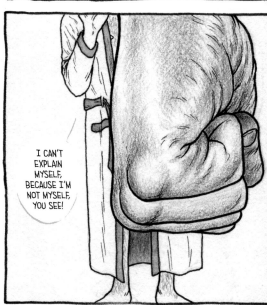

I CAN'T EXPLAIN MYSELF, BECAUSE I'M NOT MYSELF, YOU SEE!

WHAT ARE YOU EVEN SAYING?

STOP! YOU'RE HURTING ME!

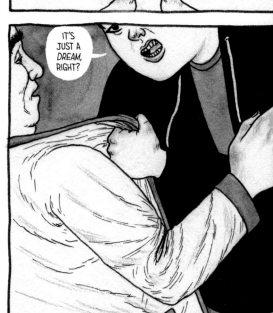

IT'S JUST A *DREAM*, RIGHT?

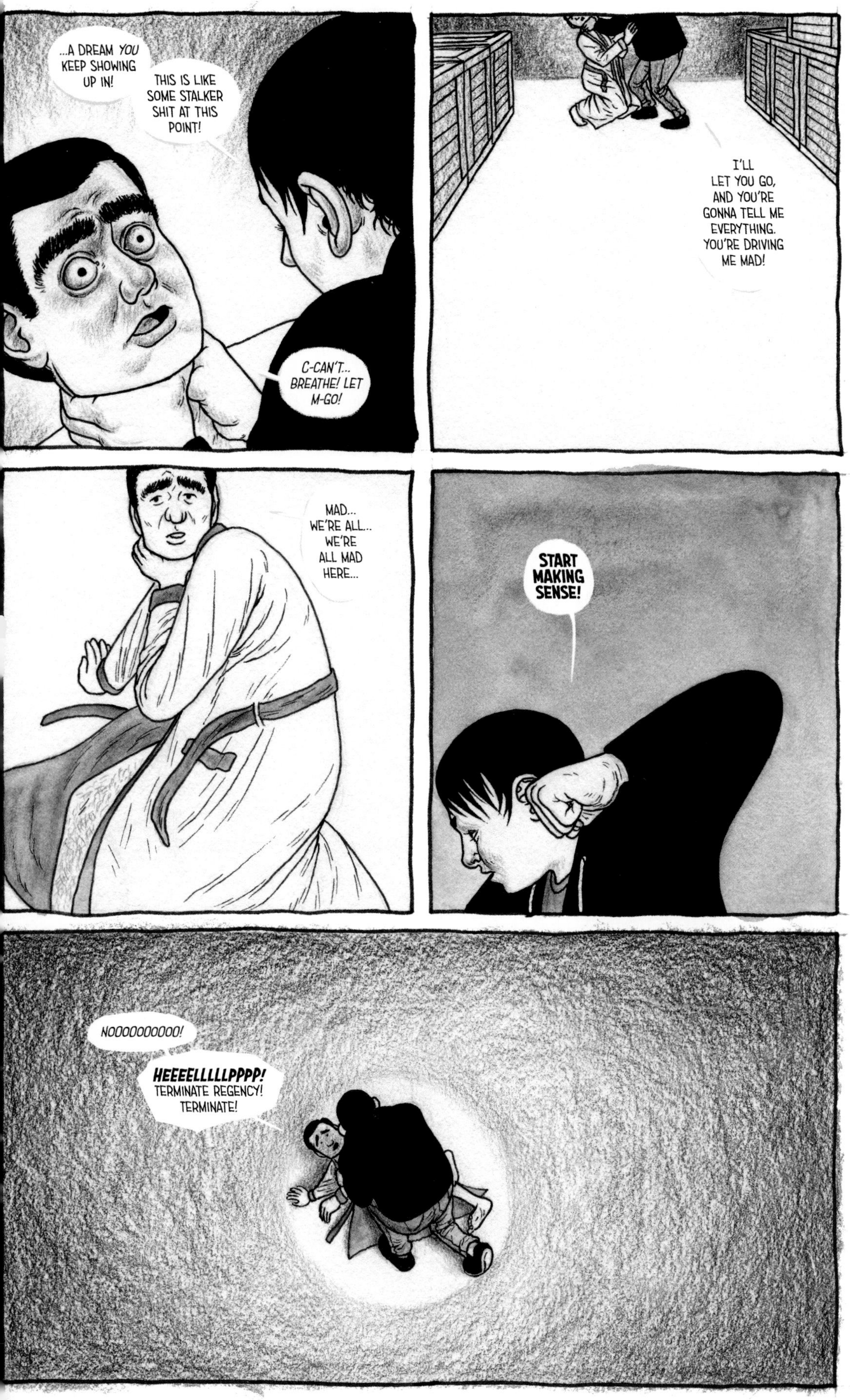

...A DREAM *YOU* KEEP SHOWING UP IN!
THIS IS LIKE SOME STALKER SHIT AT THIS POINT!
C-CAN'T... BREATHE! LET M-GO!
I'LL LET YOU GO, AND YOU'RE GONNA TELL ME EVERYTHING. YOU'RE DRIVING ME MAD!
MAD... WE'RE ALL... WE'RE ALL MAD HERE...
START MAKING SENSE!
NOOOOOOOOOO!
HEEEELLLLLPPPP! TERMINATE REGENCY! TERMINATE!

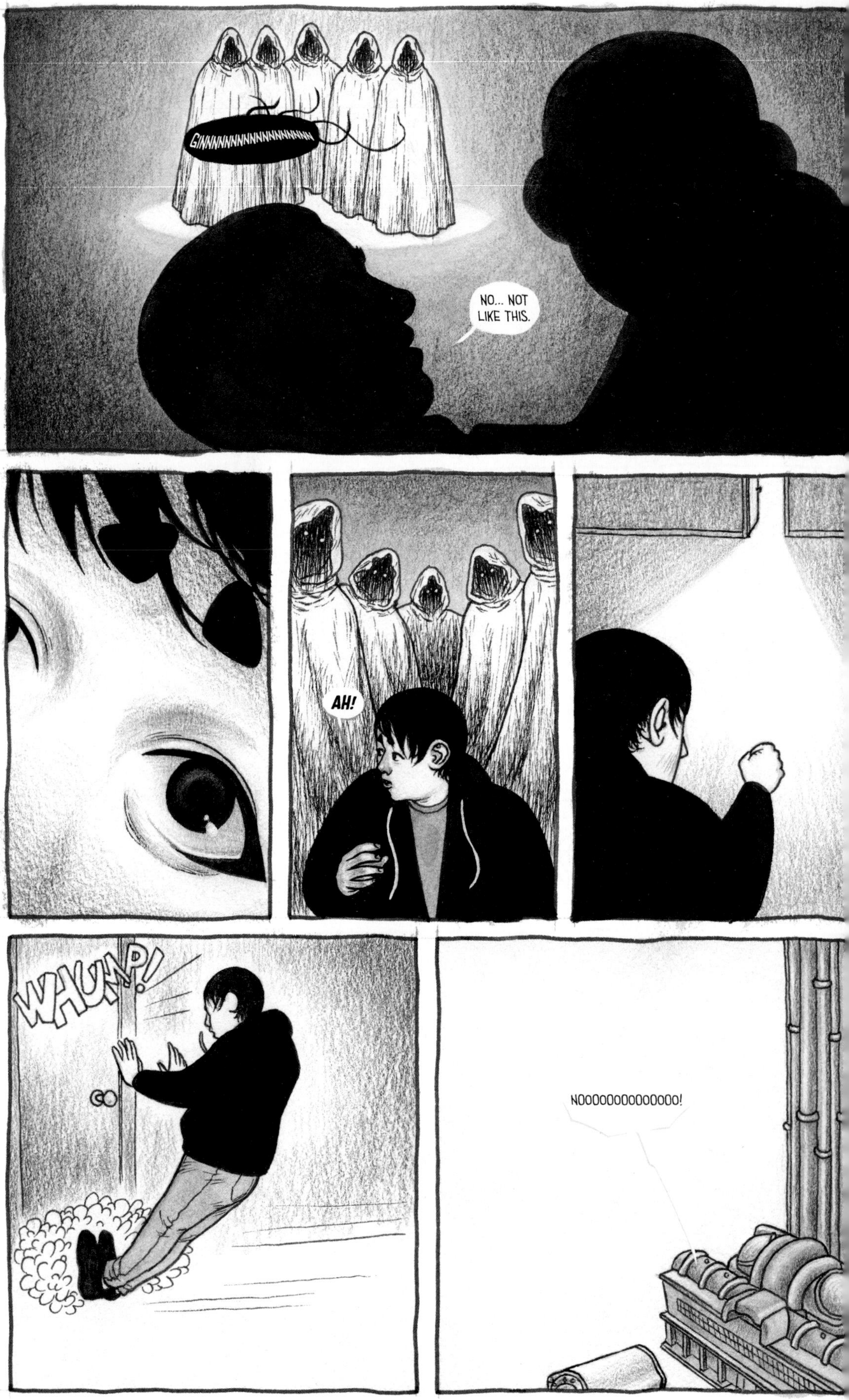
GINNNNNNNNNNNNNNNNNN
NO... NOT LIKE THIS.
AH!
WHUMP!
NOOOOOOOOOOOOOOO!

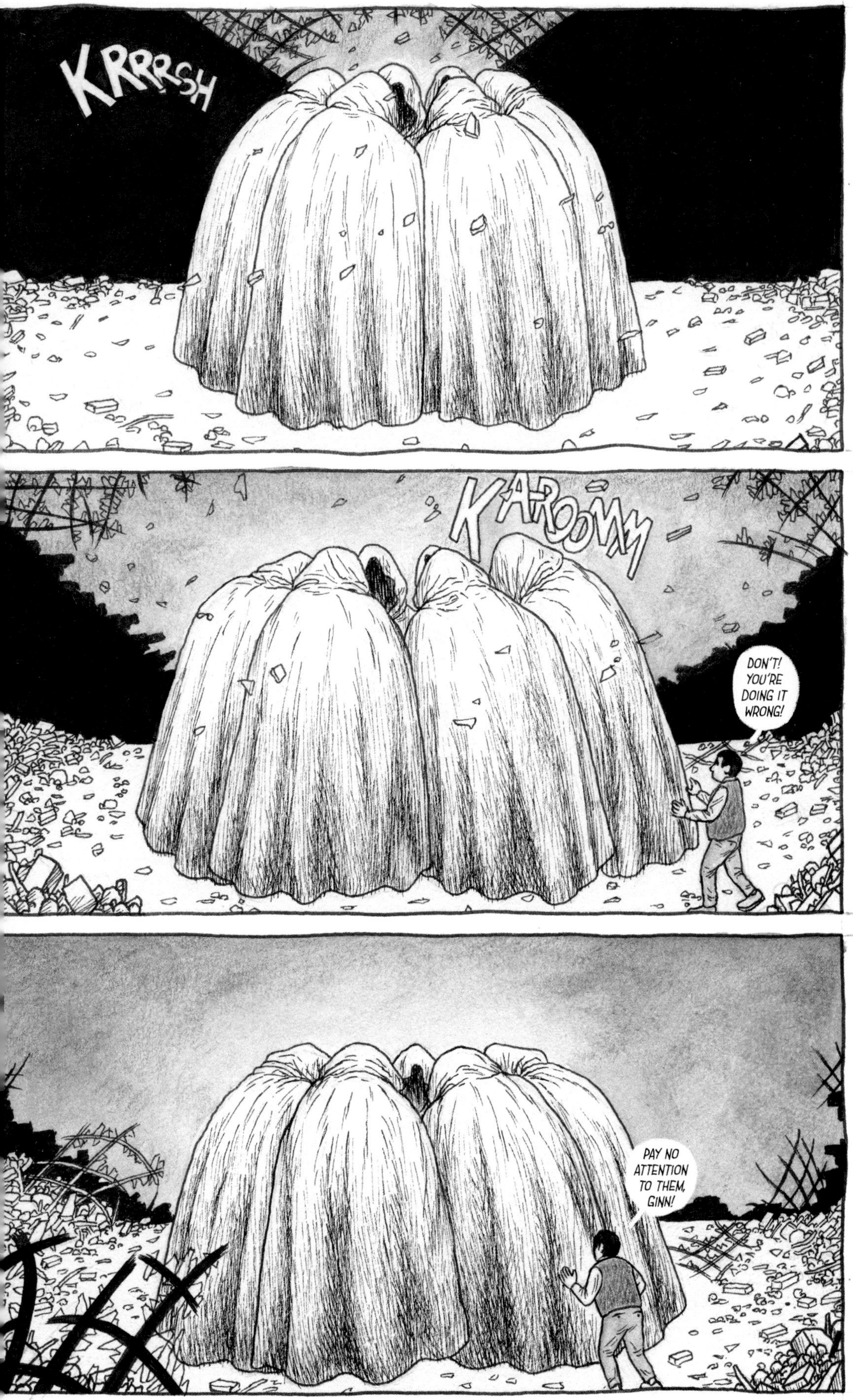
KRRRSH
KAROOMM
DON'T! YOU'RE DOING IT WRONG!
PAY NO ATTENTION TO THEM, GINN!

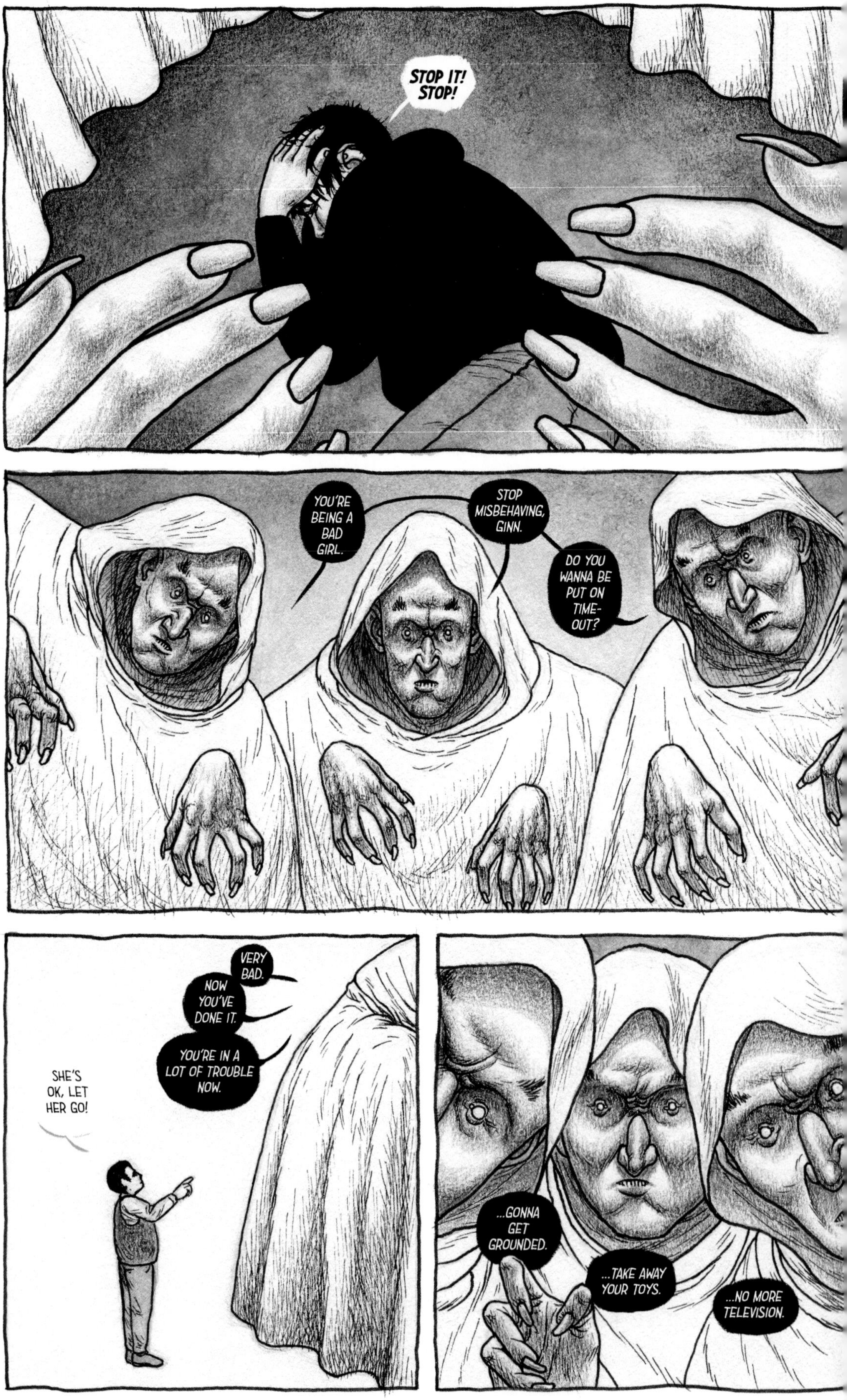
STOP IT! STOP!
YOU'RE BEING A BAD GIRL.
STOP MISBEHAVING, GINN.
DO YOU WANNA BE PUT ON TIME-OUT?
SHE'S OK, LET HER GO!
VERY BAD.
NOW YOU'VE DONE IT.
YOU'RE IN A LOT OF TROUBLE NOW.
...GONNA GET GROUNDED.
...TAKE AWAY YOUR TOYS.
...NO MORE TELEVISION.

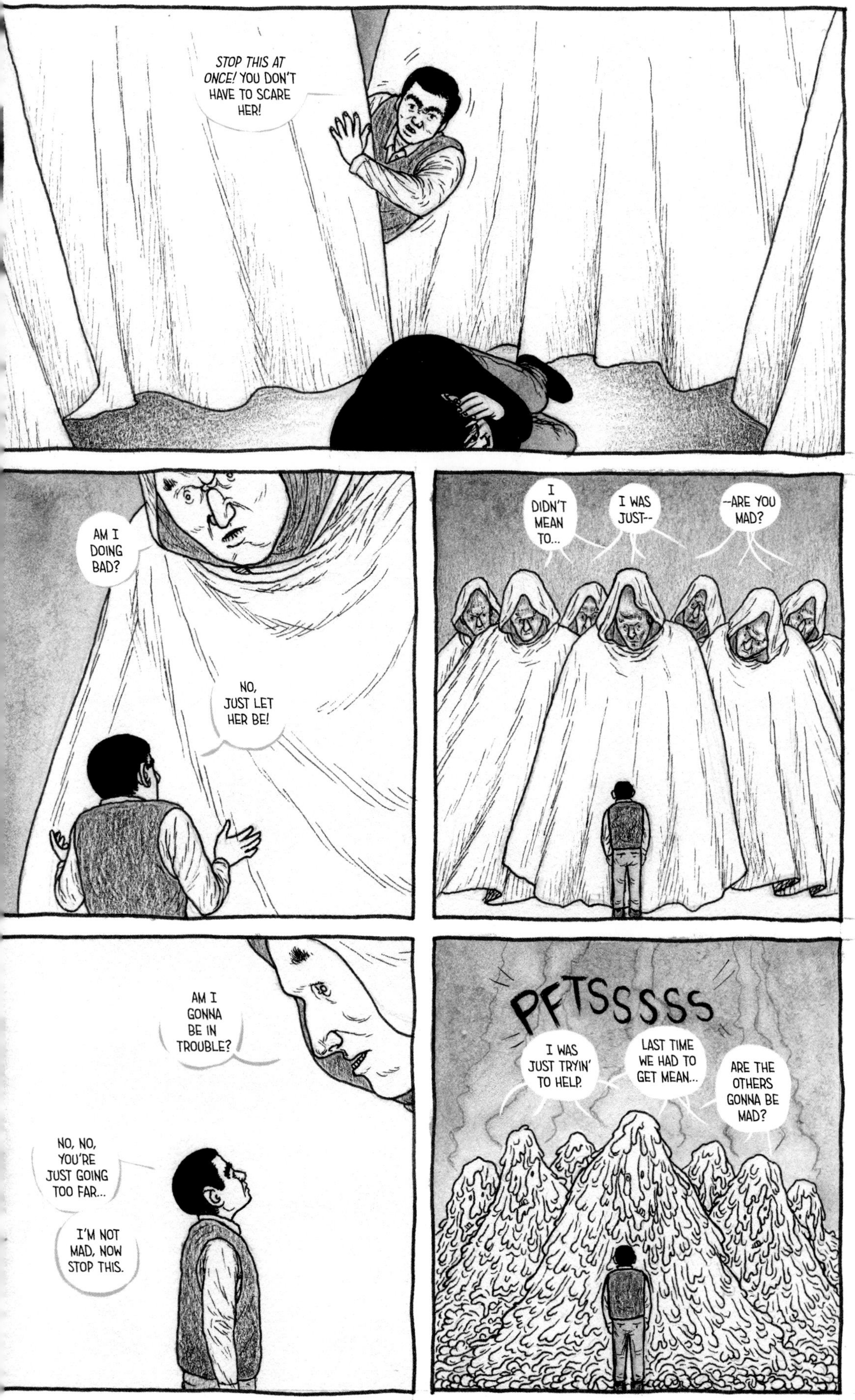
STOP THIS AT ONCE! YOU DON'T HAVE TO SCARE HER!
AM I DOING BAD?
NO, JUST LET HER BE!
I DIDN'T MEAN TO...
I WAS JUST--
--ARE YOU MAD?
AM I GONNA BE IN TROUBLE?
NO, NO, YOU'RE JUST GOING TOO FAR...
I'M NOT MAD, NOW STOP THIS.
PFTSSSSS
I WAS JUST TRYIN' TO HELP.
LAST TIME WE HAD TO GET MEAN...
ARE THE OTHERS GONNA BE MAD?

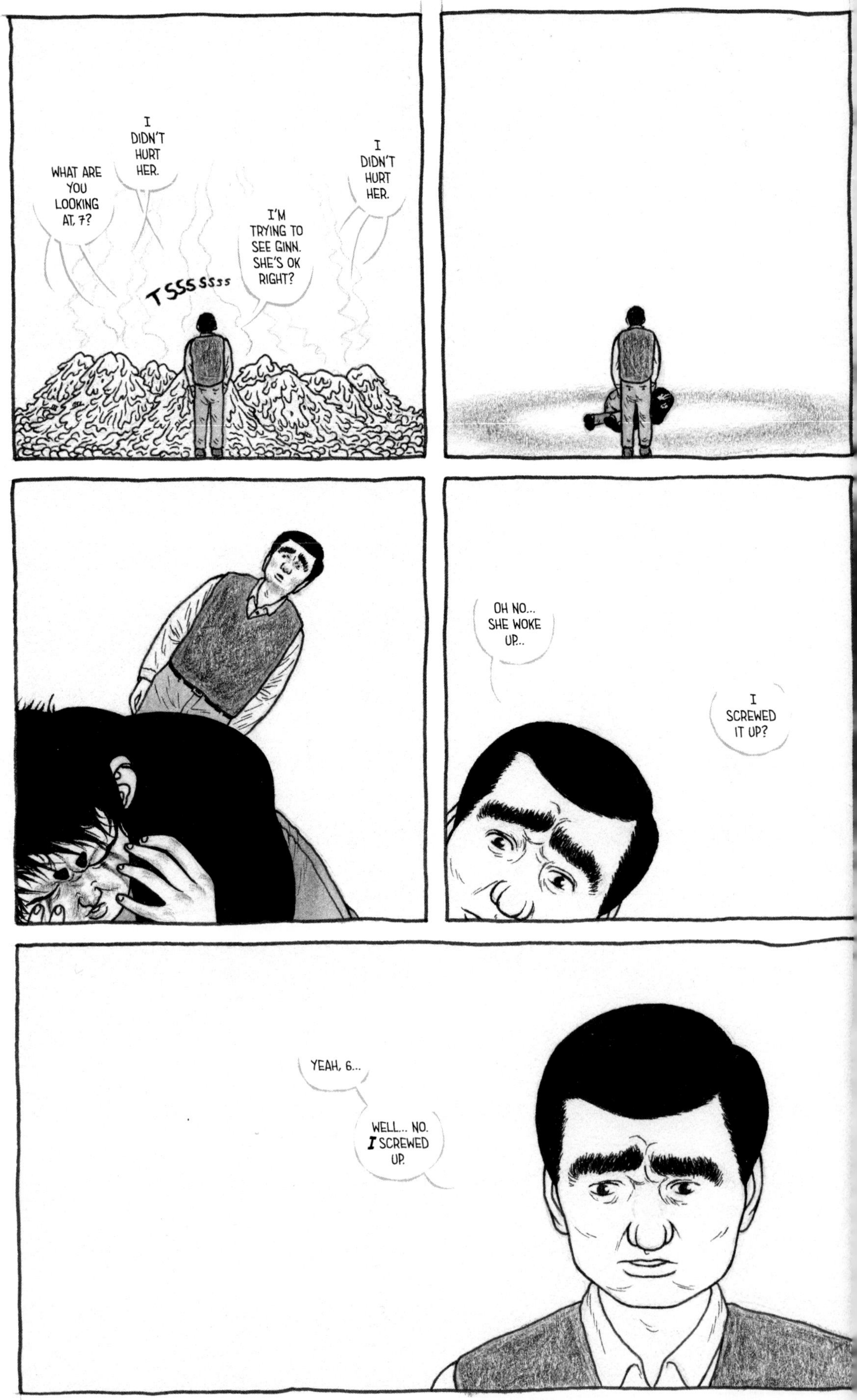
WHAT ARE YOU LOOKING AT, 7?
I DIDN'T HURT HER.
TSSSssss
I'M TRYING TO SEE GINN. SHE'S OK RIGHT?
I DIDN'T HURT HER.
OH NO... SHE WOKE UP...
I SCREWED IT UP?
YEAH, 6...
WELL... NO. *I* SCREWED UP.

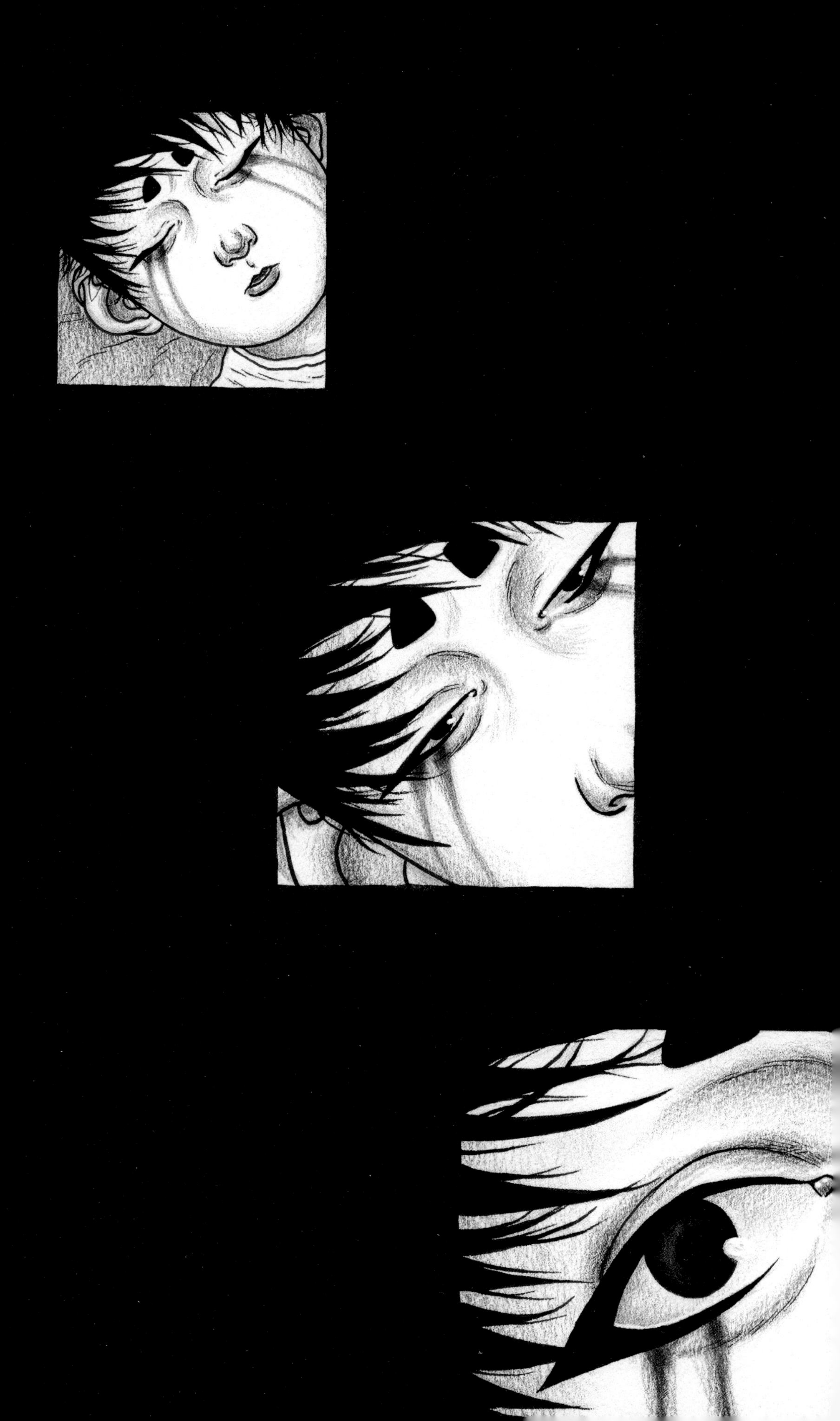

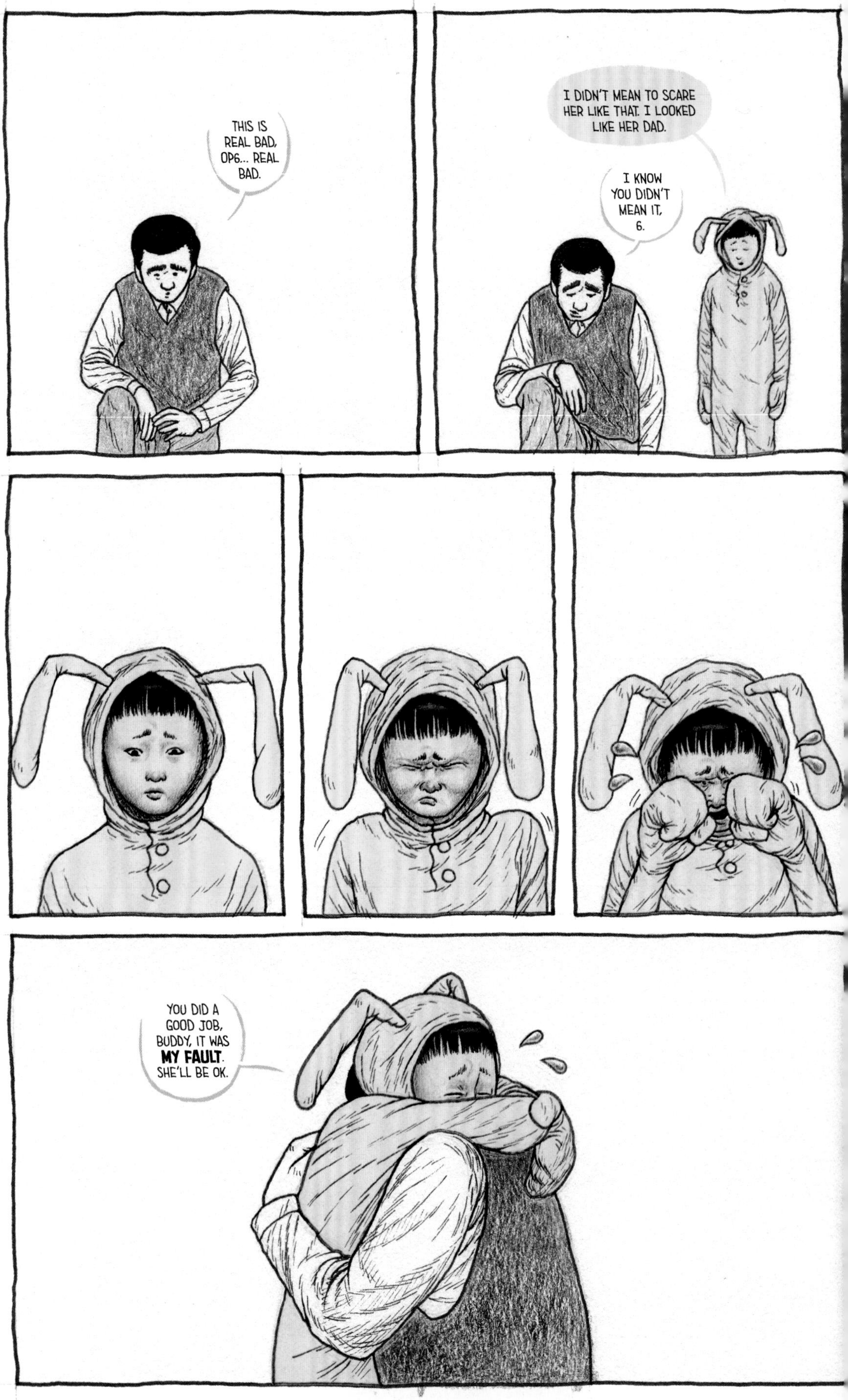
THIS IS REAL BAD, OP6... REAL BAD.
I DIDN'T MEAN TO SCARE HER LIKE THAT. I LOOKED LIKE HER DAD.
I KNOW YOU DIDN'T MEAN IT, 6.
YOU DID A GOOD JOB, BUDDY, IT WAS **MY FAULT**. SHE'LL BE OK.

YOU DID THE BEST YOU COULD. I'M GONNA MAKE SURE THAT EVERYTHING IS OK... YOU GOOD?

YEAH, I'M SORRY, 7...

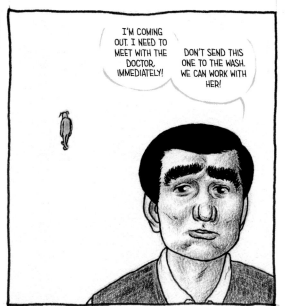

I'M COMING OUT. I NEED TO MEET WITH THE DOCTOR, IMMEDIATELY!

DON'T SEND THIS ONE TO THE WASH. WE CAN WORK WITH HER!

FINALLY COME TO? IT'S BEEN SOME TIME.

TIME IS STRANGE IN DREAMS, LISTEN, DOC... THE GIRL... GINN--

--HAS BEEN RECOVERED. WE WILL DEBRIEF ON THE DREAM AS THE FEED IS AVAILABLE.

THE THING IS...

THIS IS MY FAULT--

SHE SAW ME OUT THERE--

I BLEW IT.

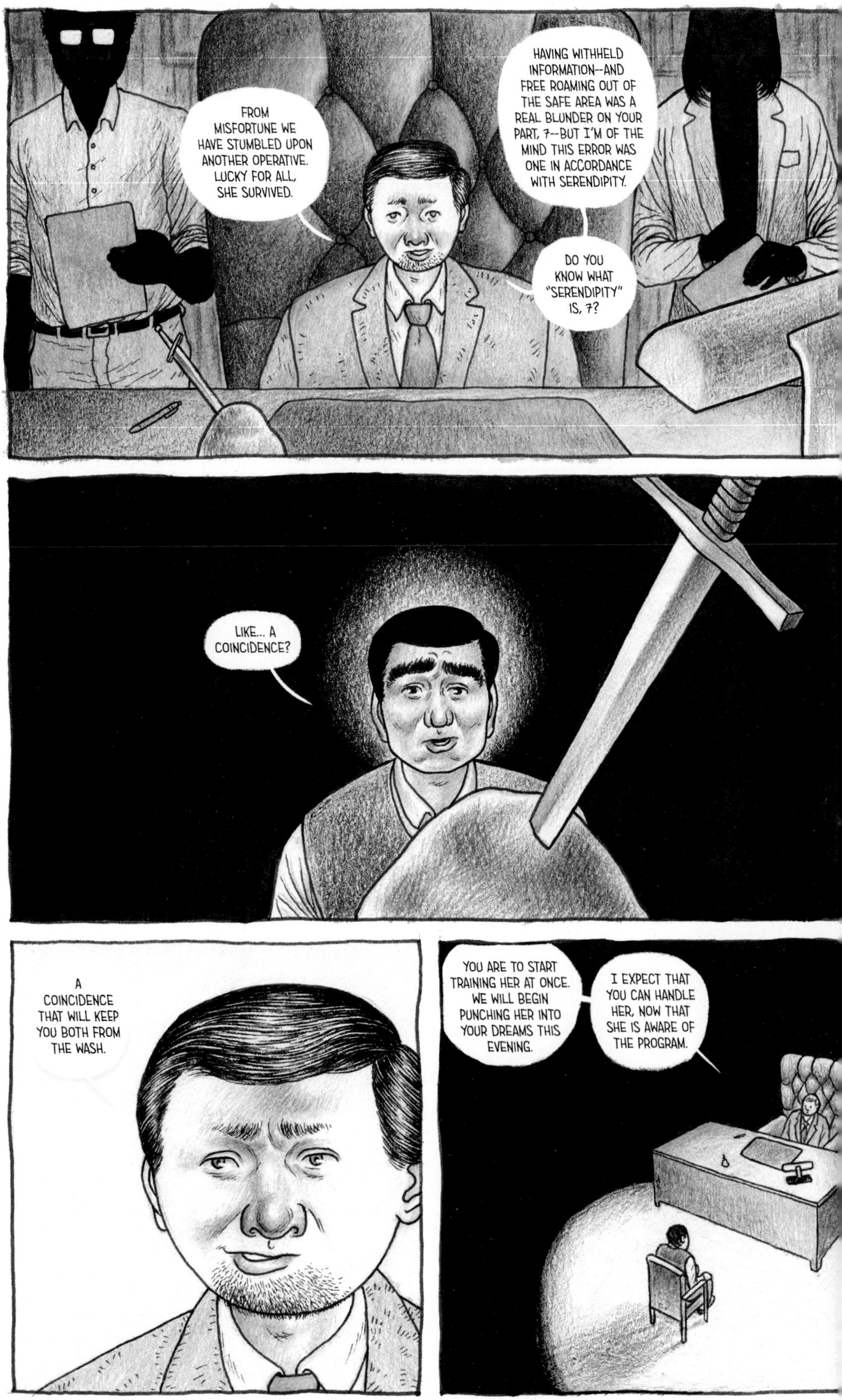
FROM MISFORTUNE WE HAVE STUMBLED UPON ANOTHER OPERATIVE. LUCKY FOR ALL, SHE SURVIVED.
HAVING WITHHELD INFORMATION--AND FREE ROAMING OUT OF THE SAFE AREA WAS A REAL BLUNDER ON YOUR PART, 7--BUT I'M OF THE MIND THIS ERROR WAS ONE IN ACCORDANCE WITH SERENDIPITY.
DO YOU KNOW WHAT "SERENDIPITY" IS, 7?
LIKE... A COINCIDENCE?
A COINCIDENCE THAT WILL KEEP YOU BOTH FROM THE WASH.
YOU ARE TO START TRAINING HER AT ONCE. WE WILL BEGIN PUNCHING HER INTO YOUR DREAMS THIS EVENING.
I EXPECT THAT YOU CAN HANDLE HER, NOW THAT SHE IS AWARE OF THE PROGRAM.

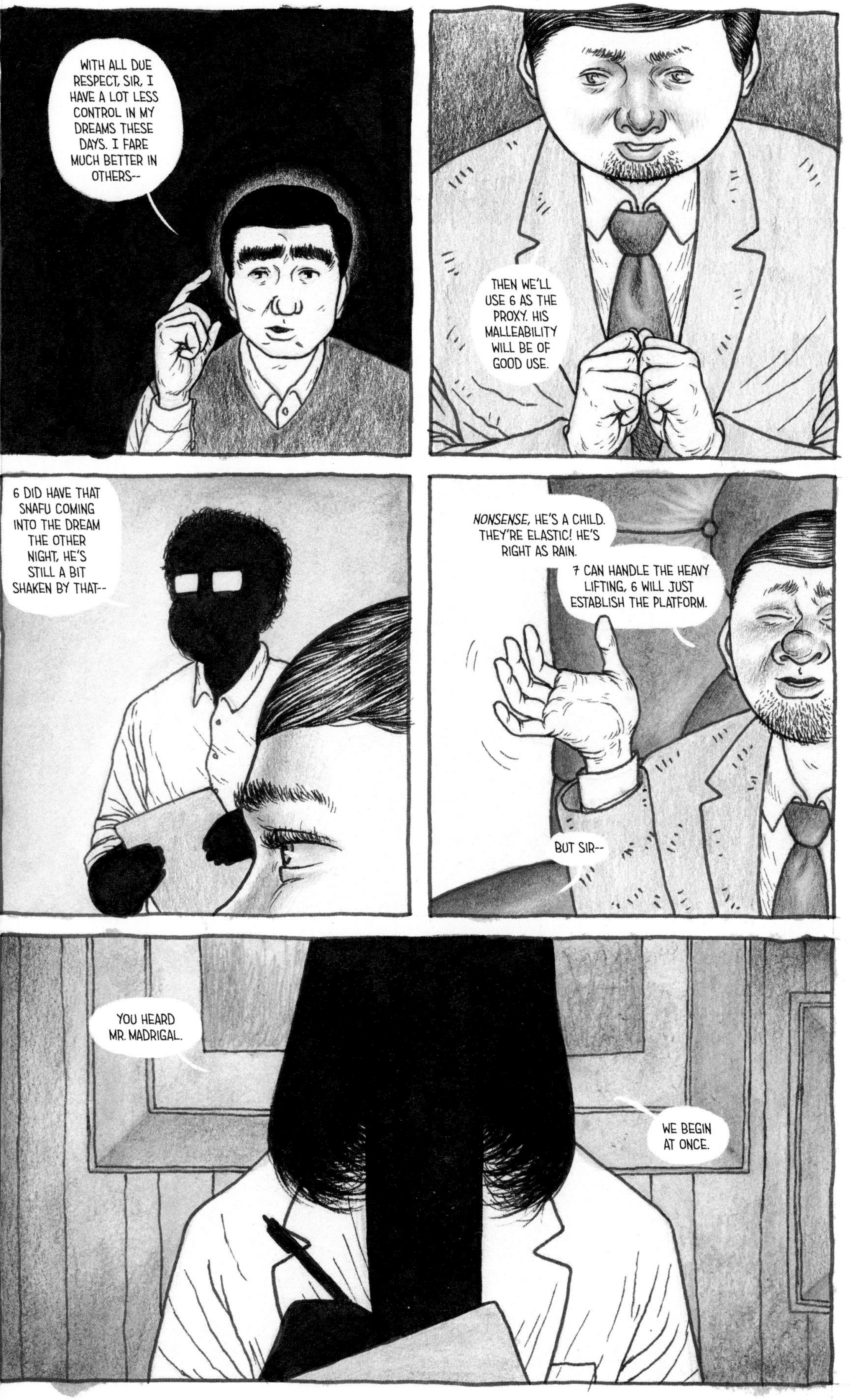
WITH ALL DUE RESPECT, SIR, I HAVE A LOT LESS CONTROL IN MY DREAMS THESE DAYS. I FARE MUCH BETTER IN OTHERS--
THEN WE'LL USE 6 AS THE PROXY. HIS MALLEABILITY WILL BE OF GOOD USE.
6 DID HAVE THAT SNAFU COMING INTO THE DREAM THE OTHER NIGHT, HE'S STILL A BIT SHAKEN BY THAT--
*NONSENSE*, HE'S A CHILD. THEY'RE ELASTIC! HE'S RIGHT AS RAIN.
7 CAN HANDLE THE HEAVY LIFTING, 6 WILL JUST ESTABLISH THE PLATFORM.
BUT SIR--
YOU HEARD MR. MADRIGAL.
WE BEGIN AT ONCE.

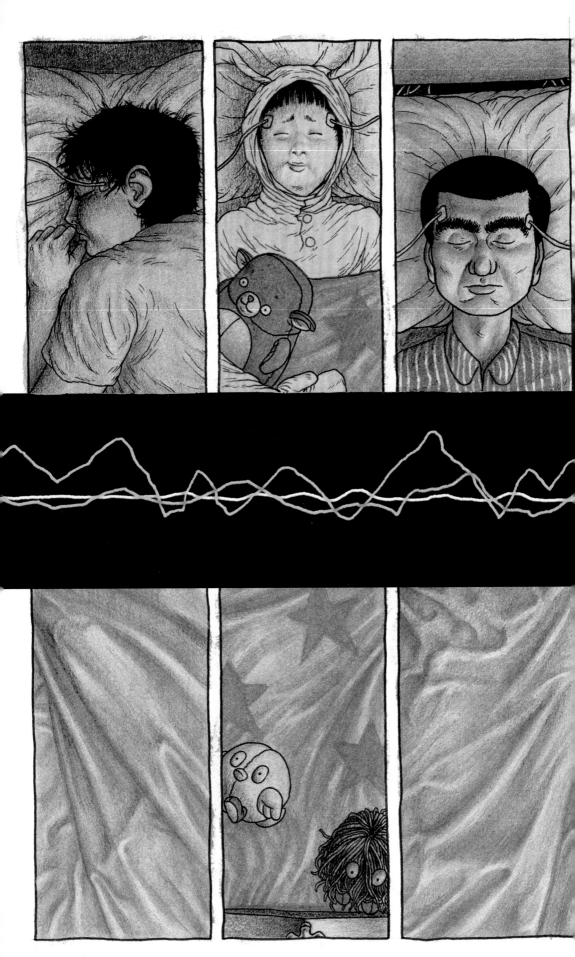

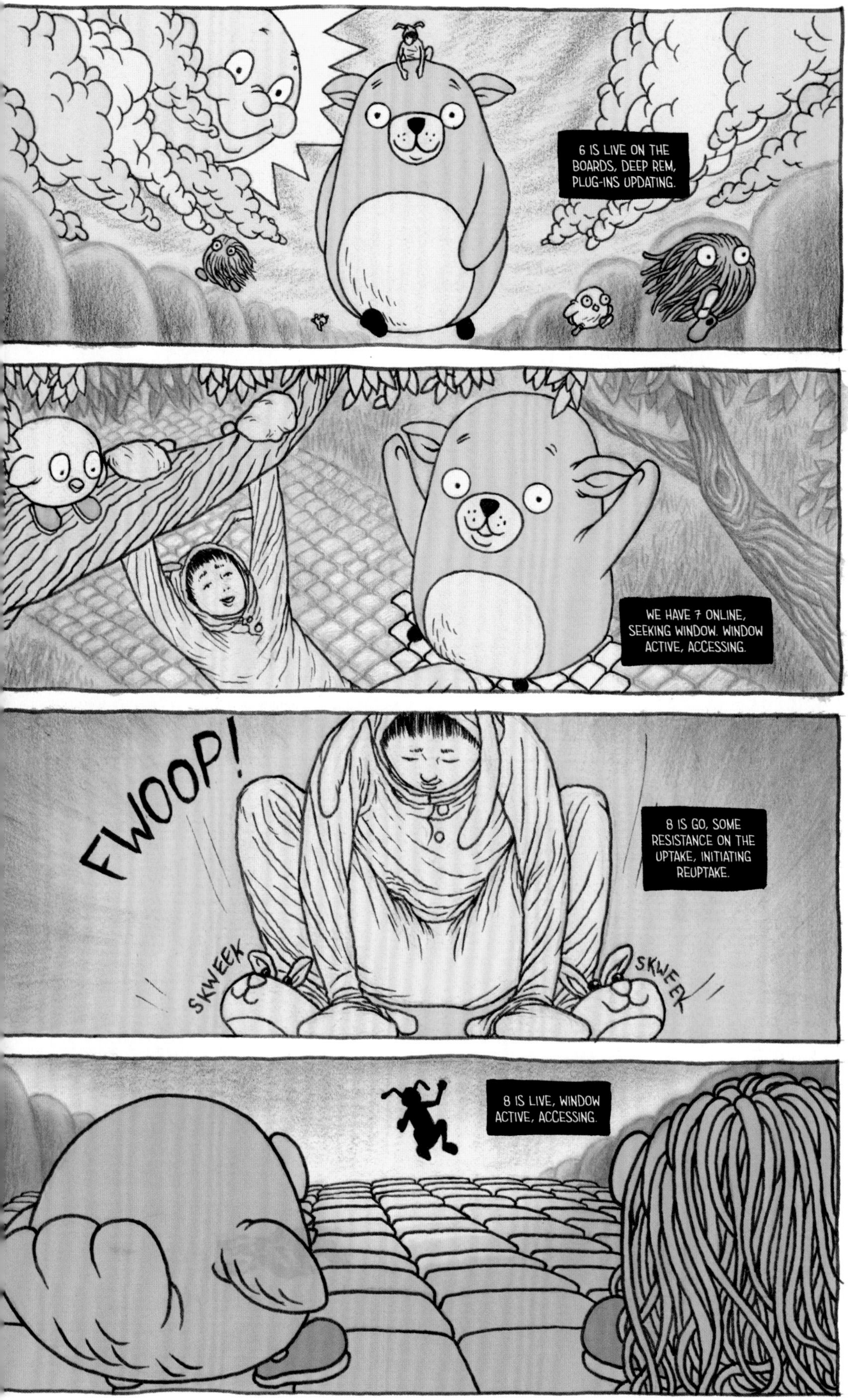

6 IS LIVE ON THE BOARDS, DEEP REM, PLUG-INS UPDATING.
WE HAVE 7 ONLINE, SEEKING WINDOW. WINDOW ACTIVE, ACCESSING.
FWOOP!
8 IS GO, SOME RESISTANCE ON THE UPTAKE, INITIATING REUPTAKE.
SKWEEK
SKWEEK
8 IS LIVE, WINDOW ACTIVE, ACCESSING.

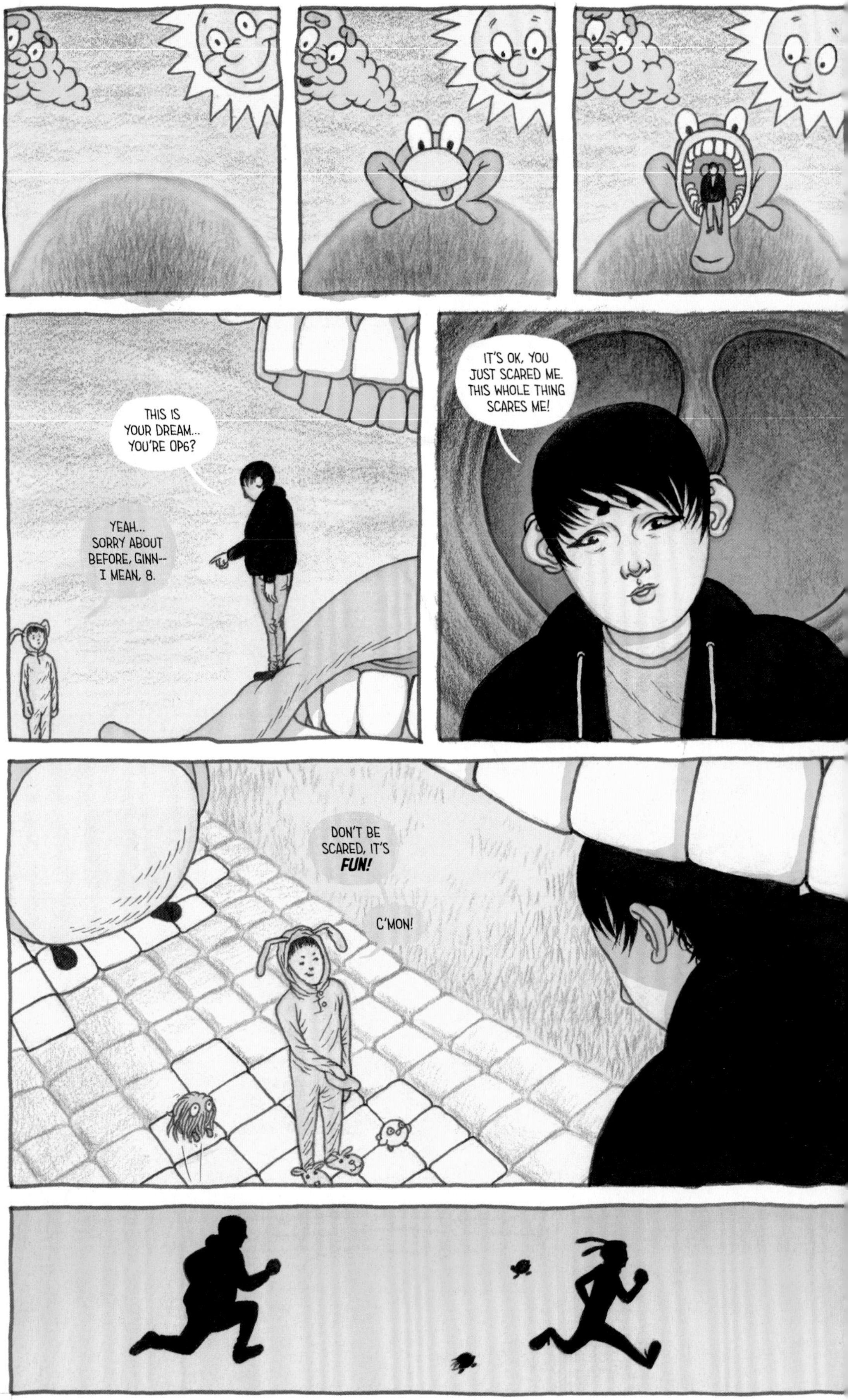
THIS IS YOUR DREAM... YOU'RE OP6?
YEAH... SORRY ABOUT BEFORE, GINN-- I MEAN, 8.
IT'S OK, YOU JUST SCARED ME. THIS WHOLE THING SCARES ME!
DON'T BE SCARED, IT'S *FUN!*
C'MON!

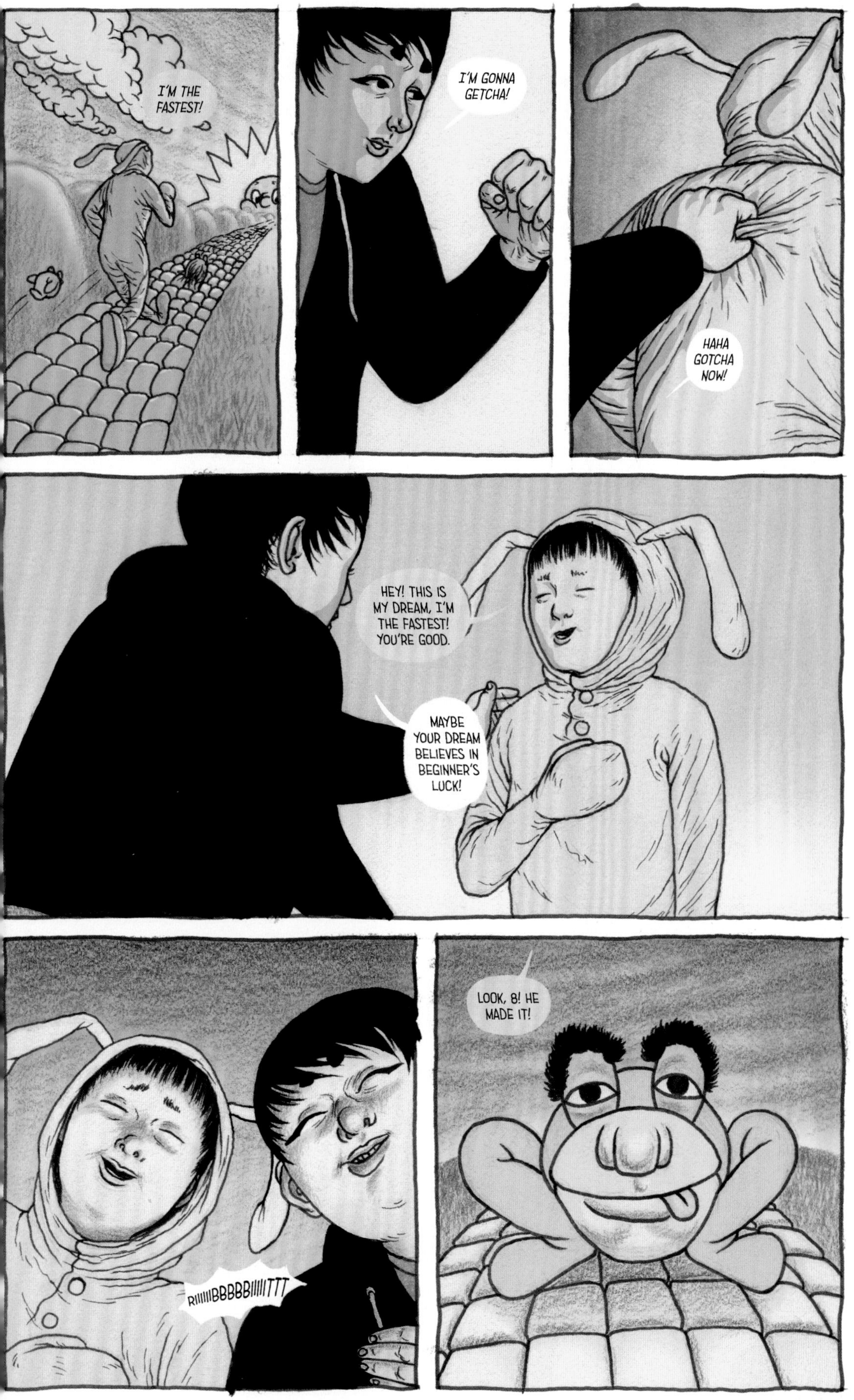
I'M THE FASTEST!
I'M GONNA GETCHA!
HAHA GOTCHA NOW!
HEY! THIS IS MY DREAM, I'M THE FASTEST! YOU'RE GOOD.
MAYBE YOUR DREAM BELIEVES IN BEGINNER'S LUCK!
RIIIIIIBBBBBIIIIIITTT
LOOK, 8! HE MADE IT!

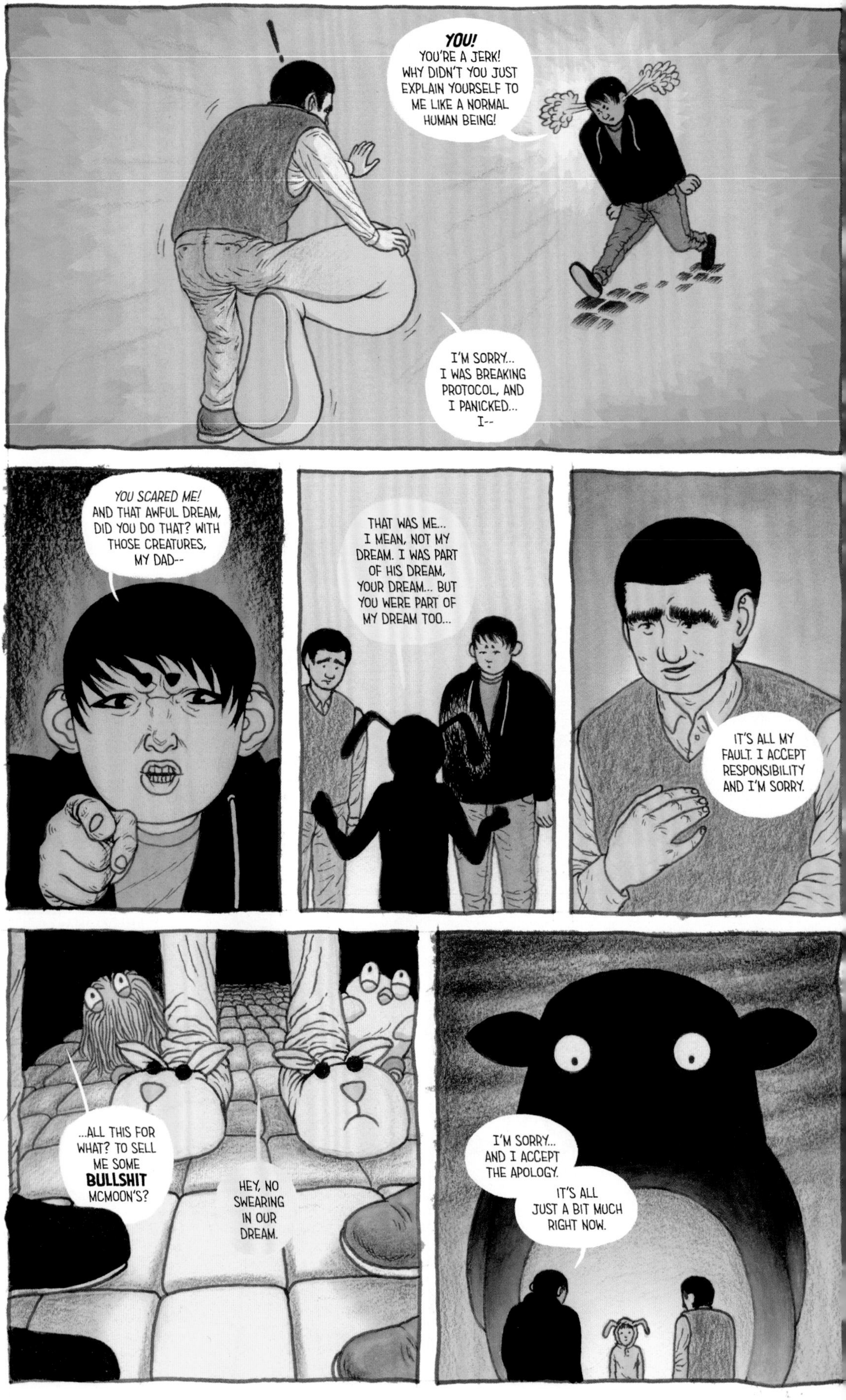

YOU! YOU'RE A JERK! WHY DIDN'T YOU JUST EXPLAIN YOURSELF TO ME LIKE A NORMAL HUMAN BEING!
I'M SORRY... I WAS BREAKING PROTOCOL, AND I PANICKED... I--
YOU SCARED ME! AND THAT AWFUL DREAM, DID YOU DO THAT? WITH THOSE CREATURES, MY DAD--
THAT WAS ME... I MEAN, NOT MY DREAM. I WAS PART OF HIS DREAM, YOUR DREAM... BUT YOU WERE PART OF MY DREAM TOO...
IT'S ALL MY FAULT. I ACCEPT RESPONSIBILITY AND I'M SORRY.
...ALL THIS FOR WHAT? TO SELL ME SOME BULLSHIT MCMOON'S?
HEY, NO SWEARING IN OUR DREAM.
I'M SORRY... AND I ACCEPT THE APOLOGY.
IT'S ALL JUST A BIT MUCH RIGHT NOW.

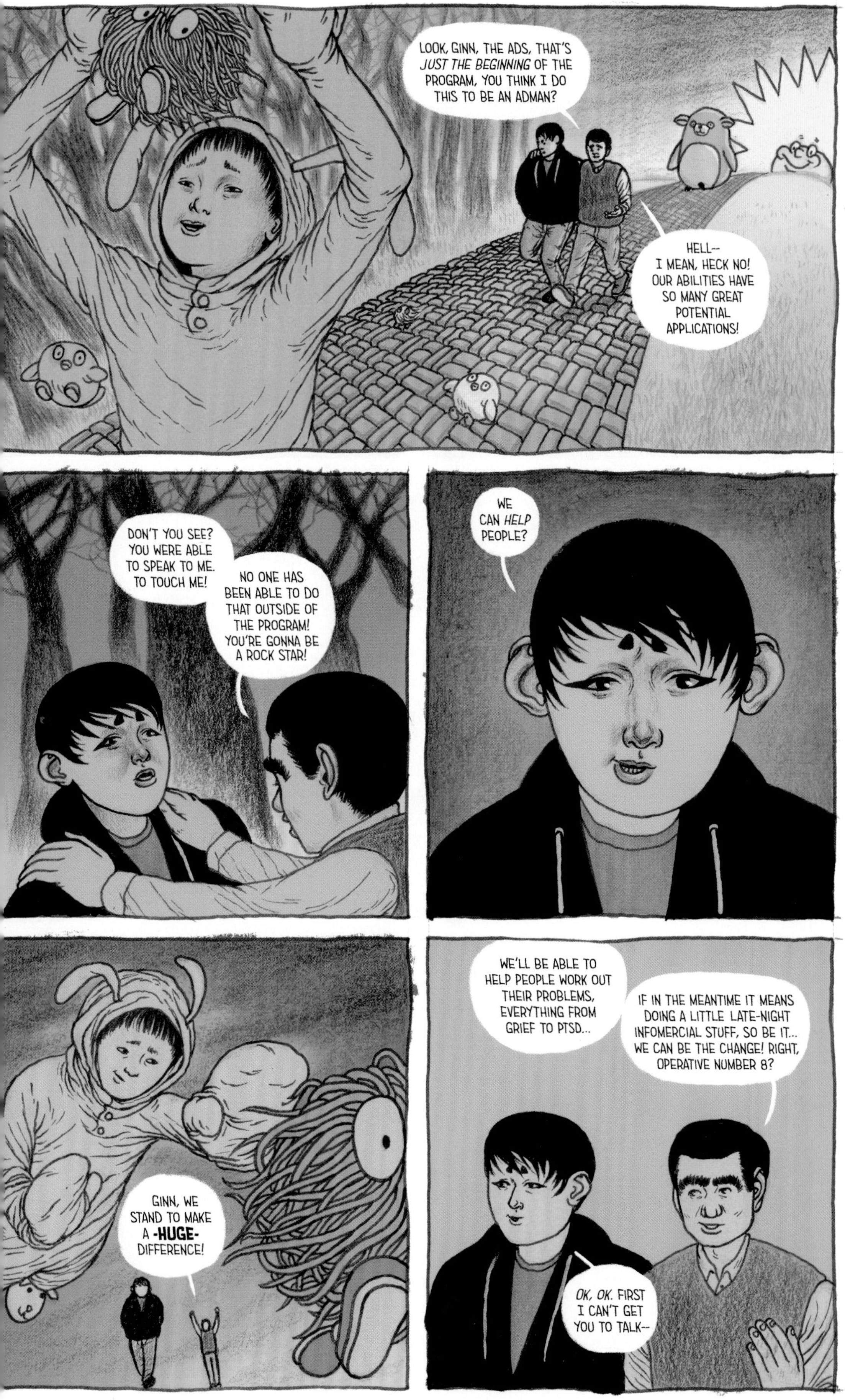
LOOK, GINN, THE ADS, THAT'S *JUST THE BEGINNING* OF THE PROGRAM, YOU THINK I DO THIS TO BE AN ADMAN?
HELL-- I MEAN, HECK NO! OUR ABILITIES HAVE SO MANY GREAT POTENTIAL APPLICATIONS!
DON'T YOU SEE? YOU WERE ABLE TO SPEAK TO ME. TO TOUCH ME!
NO ONE HAS BEEN ABLE TO DO THAT OUTSIDE OF THE PROGRAM! YOU'RE GONNA BE A ROCK STAR!
WE CAN *HELP* PEOPLE?
GINN, WE STAND TO MAKE A **-HUGE-** DIFFERENCE!
WE'LL BE ABLE TO HELP PEOPLE WORK OUT THEIR PROBLEMS, EVERYTHING FROM GRIEF TO PTSD...
IF IN THE MEANTIME IT MEANS DOING A LITTLE LATE-NIGHT INFOMERCIAL STUFF, SO BE IT... WE CAN BE THE CHANGE! RIGHT, OPERATIVE NUMBER 8?
*OK, OK.* FIRST I CAN'T GET YOU TO TALK--

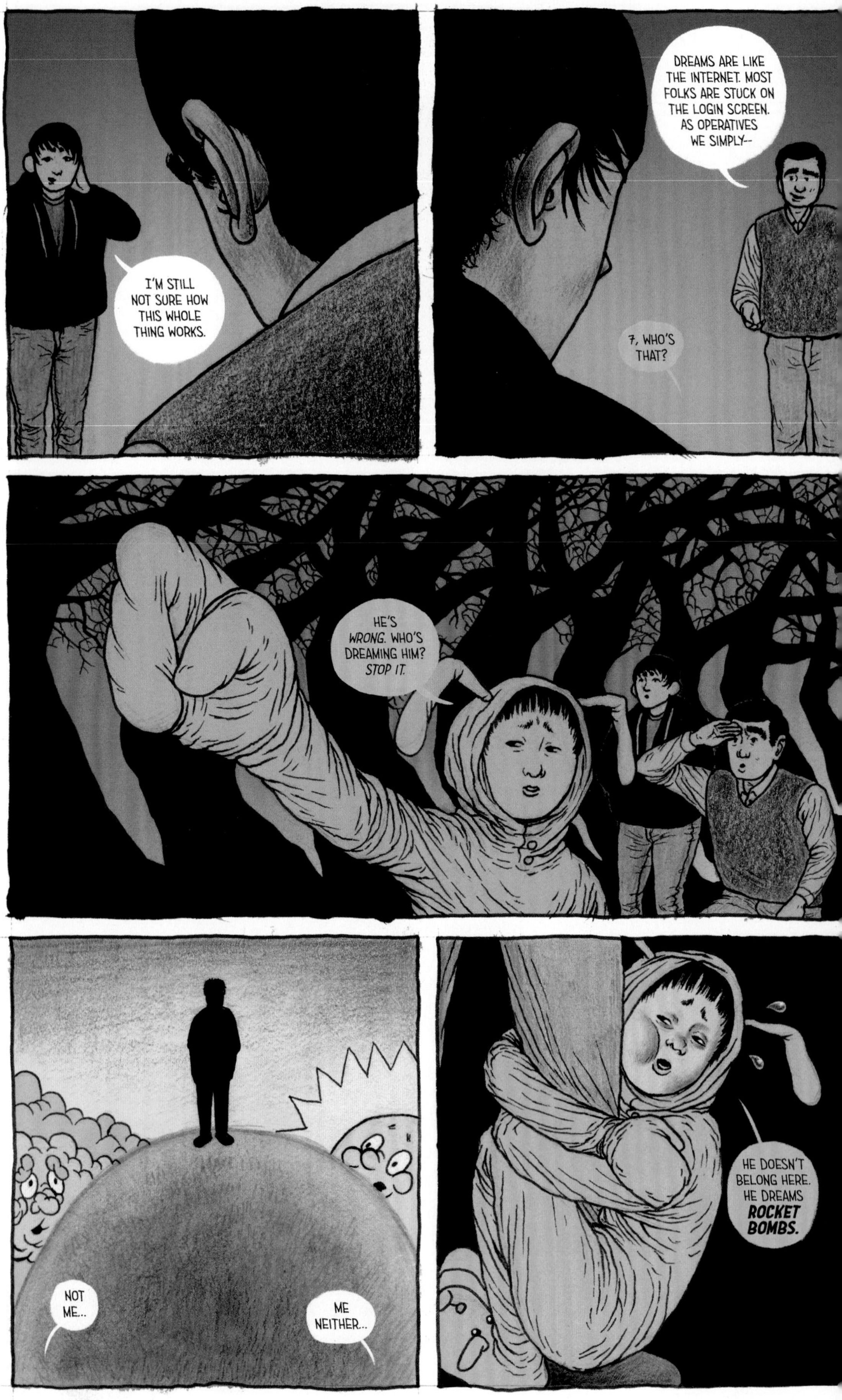
I'M STILL NOT SURE HOW THIS WHOLE THING WORKS.
DREAMS ARE LIKE THE INTERNET. MOST FOLKS ARE STUCK ON THE LOGIN SCREEN. AS OPERATIVES WE SIMPLY--
7, WHO'S THAT?
HE'S *WRONG*. WHO'S DREAMING HIM? *STOP IT.*
NOT ME...
ME NEITHER...
HE DOESN'T BELONG HERE. HE DREAMS **ROCKET BOMBS.**

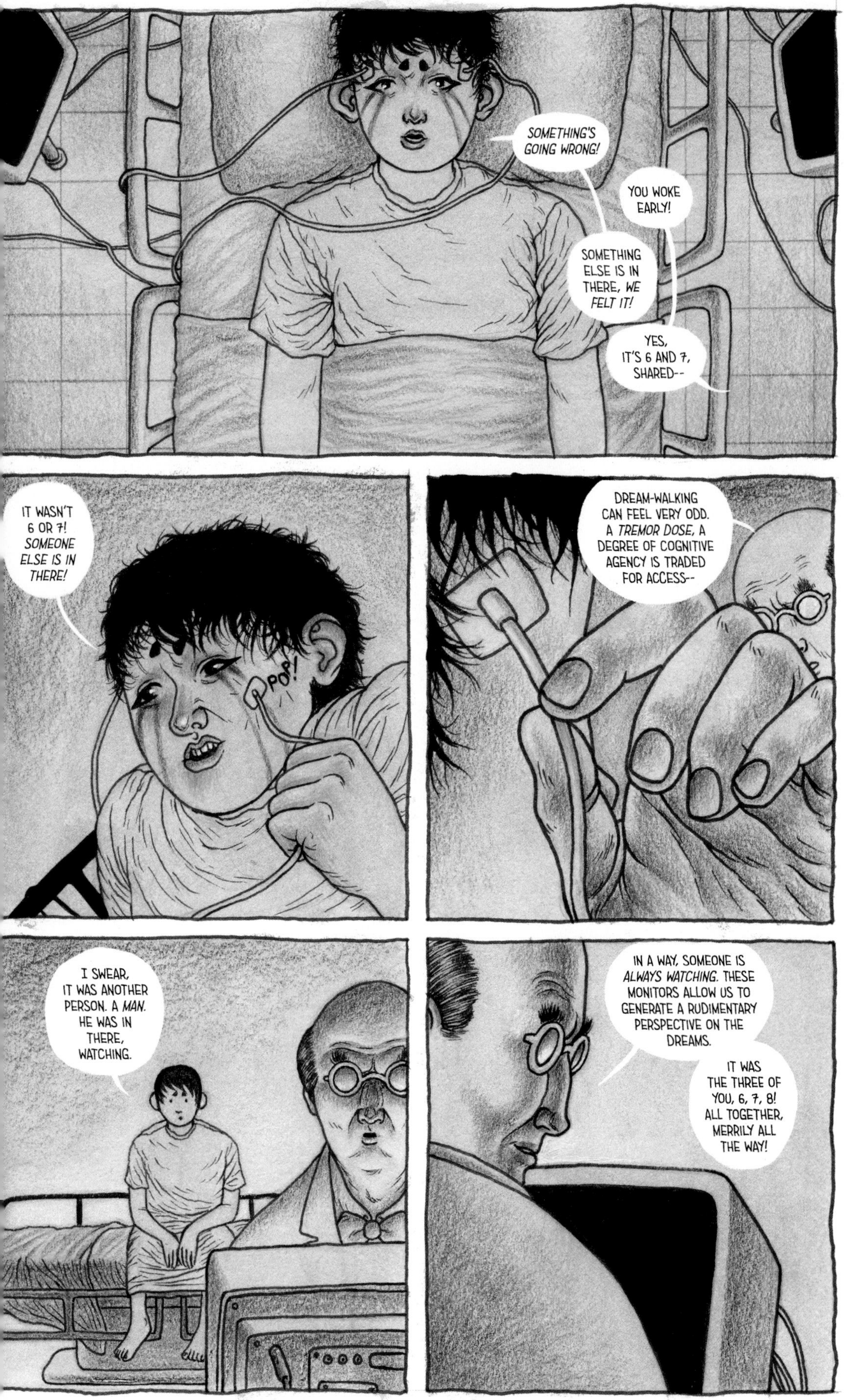
SOMETHING'S GOING WRONG!
YOU WOKE EARLY!
SOMETHING ELSE IS IN THERE, WE FELT IT!
YES, IT'S 6 AND 7, SHARED--
IT WASN'T 6 OR 7! SOMEONE ELSE IS IN THERE!
POP!
DREAM-WALKING CAN FEEL VERY ODD. A TREMOR DOSE, A DEGREE OF COGNITIVE AGENCY IS TRADED FOR ACCESS--
I SWEAR, IT WAS ANOTHER PERSON. A MAN. HE WAS IN THERE, WATCHING.
IN A WAY, SOMEONE IS ALWAYS WATCHING. THESE MONITORS ALLOW US TO GENERATE A RUDIMENTARY PERSPECTIVE ON THE DREAMS.
IT WAS THE THREE OF YOU, 6, 7, 8! ALL TOGETHER, MERRILY ALL THE WAY!

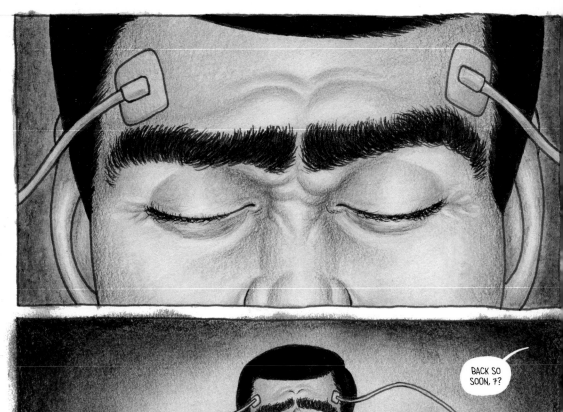

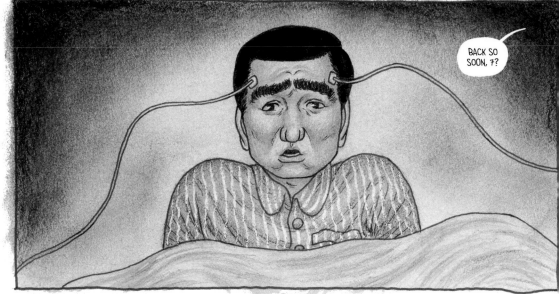

BACK SO SOON, 7?

6...
I GOTTA CHECK ON 6.

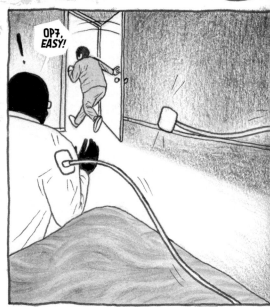

OP7, EASY!

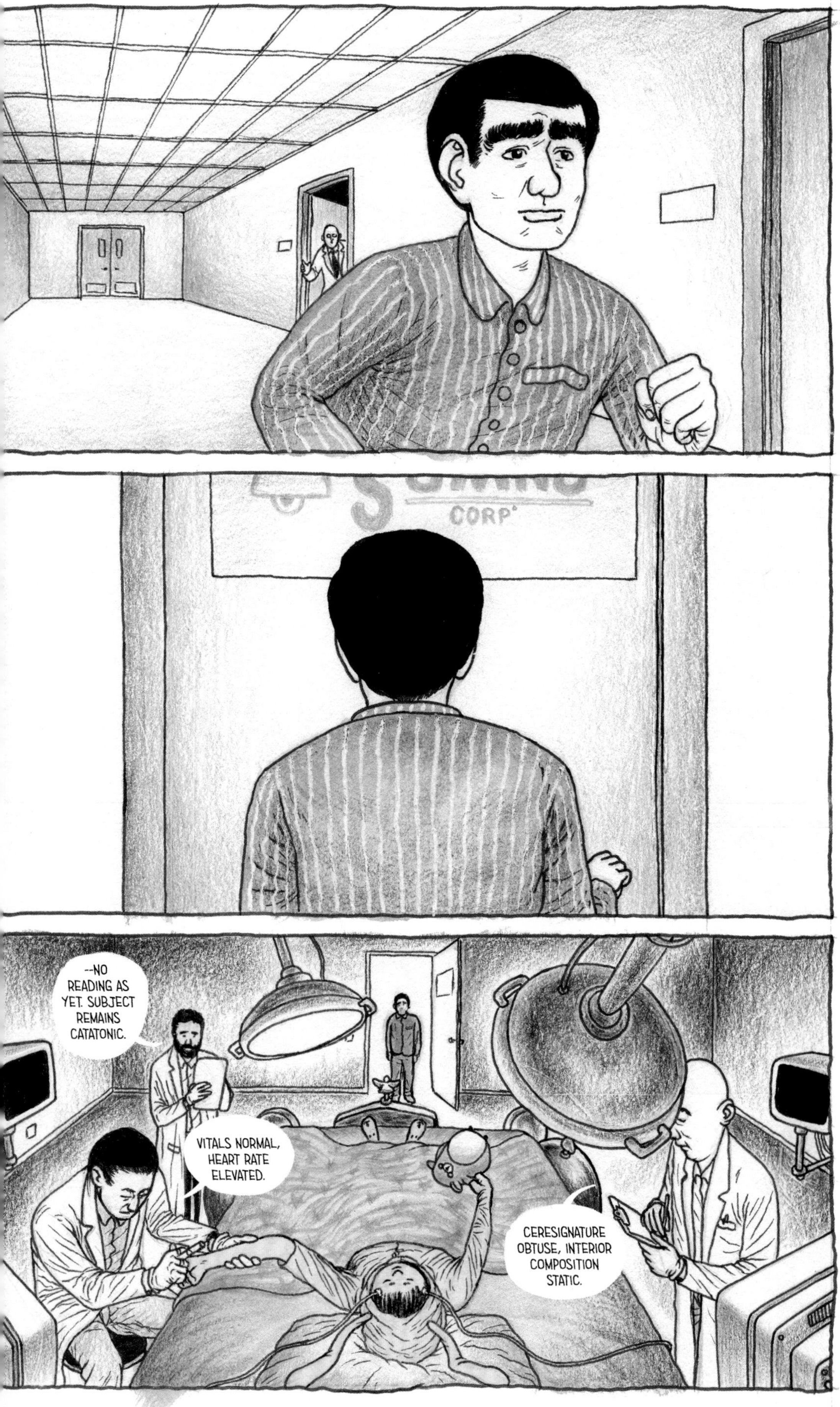
CORP
--NO READING AS YET. SUBJECT REMAINS CATATONIC.
VITALS NORMAL, HEART RATE ELEVATED.
CERESIGNATURE OBTUSE, INTERIOR COMPOSITION STATIC.

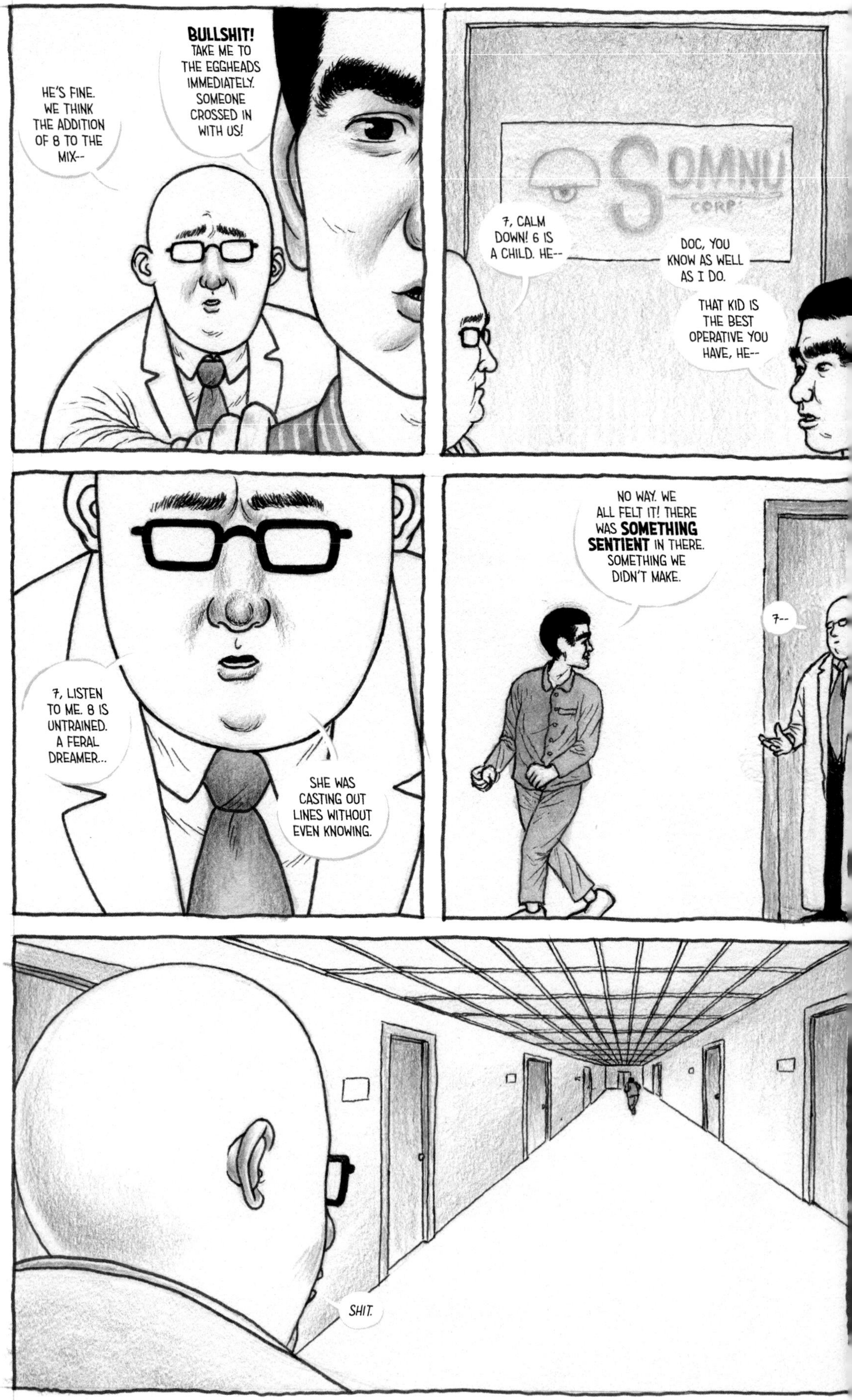
HE'S FINE. WE THINK THE ADDITION OF 8 TO THE MIX--
**BULLSHIT!** TAKE ME TO THE EGGHEADS IMMEDIATELY. SOMEONE CROSSED IN WITH US!
SOMNU CORP
7, CALM DOWN! 6 IS A CHILD. HE--
DOC, YOU KNOW AS WELL AS I DO.
THAT KID IS THE BEST OPERATIVE YOU HAVE, HE--
7, LISTEN TO ME. 8 IS UNTRAINED. A FERAL DREAMER...
SHE WAS CASTING OUT LINES WITHOUT EVEN KNOWING.
NO WAY. WE ALL FELT IT! THERE WAS **SOMETHING SENTIENT** IN THERE. SOMETHING WE DIDN'T MAKE.
7--
SHIT.

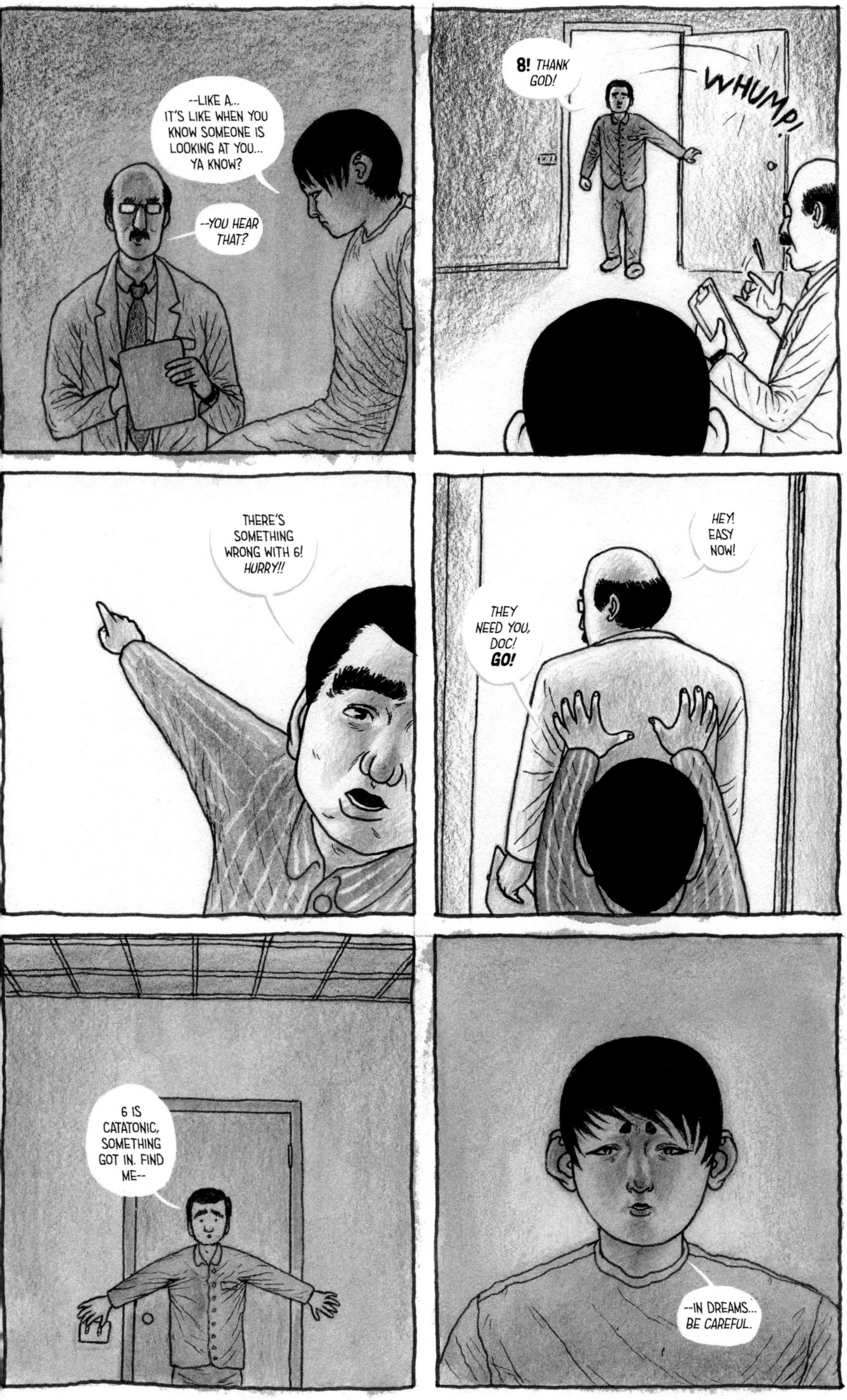
--LIKE A... IT'S LIKE WHEN YOU KNOW SOMEONE IS LOOKING AT YOU... YA KNOW?
--YOU HEAR THAT?
8! THANK GOD!
WHUMP!
THERE'S SOMETHING WRONG WITH 6! HURRY!!
HEY! EASY NOW!
THEY NEED YOU, DOC! GO!
6 IS CATATONIC, SOMETHING GOT IN. FIND ME--
--IN DREAMS... BE CAREFUL.

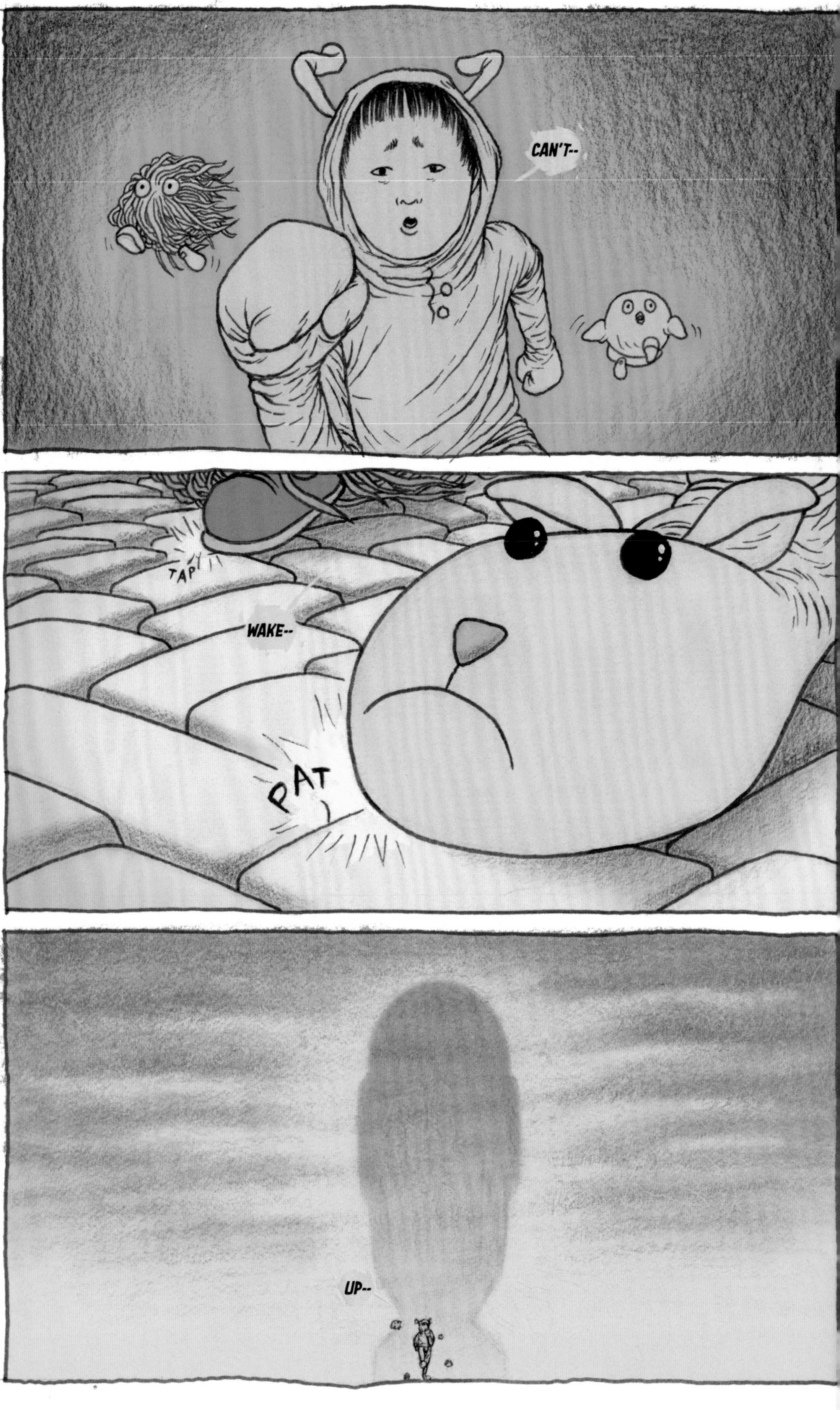
CAN'T--
TAP
WAKE--
PAT
UP--

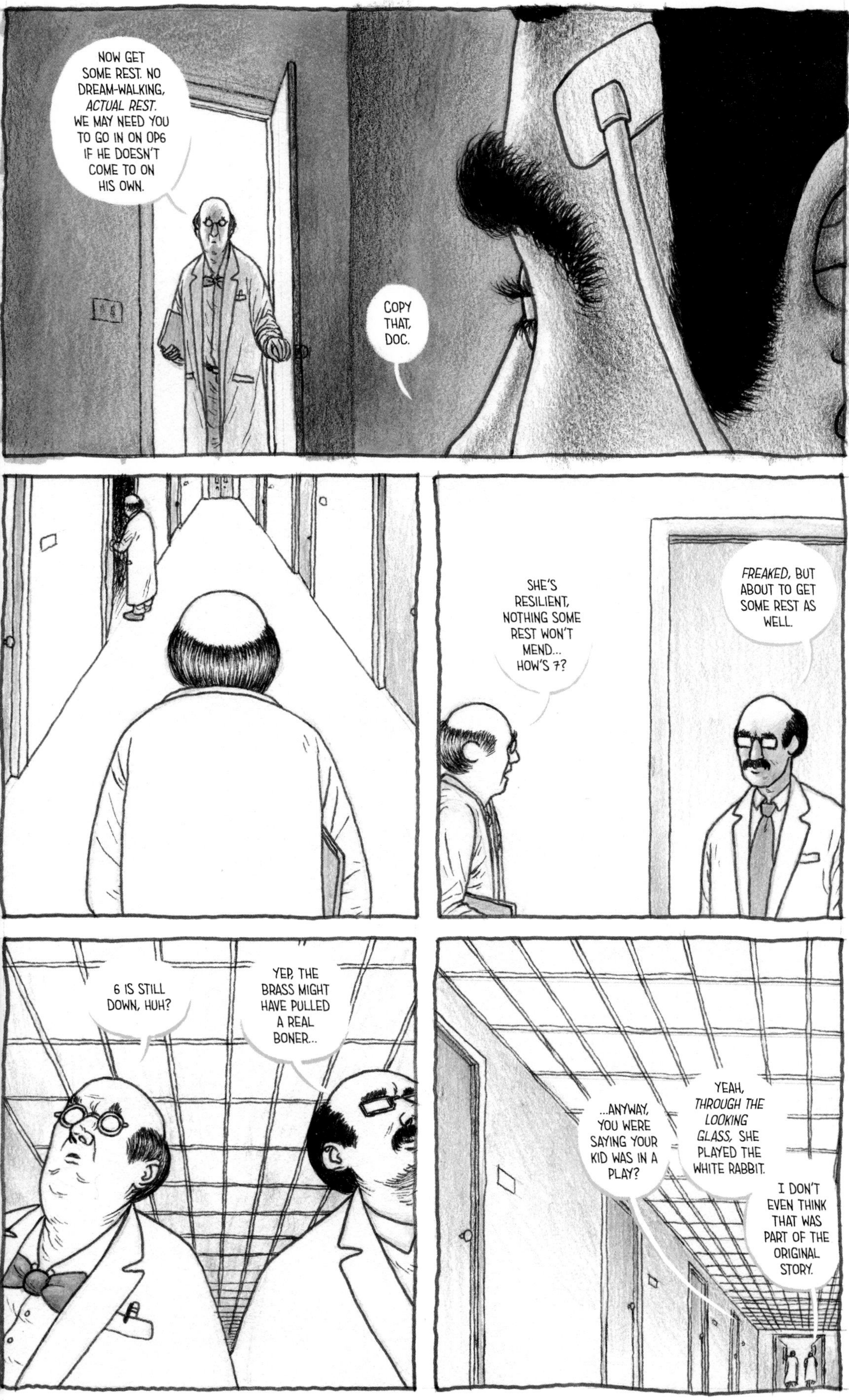
NOW GET SOME REST. NO DREAM-WALKING, *ACTUAL REST.* WE MAY NEED YOU TO GO IN ON OP6 IF HE DOESN'T COME TO ON HIS OWN.
COPY THAT, DOC.
SHE'S RESILIENT, NOTHING SOME REST WON'T MEND... HOW'S 7?
*FREAKED,* BUT ABOUT TO GET SOME REST AS WELL.
6 IS STILL DOWN, HUH?
YEP, THE BRASS MIGHT HAVE PULLED A REAL BONER...
...ANYWAY, YOU WERE SAYING YOUR KID WAS IN A PLAY?
YEAH, *THROUGH THE LOOKING GLASS,* SHE PLAYED THE WHITE RABBIT.
I DON'T EVEN THINK THAT WAS PART OF THE ORIGINAL STORY.

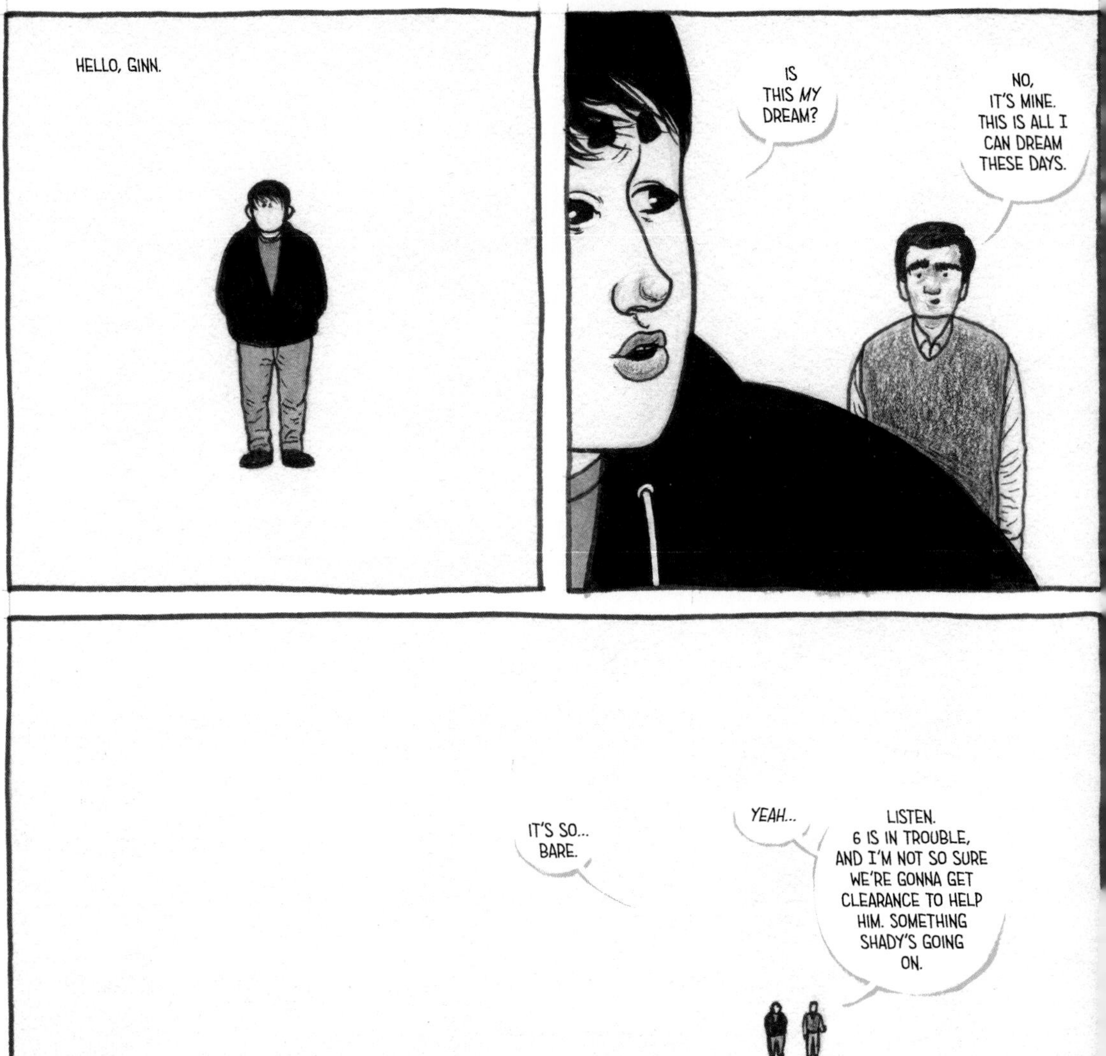
HELLO, GINN.
IS THIS MY DREAM?
NO, IT'S MINE. THIS IS ALL I CAN DREAM THESE DAYS.
IT'S SO... BARE.
YEAH...
LISTEN. 6 IS IN TROUBLE, AND I'M NOT SO SURE WE'RE GONNA GET CLEARANCE TO HELP HIM. SOMETHING SHADY'S GOING ON.
BUT... HOW?
WELL...
DOWN THE RABBIT HOLE.

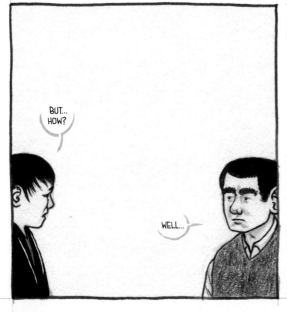

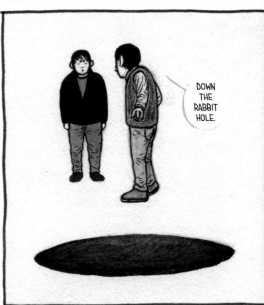

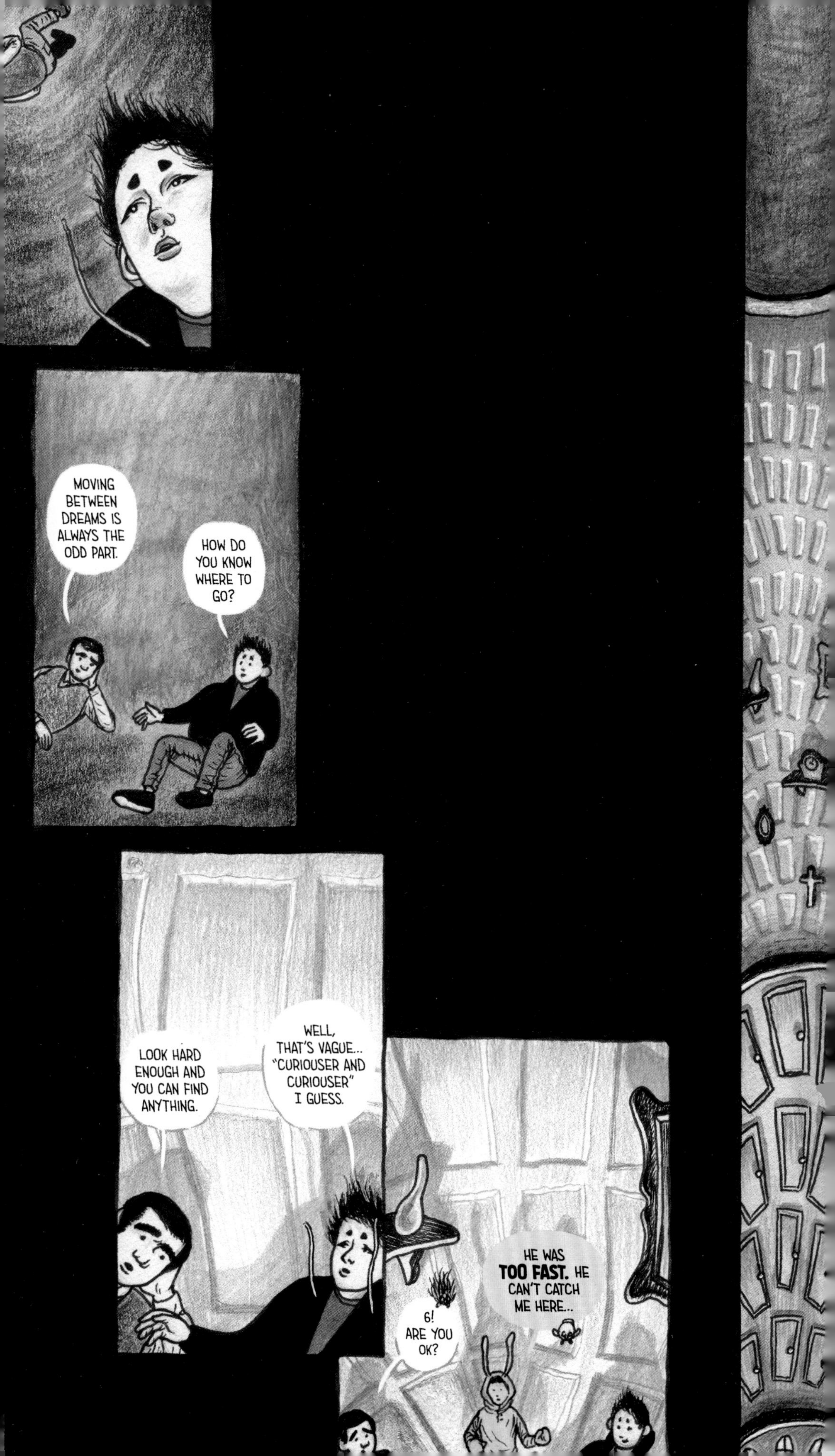
MOVING BETWEEN DREAMS IS ALWAYS THE ODD PART.
HOW DO YOU KNOW WHERE TO GO?
LOOK HARD ENOUGH AND YOU CAN FIND ANYTHING.
WELL, THAT'S VAGUE... "CURIOUSER AND CURIOUSER" I GUESS.
HE WAS TOO FAST. HE CAN'T CATCH ME HERE...
6! ARE YOU OK?

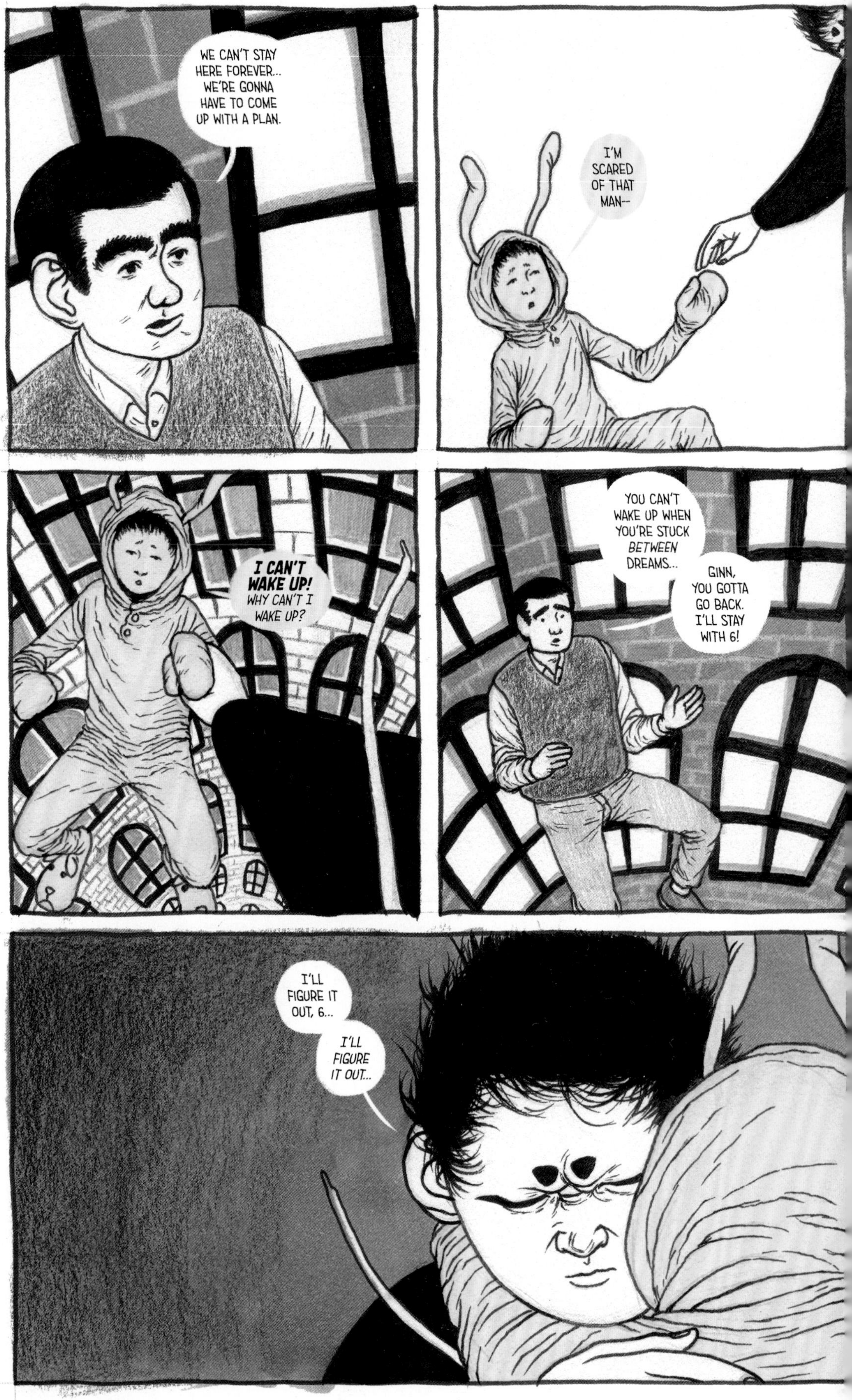
WE CAN'T STAY HERE FOREVER... WE'RE GONNA HAVE TO COME UP WITH A PLAN.
I'M SCARED OF THAT MAN--
I CAN'T WAKE UP! WHY CAN'T I WAKE UP?
YOU CAN'T WAKE UP WHEN YOU'RE STUCK BETWEEN DREAMS...
GINN, YOU GOTTA GO BACK. I'LL STAY WITH 6!
I'LL FIGURE IT OUT, 6...
I'LL FIGURE IT OUT...

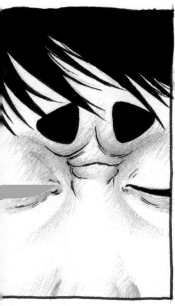

--AND THAT'S THE LATEST DREAM. CRAZY, RIGHT?

I'VE NEVER MET YOU BEFORE, BUT UP UNTIL THIS VERY MOMENT I'VE ALREADY EXPERIENCED ALL OF THIS...

THIS IS BIZARRE, GINN, MAYBE YOU SAW US PRIOR TO THIS MEETING--

NO.

--NO. I'VE NEVER SEEN *EITHER OF YOU* OUTSIDE OF MY DREAMS.

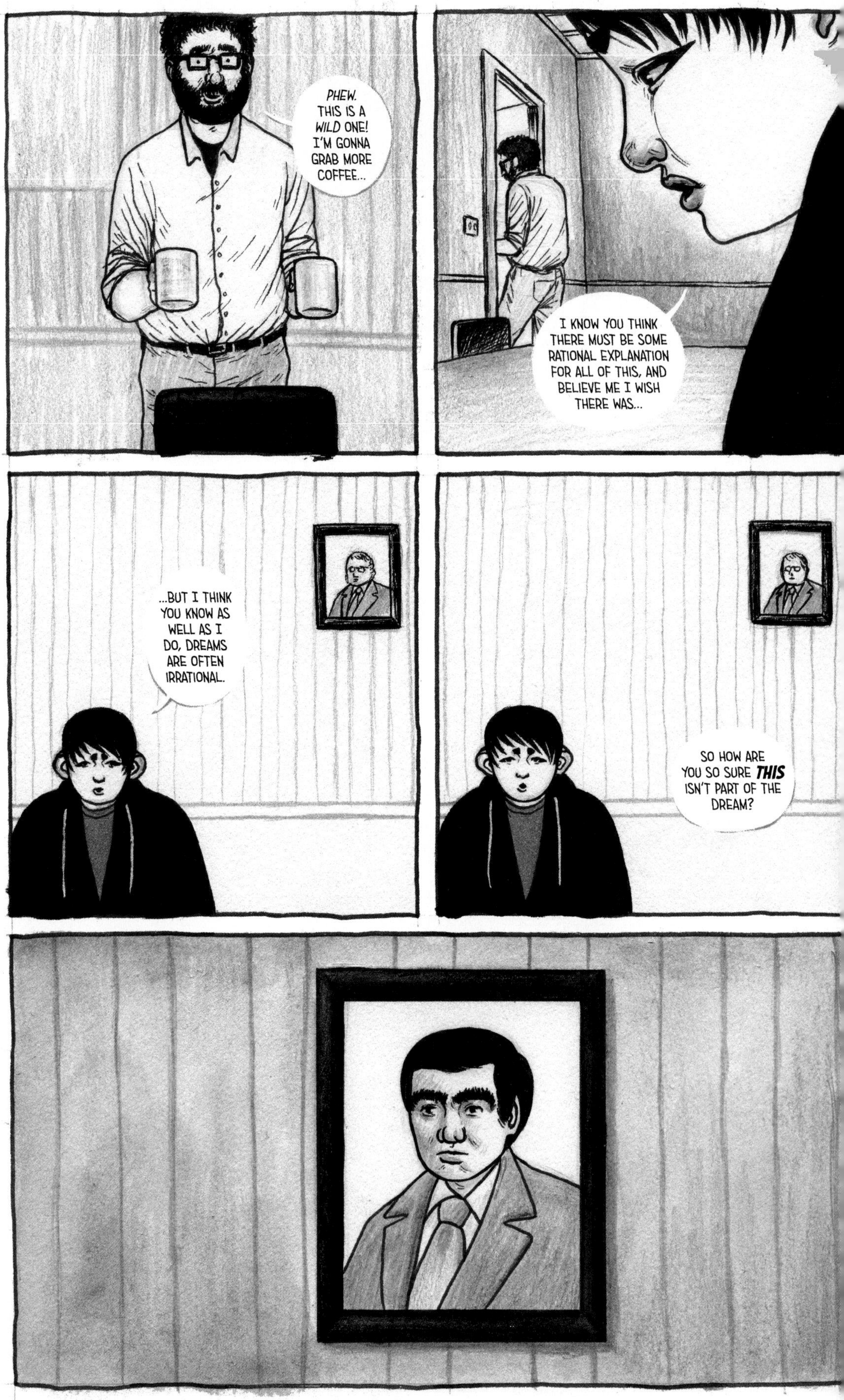
PHEW. THIS IS A *WILD* ONE! I'M GONNA GRAB MORE COFFEE...
I KNOW YOU THINK THERE MUST BE SOME RATIONAL EXPLANATION FOR ALL OF THIS, AND BELIEVE ME I WISH THERE WAS...
...BUT I THINK YOU KNOW AS WELL AS I DO, DREAMS ARE OFTEN IRRATIONAL.
SO HOW ARE YOU SO SURE ***THIS*** ISN'T PART OF THE DREAM?

TWO MORE HOT CUPS OF--

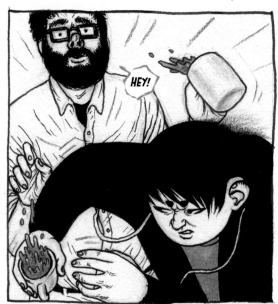

HEY!

OP8! STOP!

AHHH!

SPLSSSH!

AHHH!

WHAT ARE YOU PEOPLE DOING TO US?!

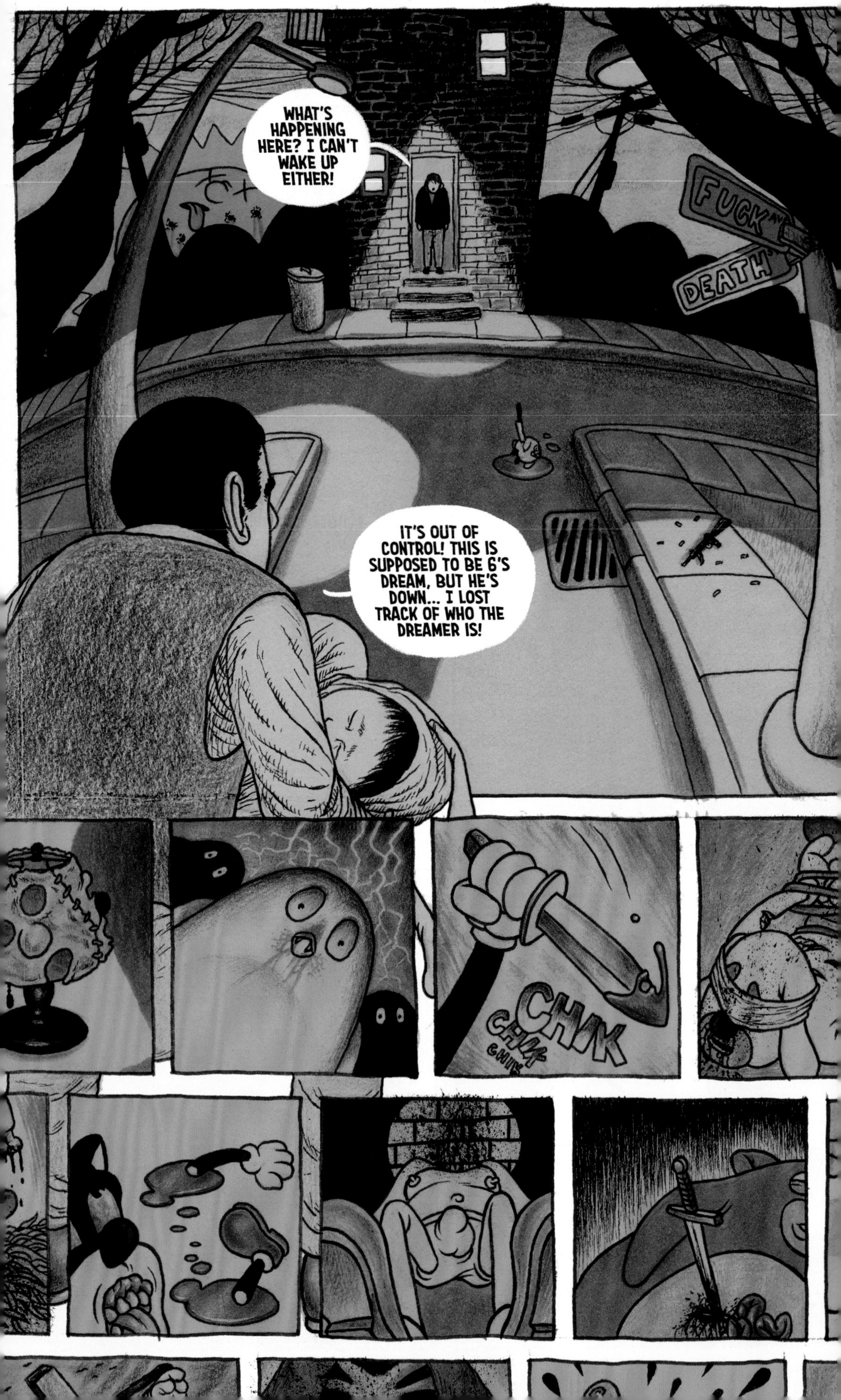
WHAT'S HAPPENING HERE? I CAN'T WAKE UP EITHER!
FUCK AV
DEATH
IT'S OUT OF CONTROL! THIS IS SUPPOSED TO BE 6'S DREAM, BUT HE'S DOWN... I LOST TRACK OF WHO THE DREAMER IS!
CHIK
CHIK
CHIK

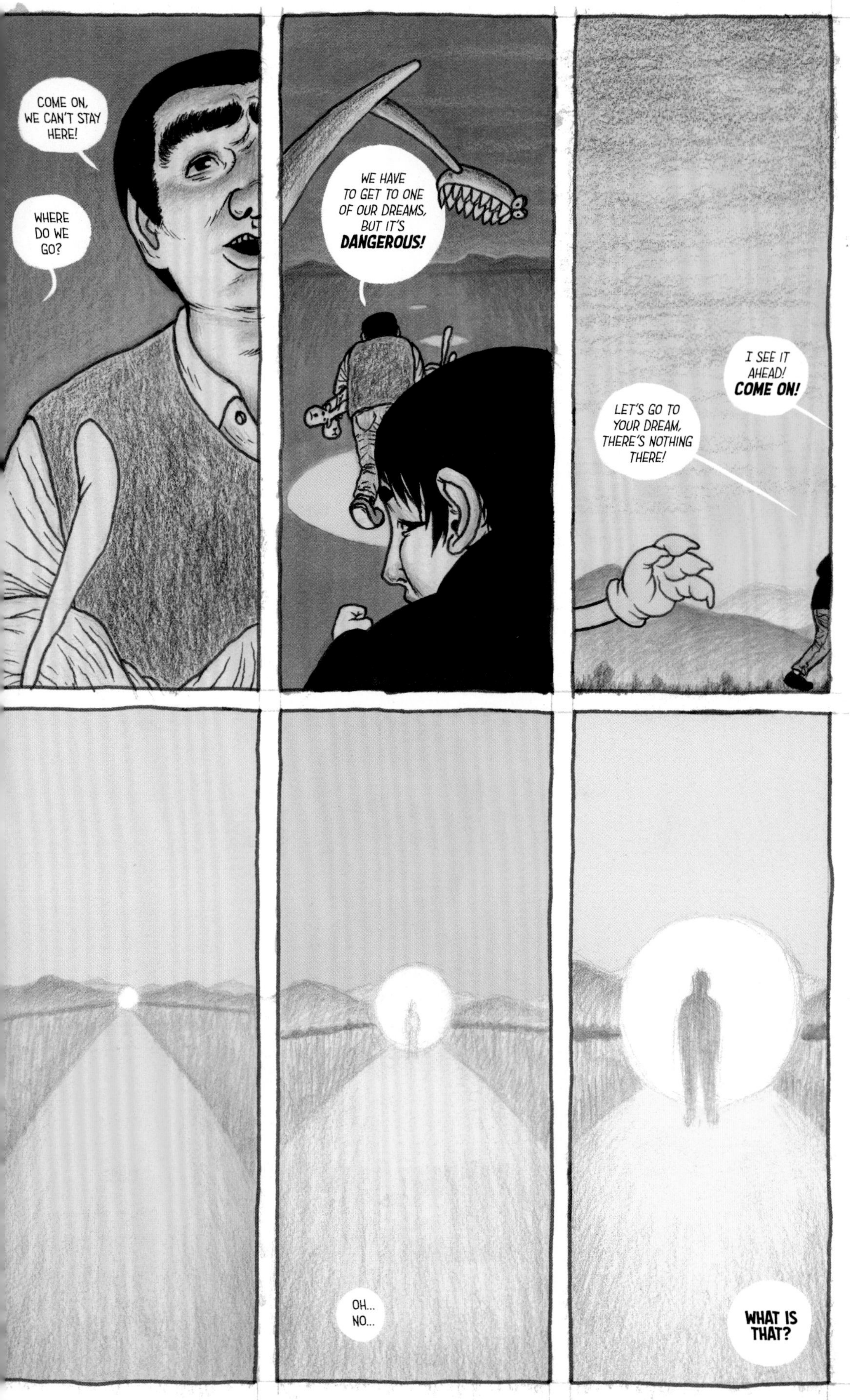
COME ON, WE CAN'T STAY HERE!
WHERE DO WE GO?
WE HAVE TO GET TO ONE OF OUR DREAMS, BUT IT'S **DANGEROUS!**
I SEE IT AHEAD! **COME ON!**
LET'S GO TO YOUR DREAM, THERE'S NOTHING THERE!
OH... NO...
WHAT IS THAT?

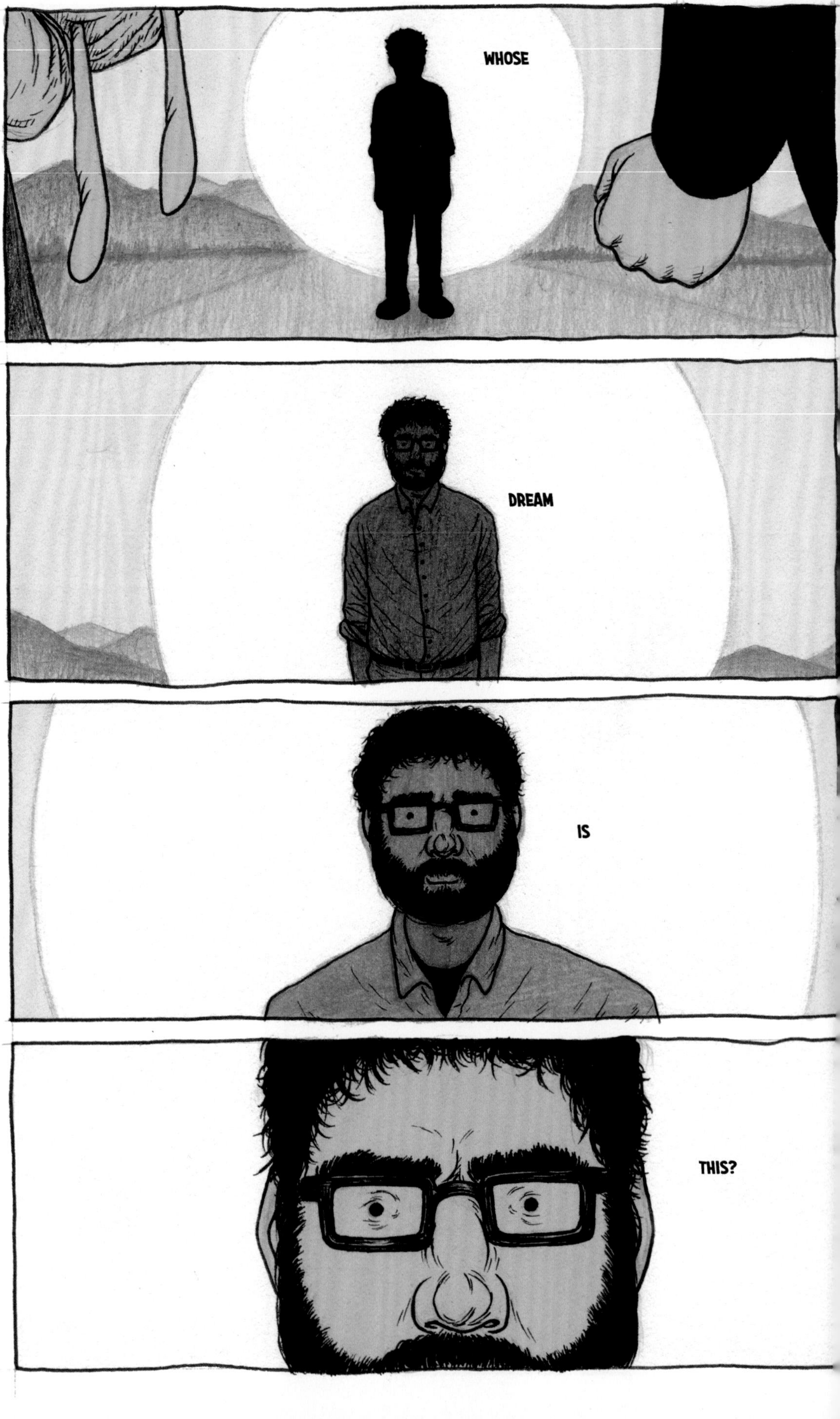
WHOSE
DREAM
IS
THIS?

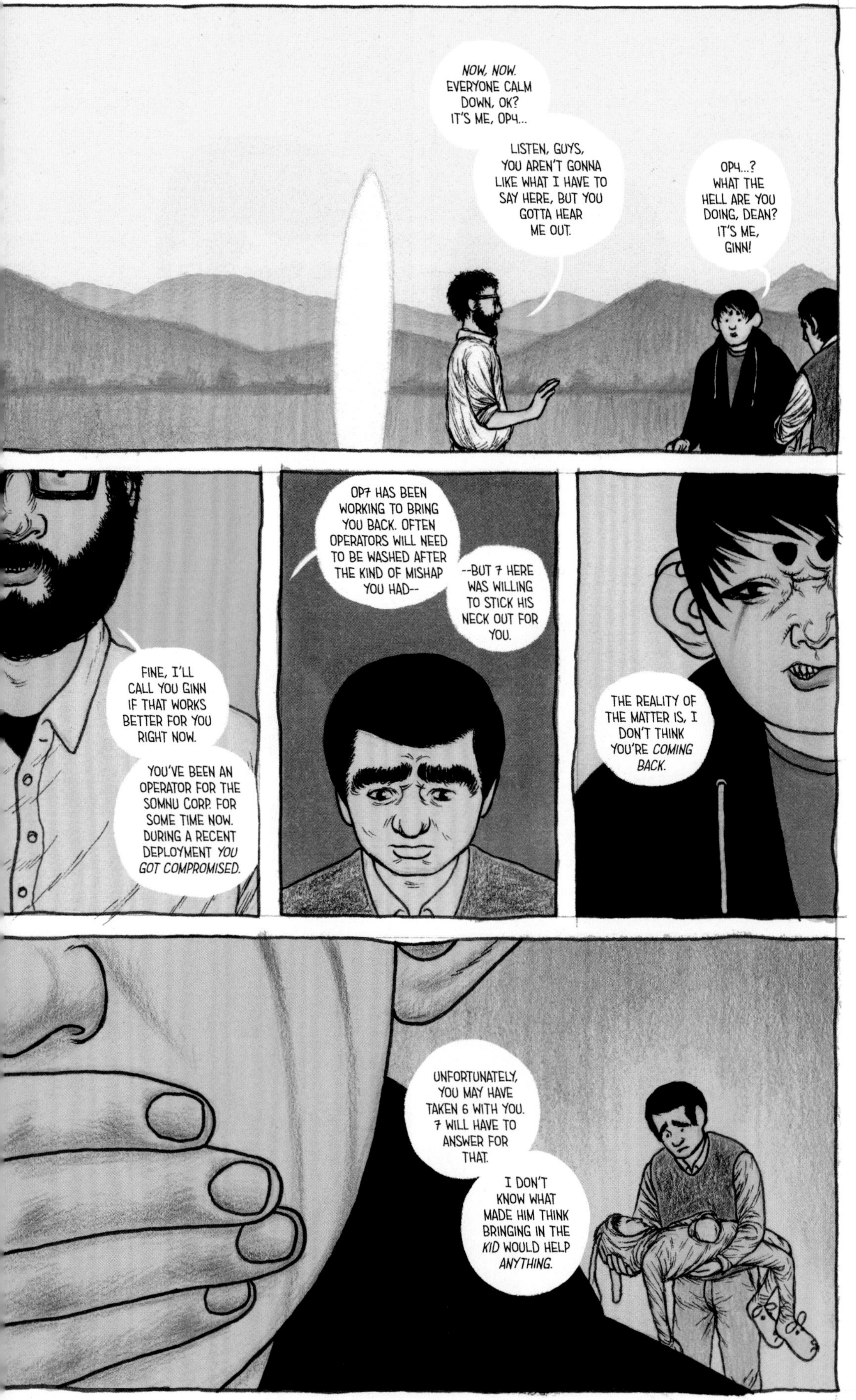
NOW, NOW. EVERYONE CALM DOWN, OK? IT'S ME, OP4...
LISTEN, GUYS, YOU AREN'T GONNA LIKE WHAT I HAVE TO SAY HERE, BUT YOU GOTTA HEAR ME OUT.
OP4...? WHAT THE HELL ARE YOU DOING, DEAN? IT'S ME, GINN!
FINE, I'LL CALL YOU GINN IF THAT WORKS BETTER FOR YOU RIGHT NOW.
YOU'VE BEEN AN OPERATOR FOR THE SOMNU CORP. FOR SOME TIME NOW. DURING A RECENT DEPLOYMENT YOU GOT COMPROMISED.
OP7 HAS BEEN WORKING TO BRING YOU BACK. OFTEN OPERATORS WILL NEED TO BE WASHED AFTER THE KIND OF MISHAP YOU HAD--
--BUT 7 HERE WAS WILLING TO STICK HIS NECK OUT FOR YOU.
THE REALITY OF THE MATTER IS, I DON'T THINK YOU'RE COMING BACK.
UNFORTUNATELY, YOU MAY HAVE TAKEN 6 WITH YOU. 7 WILL HAVE TO ANSWER FOR THAT.
I DON'T KNOW WHAT MADE HIM THINK BRINGING IN THE KID WOULD HELP ANYTHING.

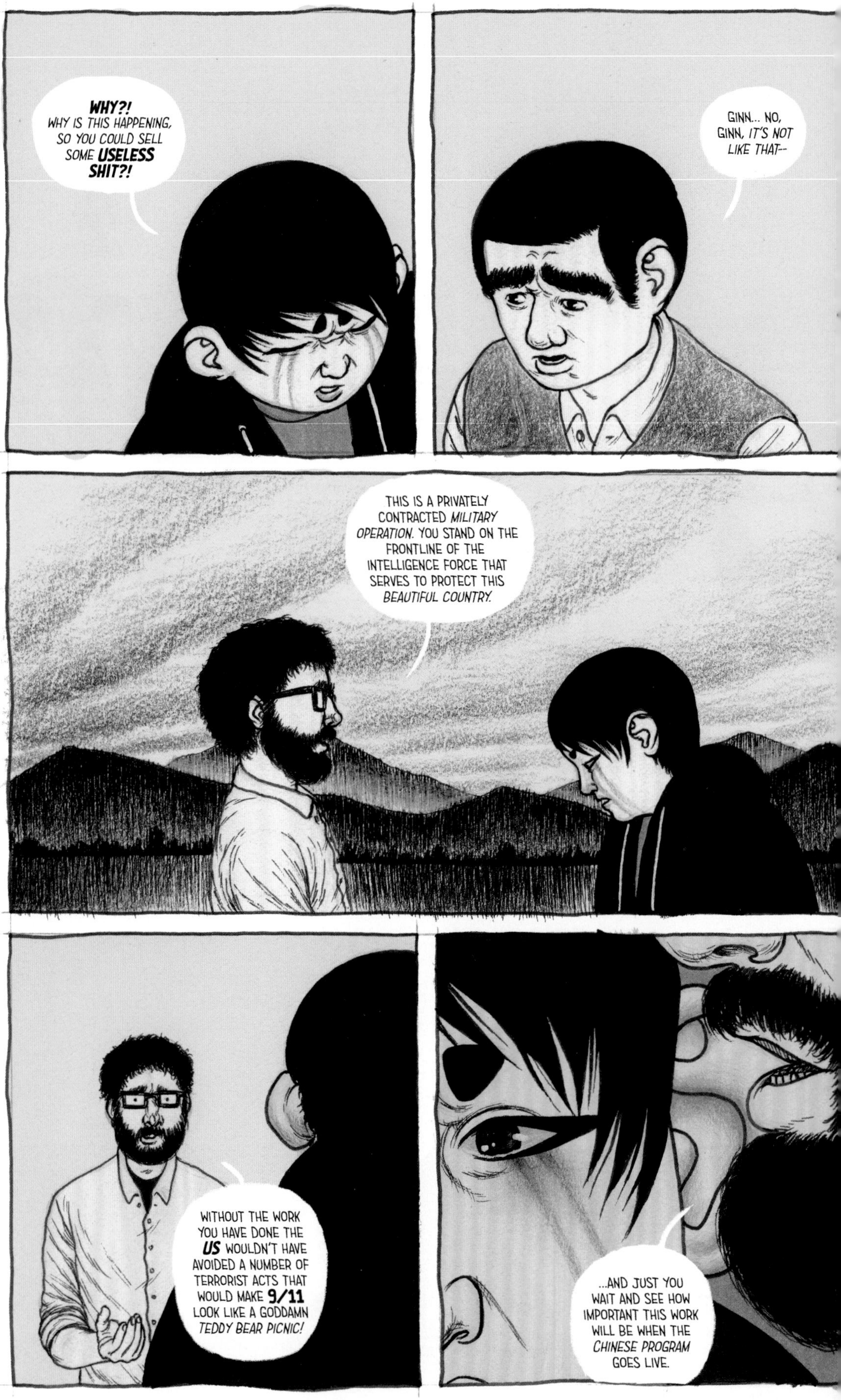
WHY?! WHY IS THIS HAPPENING, SO YOU COULD SELL SOME USELESS SHIT?!
GINN... NO, GINN, IT'S NOT LIKE THAT--
THIS IS A PRIVATELY CONTRACTED MILITARY OPERATION. YOU STAND ON THE FRONTLINE OF THE INTELLIGENCE FORCE THAT SERVES TO PROTECT THIS BEAUTIFUL COUNTRY.
WITHOUT THE WORK YOU HAVE DONE THE US WOULDN'T HAVE AVOIDED A NUMBER OF TERRORIST ACTS THAT WOULD MAKE 9/11 LOOK LIKE A GODDAMN TEDDY BEAR PICNIC!
...AND JUST YOU WAIT AND SEE HOW IMPORTANT THIS WORK WILL BE WHEN THE CHINESE PROGRAM GOES LIVE.

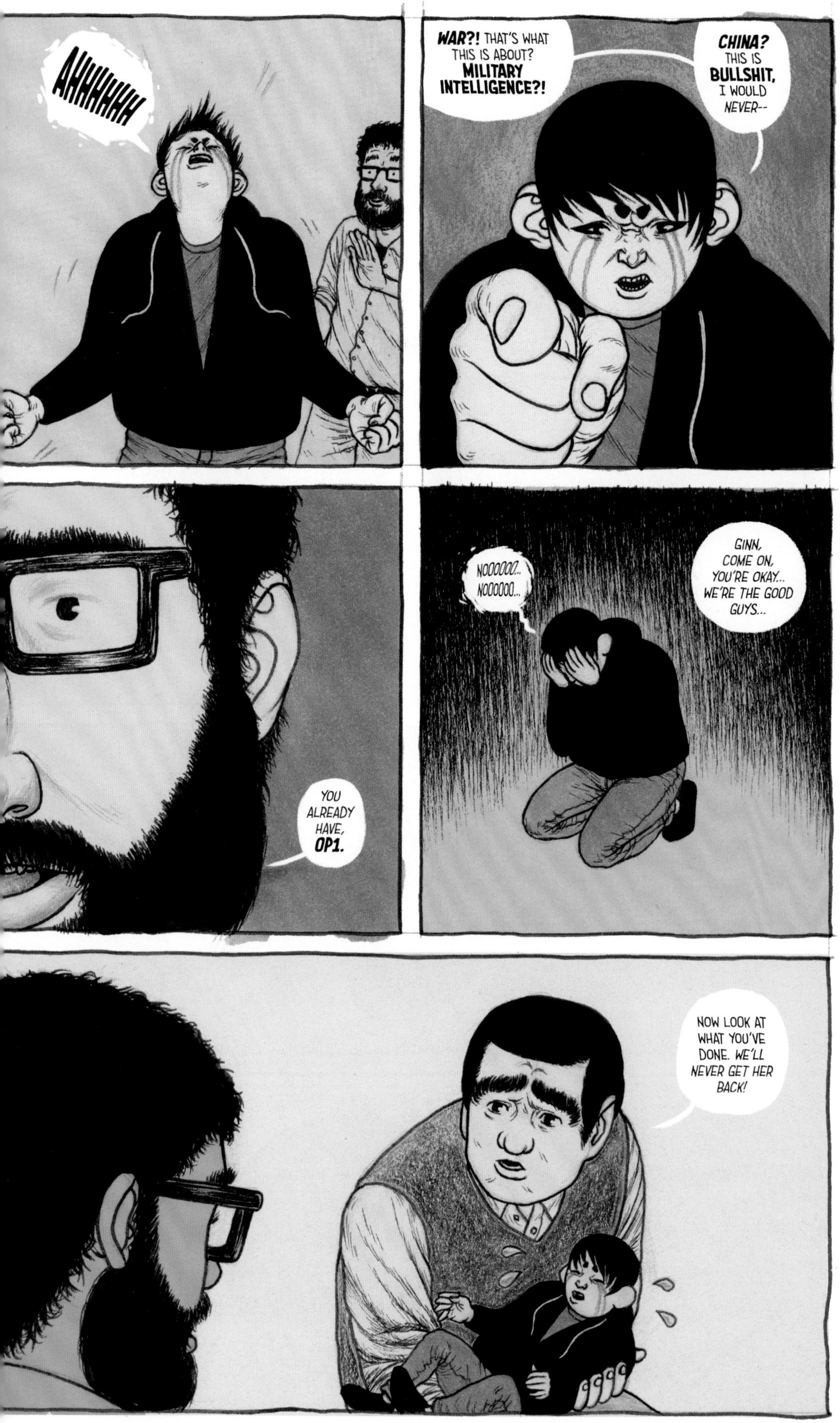
AHHHHHH
WAR?! THAT'S WHAT THIS IS ABOUT? MILITARY INTELLIGENCE?!
CHINA? THIS IS BULLSHIT, I WOULD NEVER--
YOU ALREADY HAVE, OP1.
NOOOOOO... NOOOOOO...
GINN, COME ON, YOU'RE OKAY... WE'RE THE GOOD GUYS...
NOW LOOK AT WHAT YOU'VE DONE. WE'LL NEVER GET HER BACK!

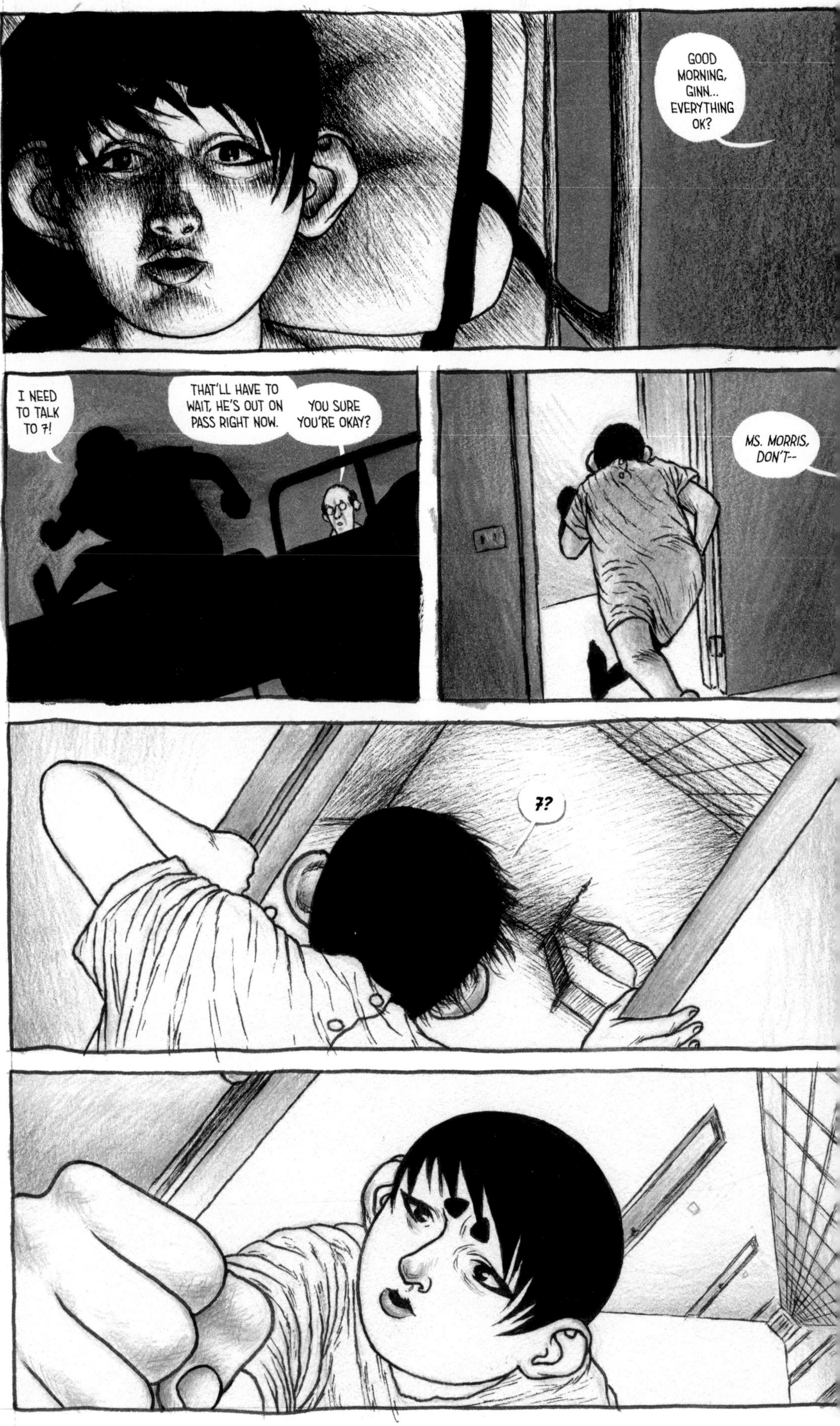
GOOD MORNING, GINN... EVERYTHING OK?
I NEED TO TALK TO 7!
THAT'LL HAVE TO WAIT, HE'S OUT ON PASS RIGHT NOW.
YOU SURE YOU'RE OKAY?
MS. MORRIS, DON'T--
7?

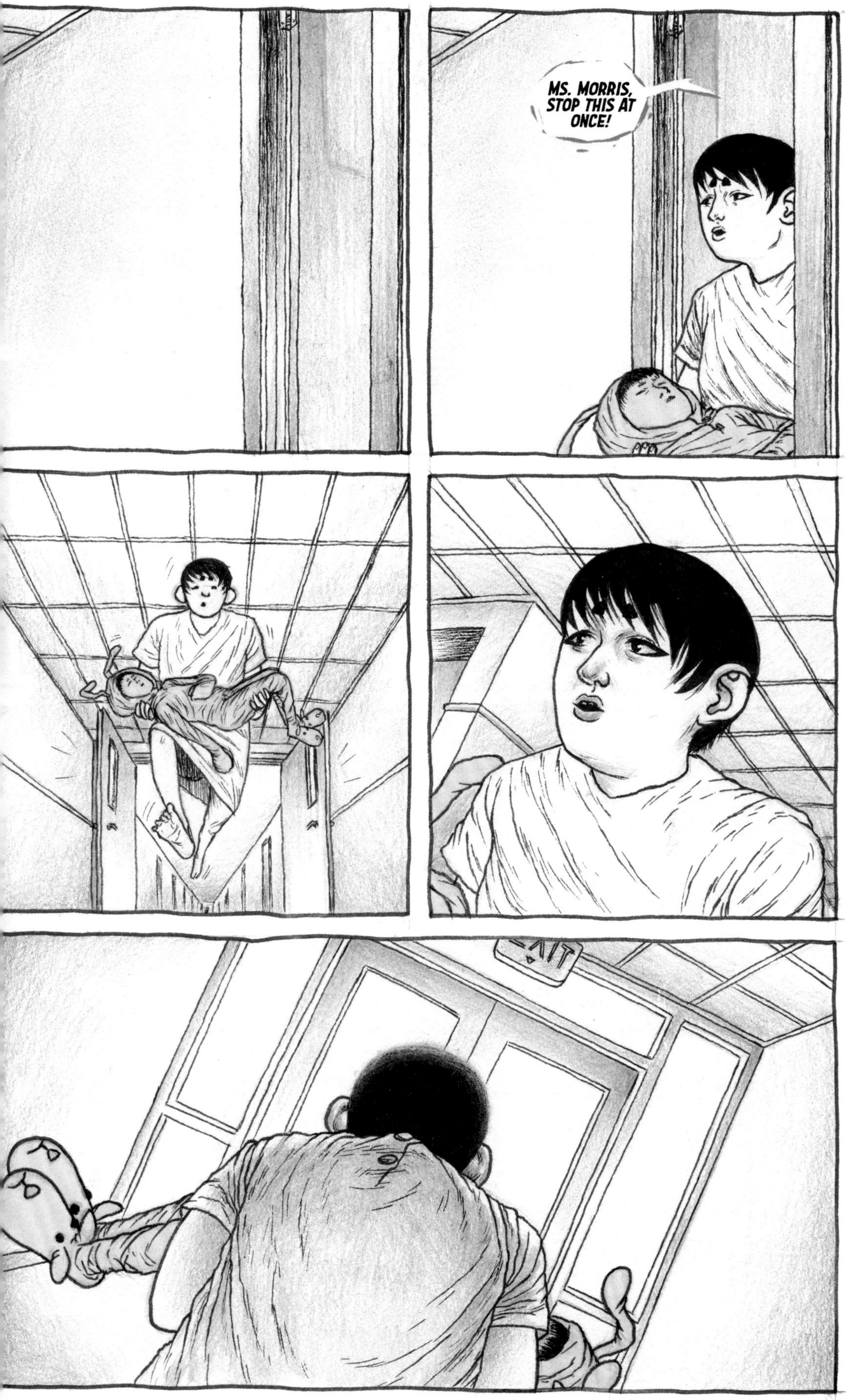
MS. MORRIS, STOP THIS AT ONCE!

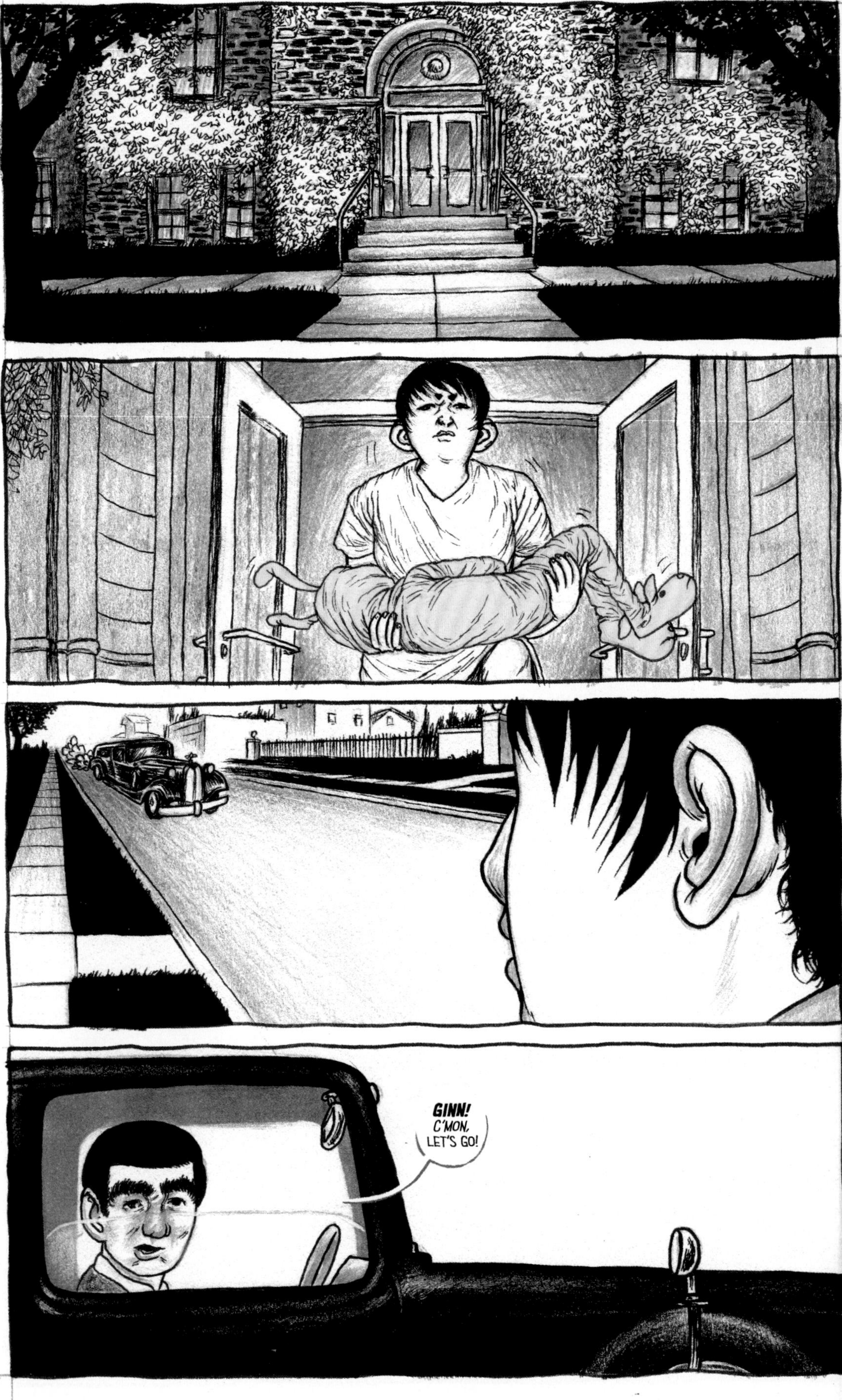
GINN! C'MON, LET'S GO!

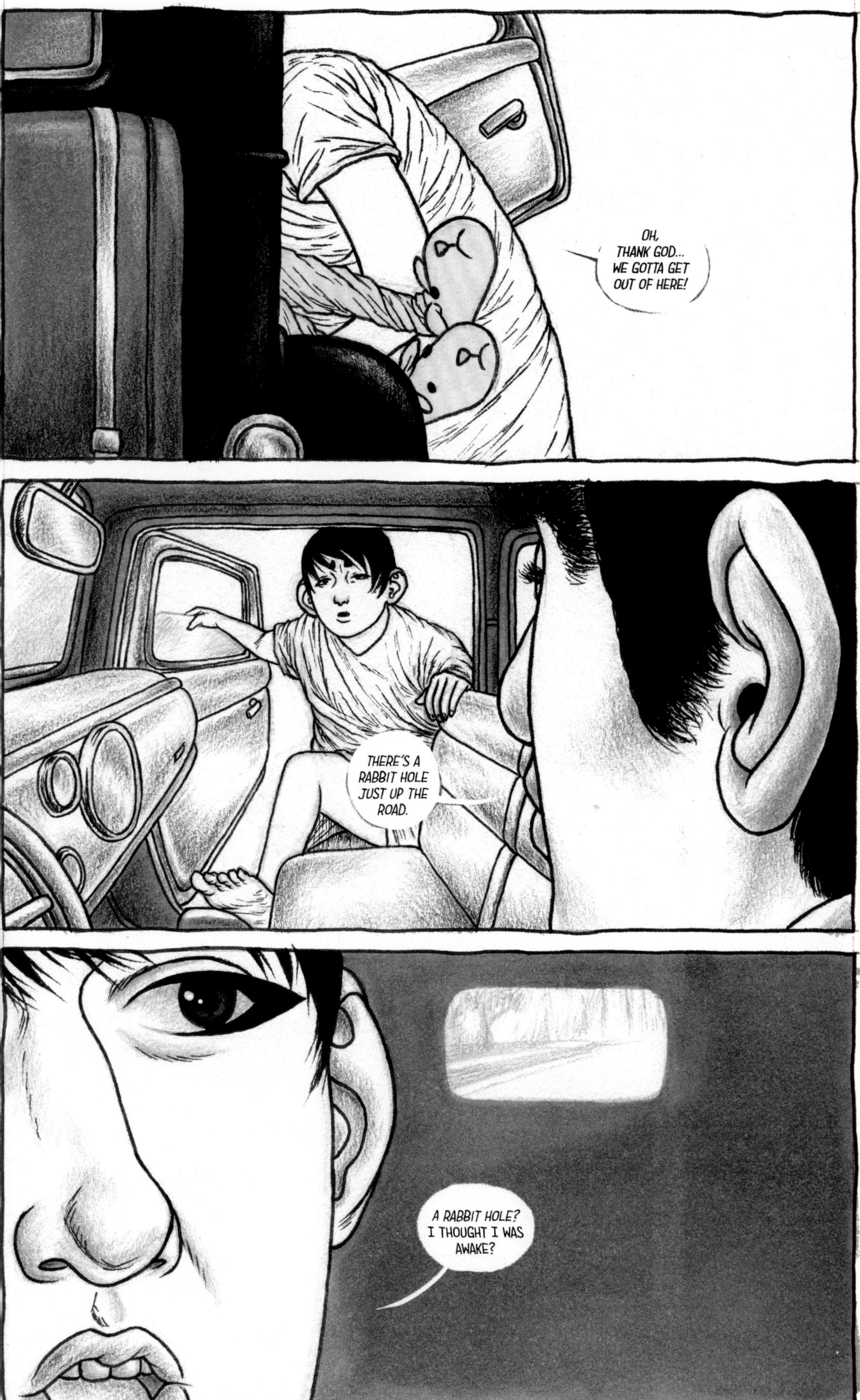
OH, THANK GOD... WE GOTTA GET OUT OF HERE!
THERE'S A RABBIT HOLE JUST UP THE ROAD.
A RABBIT HOLE? I THOUGHT I WAS AWAKE?

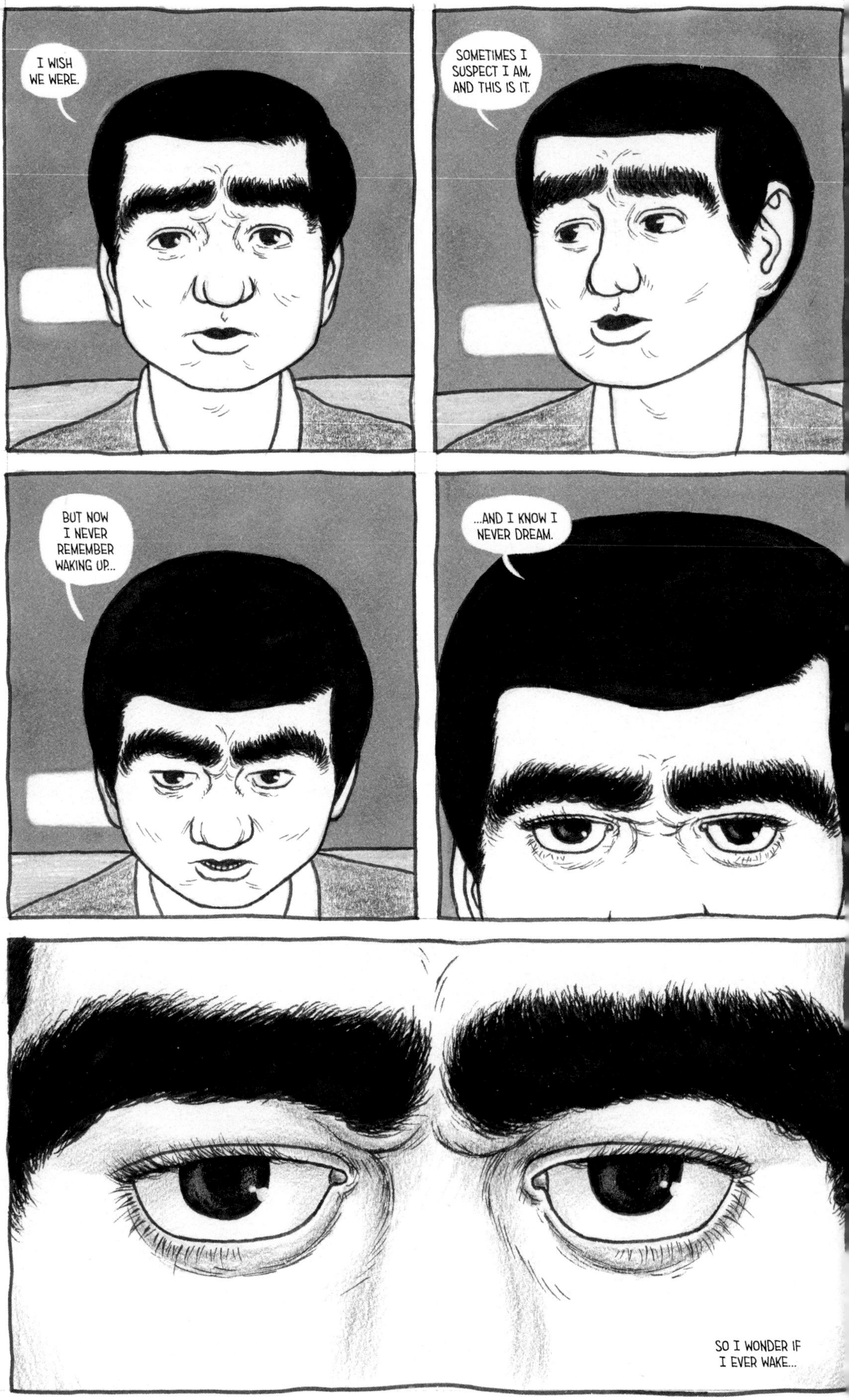
I WISH WE WERE.
SOMETIMES I SUSPECT I AM, AND THIS IS IT.
BUT NOW I NEVER REMEMBER WAKING UP...
...AND I KNOW I NEVER DREAM.
SO I WONDER IF I EVER WAKE...

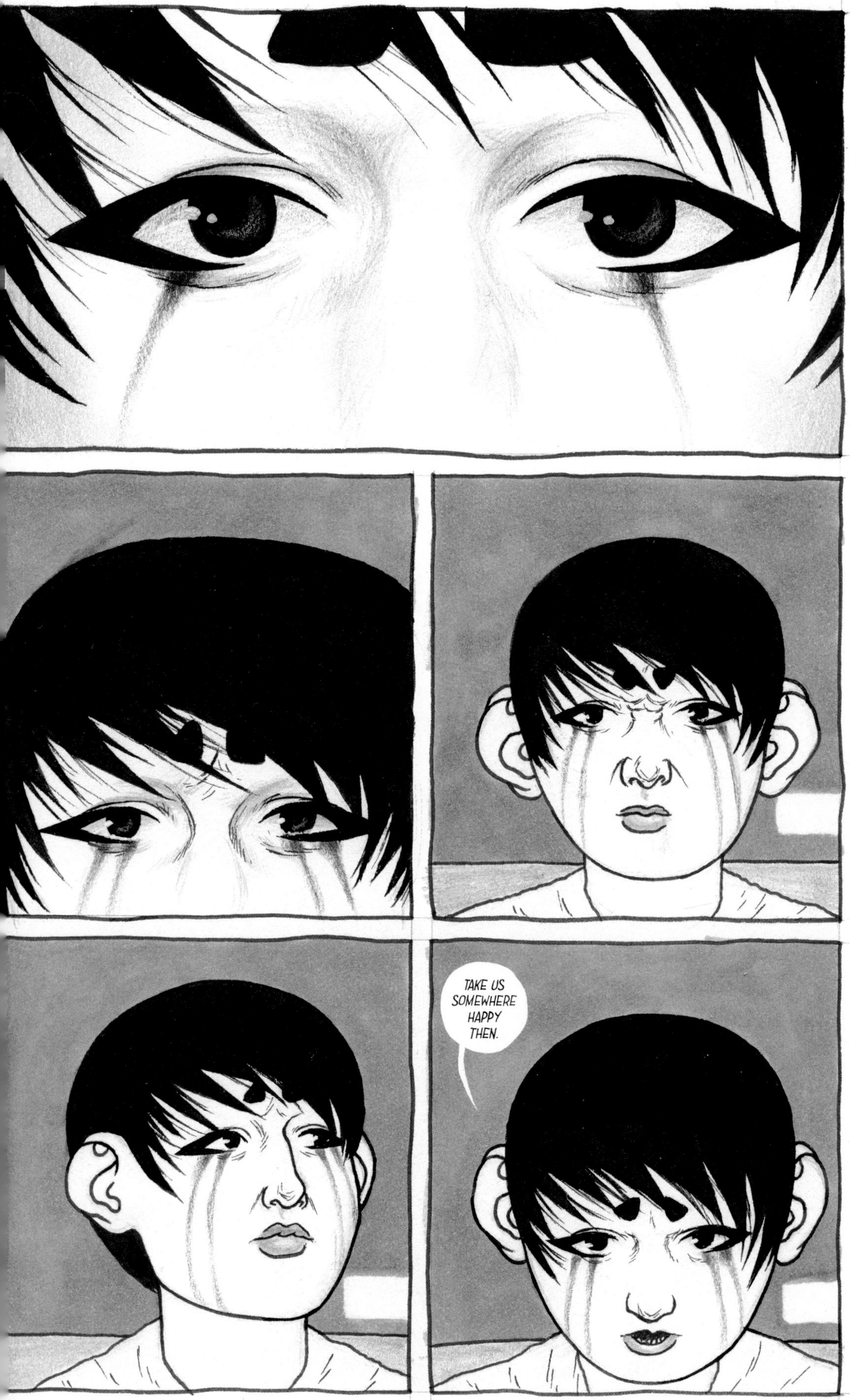
TAKE US SOMEWHERE HAPPY THEN.

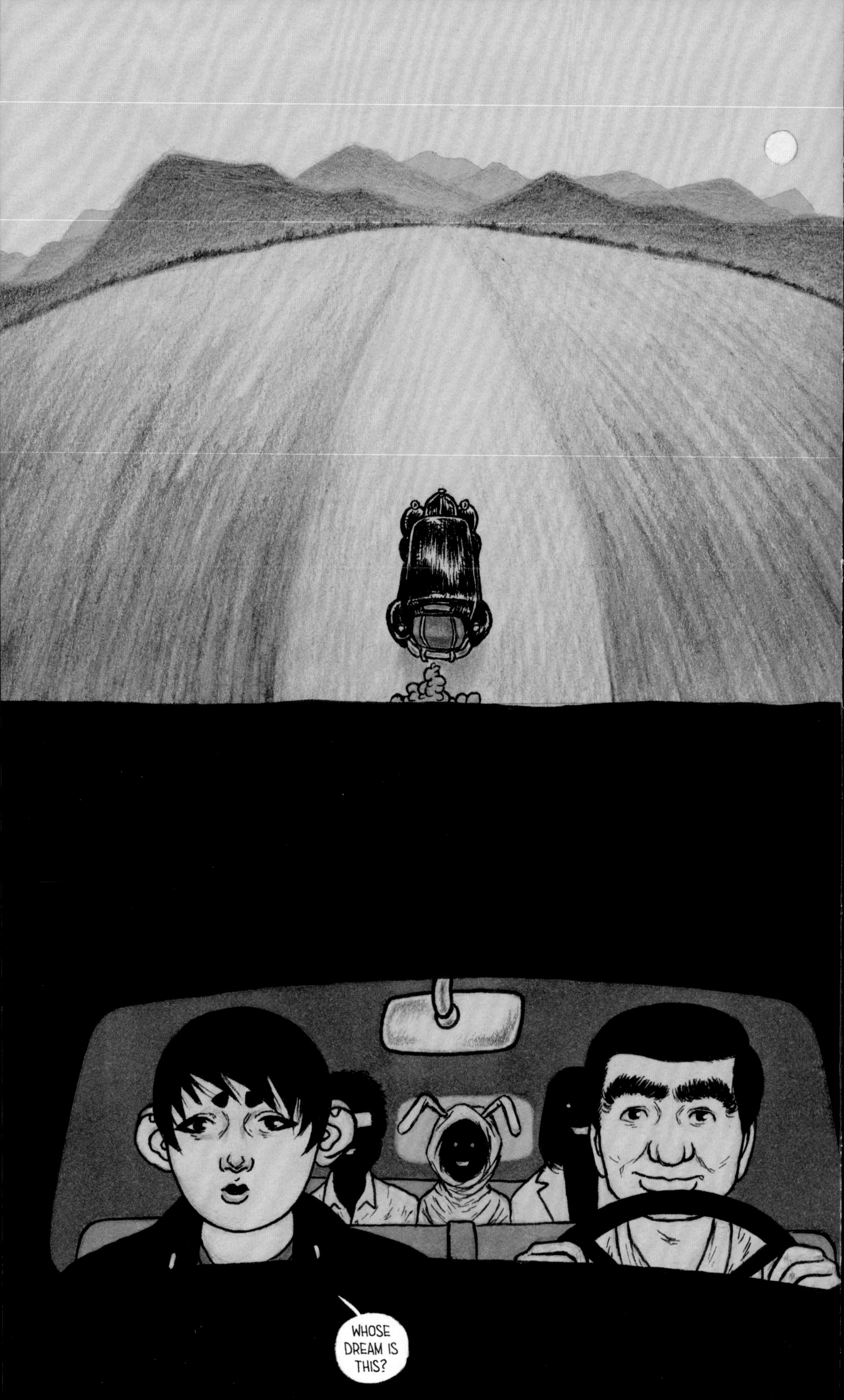
WHOSE DREAM IS THIS?

# EPILOGUE

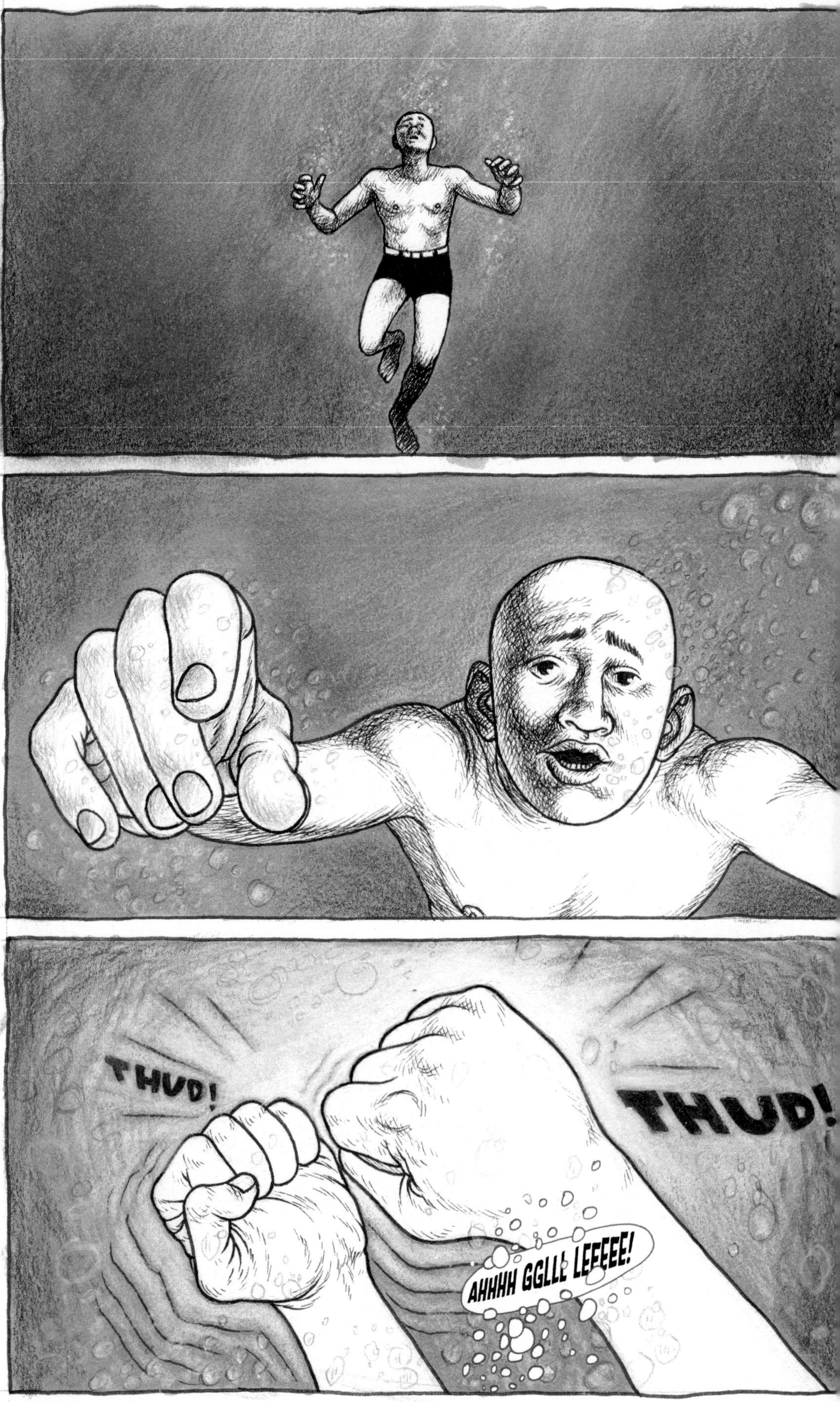
THUD!
THUD!
AHHHH GGLLL LEEEEE!

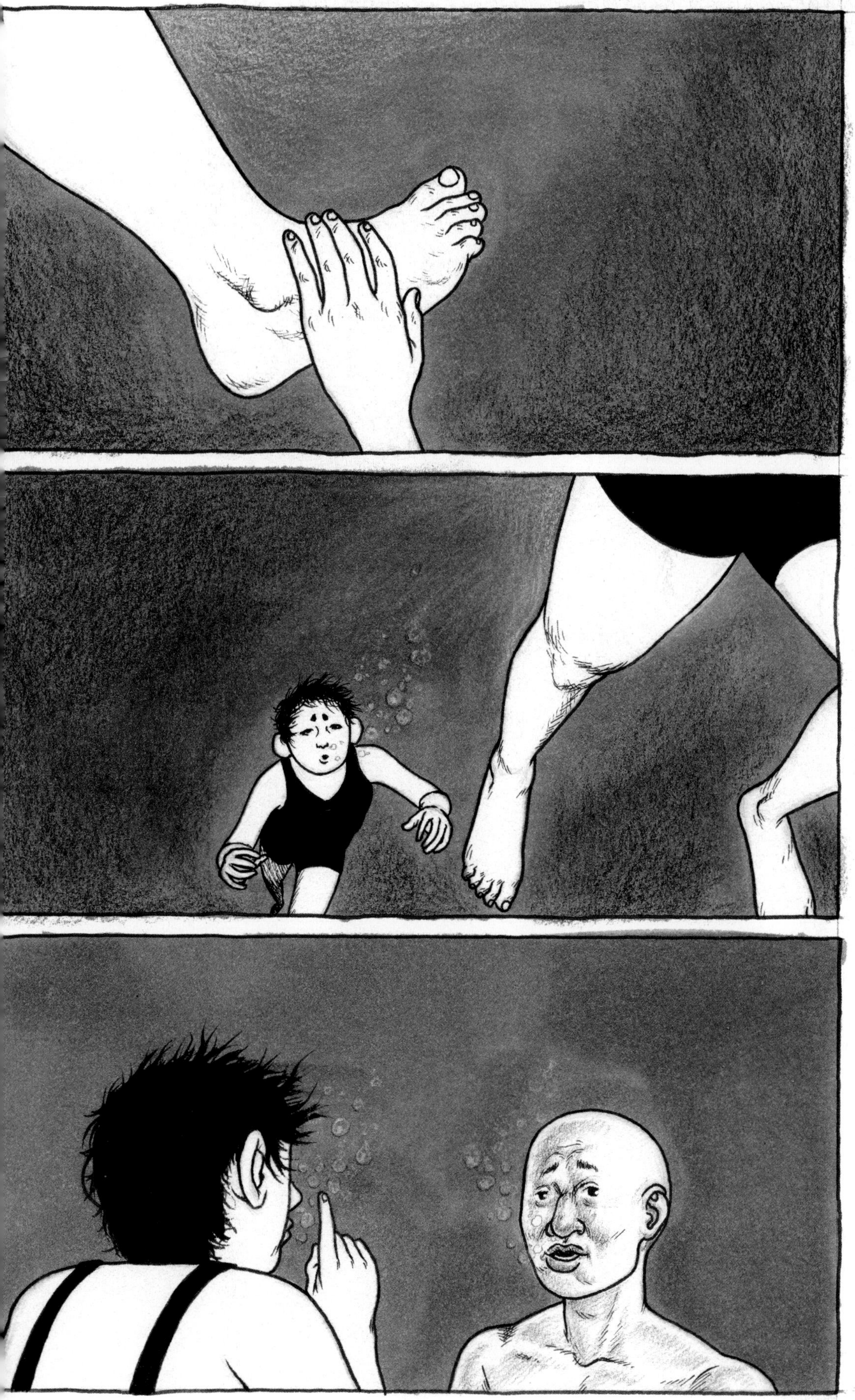

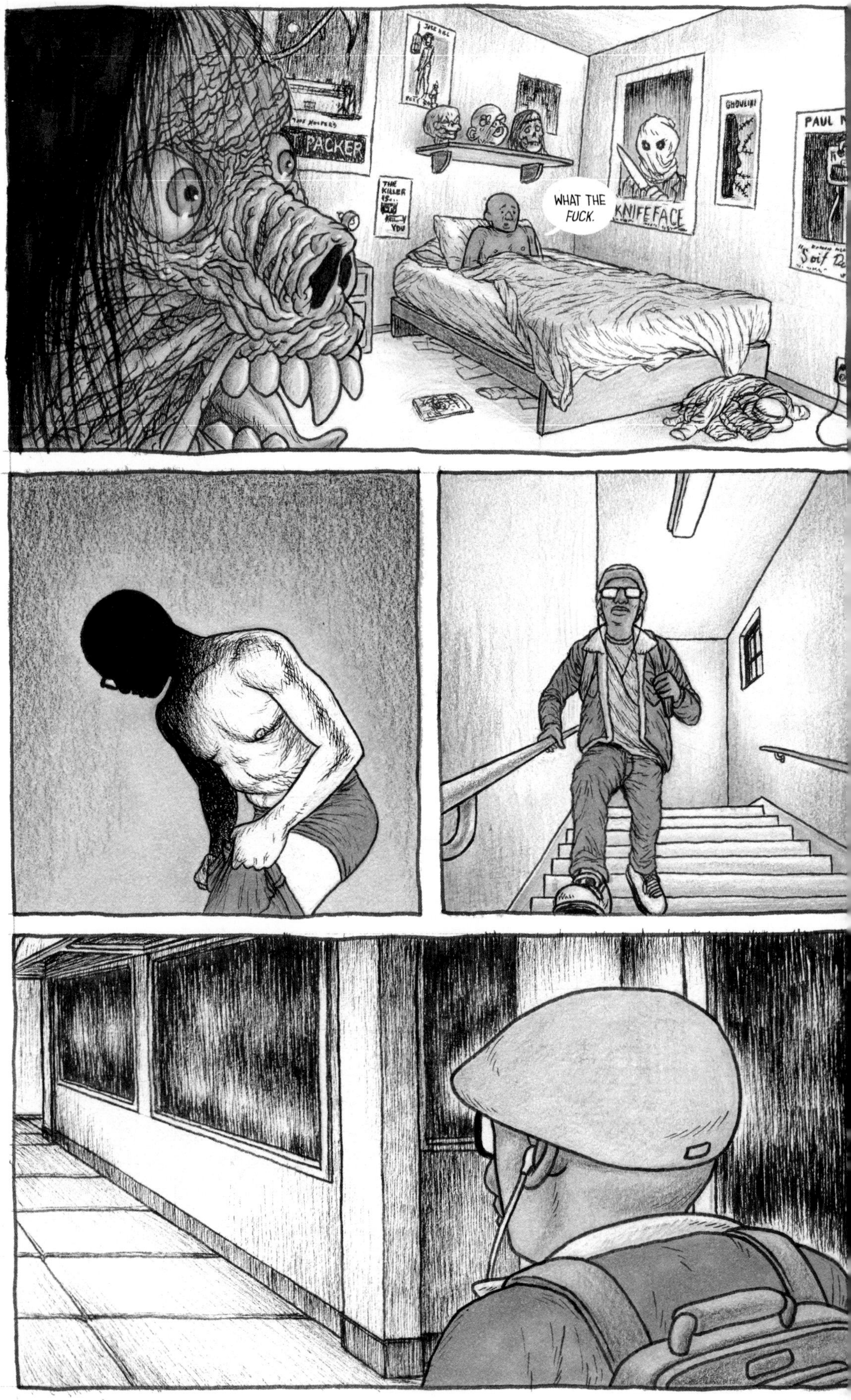
PACKER
THE KILLER IS...
KNIFEFACE
WHAT THE FUCK.

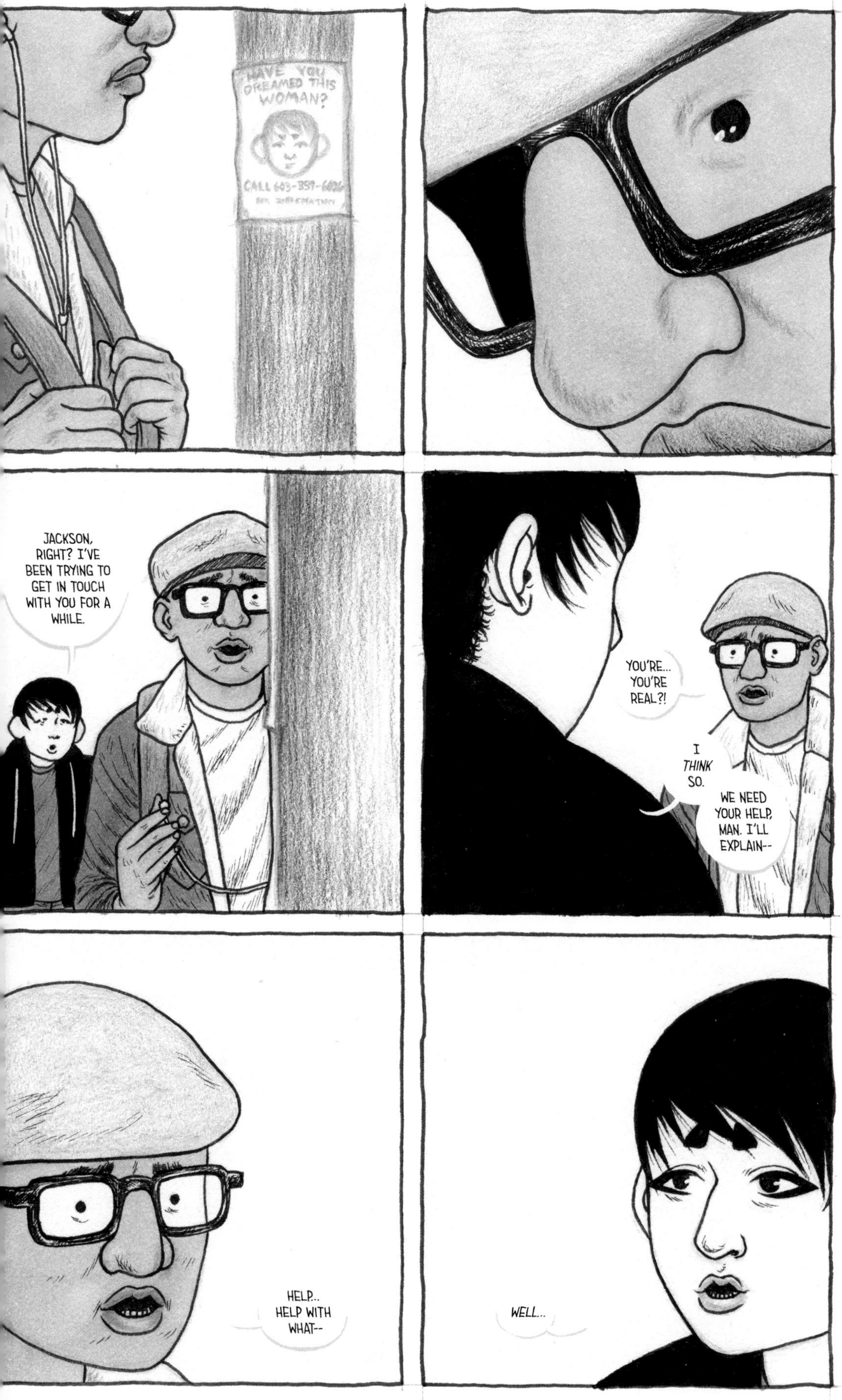
HAVE YOU DREAMED THIS WOMAN?
CALL 603-359-6026
JACKSON, RIGHT? I'VE BEEN TRYING TO GET IN TOUCH WITH YOU FOR A WHILE.
YOU'RE... YOU'RE REAL?!
I *THINK* SO.
WE NEED YOUR HELP, MAN. I'LL EXPLAIN--
HELP... HELP WITH WHAT--
WELL...

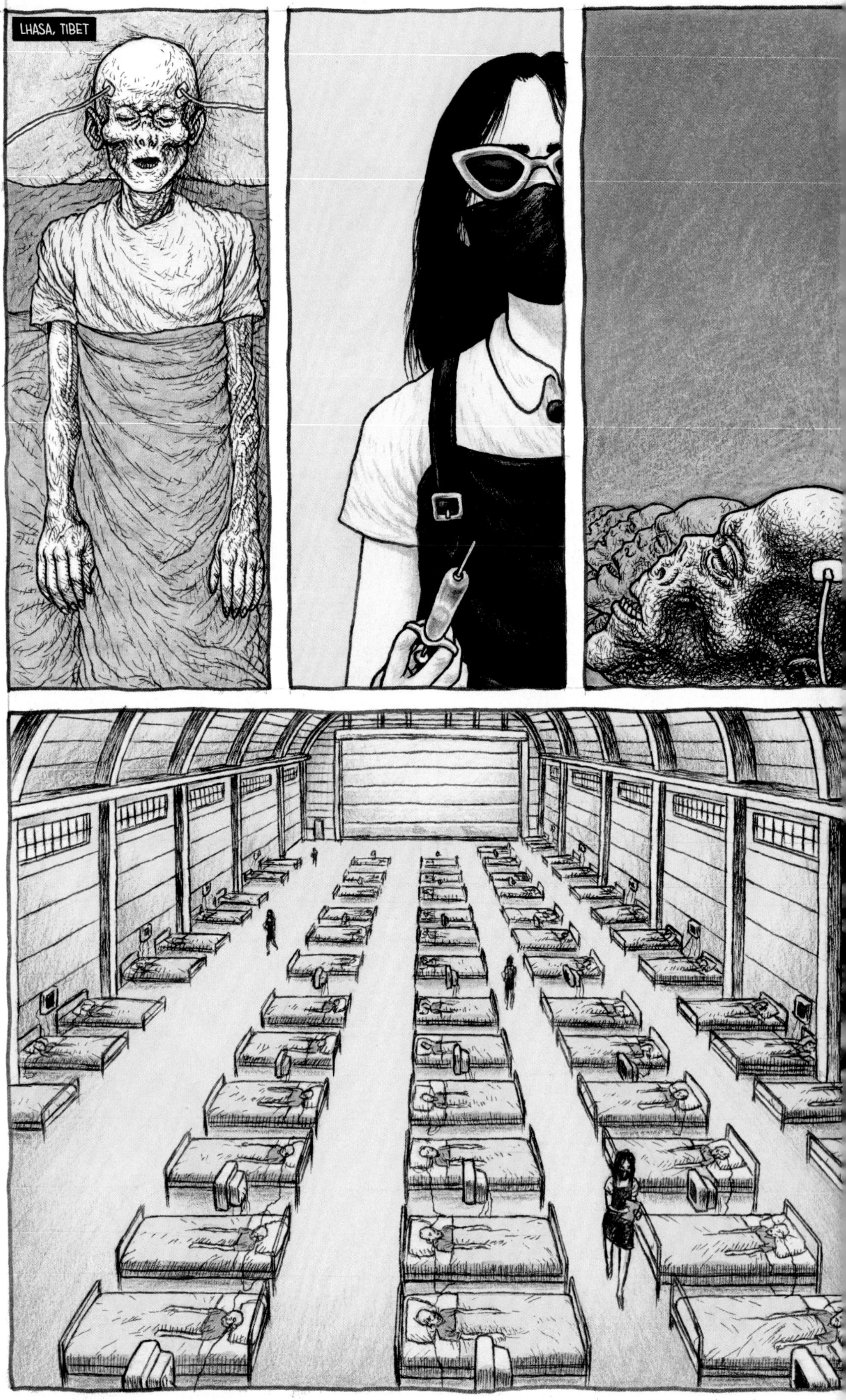
LHASA, TIBET

I killed a classmate in a lucid dream when I was ten years old. I rarely speak of it, and frankly I'm not very comfortable sharing it here, but it's important to know that this event led me to have an interest in the power of dreams. I am not at all an authority on dreaming and wouldn't wish to convince you otherwise, but *Tremor Dose* has very much been influenced by this interest and the research that I have done over the years.

I'm not the kind of writer who often finds viable narrative elements in my dreams. My dreams are usually little more than mundane expressions of anxiety played out in an obtuse and often nonlinear manner. One of the theories about dreams is that they are a means with which people untangle unresolved issues from their waking life, in my case it feels more like a meditation on these. In my dreams things don't often get solved, hell, the stressors are rarely even identified, it's simply understood that something is awry.

If Noah and I have done it right *Tremor Dose* should give all the key information to provide the answers to the questions it raises. Unlike my dreams everything in the book exists for a reason and we have taken effort to avoid red herrings. At first blush something might seem out of place or incongruent, but I promise you, everything is right where it belongs.

There were times during the creation of this book that I have felt like we were going crazy. Our story didn't fit a genre and Noah's art looks like no one else in comics. We were "crazy" or we were on to something completely original and divergent from the common expectations of what makes a good comic. We lack fisticuffs, overtly attractive characters, political agendas, and a simple elevator pitch. In the process of making this I had at times considered sexing it up through using such elements, but in the end we followed our hearts. During the pitches we did with ComiXology Originals I struggled to explain what exactly this story was saying. I knew that for us the story was about [redacted] but I have had zero interest in telling you, the reader, what to think or feel. In the end I will be very happy if you enjoy the art and the story, the rest is up to you.

The fact is ComiXology Originals took a big chance on this one. I understood this when I was told by Chip Mosher and Ivan Salazar (our champions over there) that this would be "by far the weirdest book ComiXology Originals has done" . . . upon hearing this I immediately called Noah and let him know that it had worked. We had created something that was too compelling to walk away from. We made no effort to intentionally go weird, but weird is what happens when creators like us are allowed to have a voice unclouded by a room full of suits with no vision. We truly owe them a huge debt, without their belief in us this book would likely have never found you.

We hope you enjoyed it. We fell in love with these characters and this world. With any luck at some point you will wake feeling like someone has found a way into your dreams, or like you have entered someone else's. If this is the case, be sure to behave with care and compassion always (unlike the young/angry me), there's a war going on and it's only won when we realize that we all share the same dreams.

With Love—
Michael Conrad

# SKETCHES

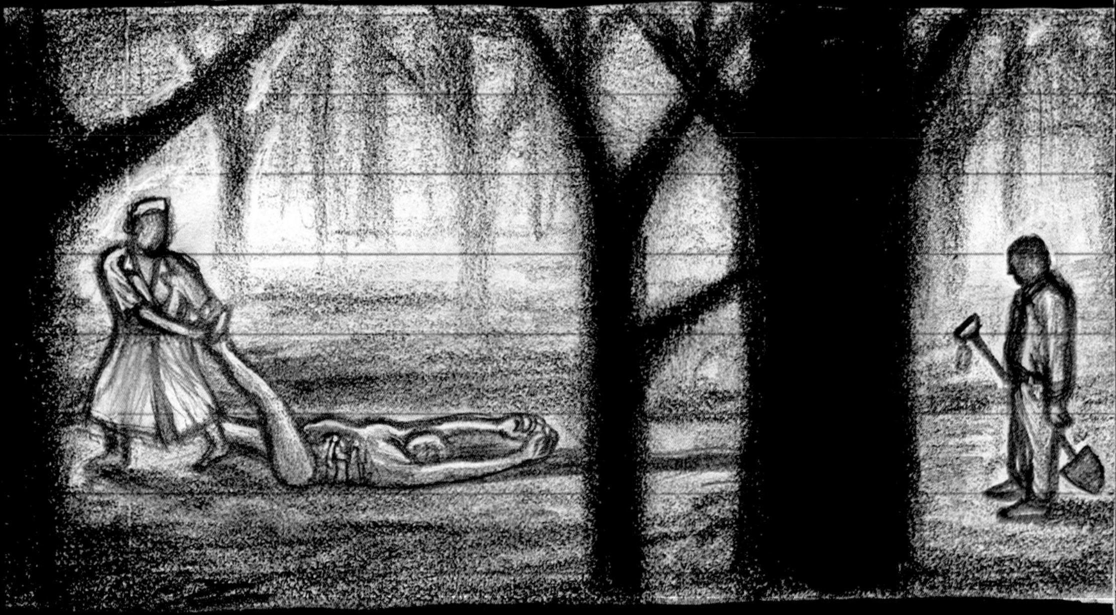

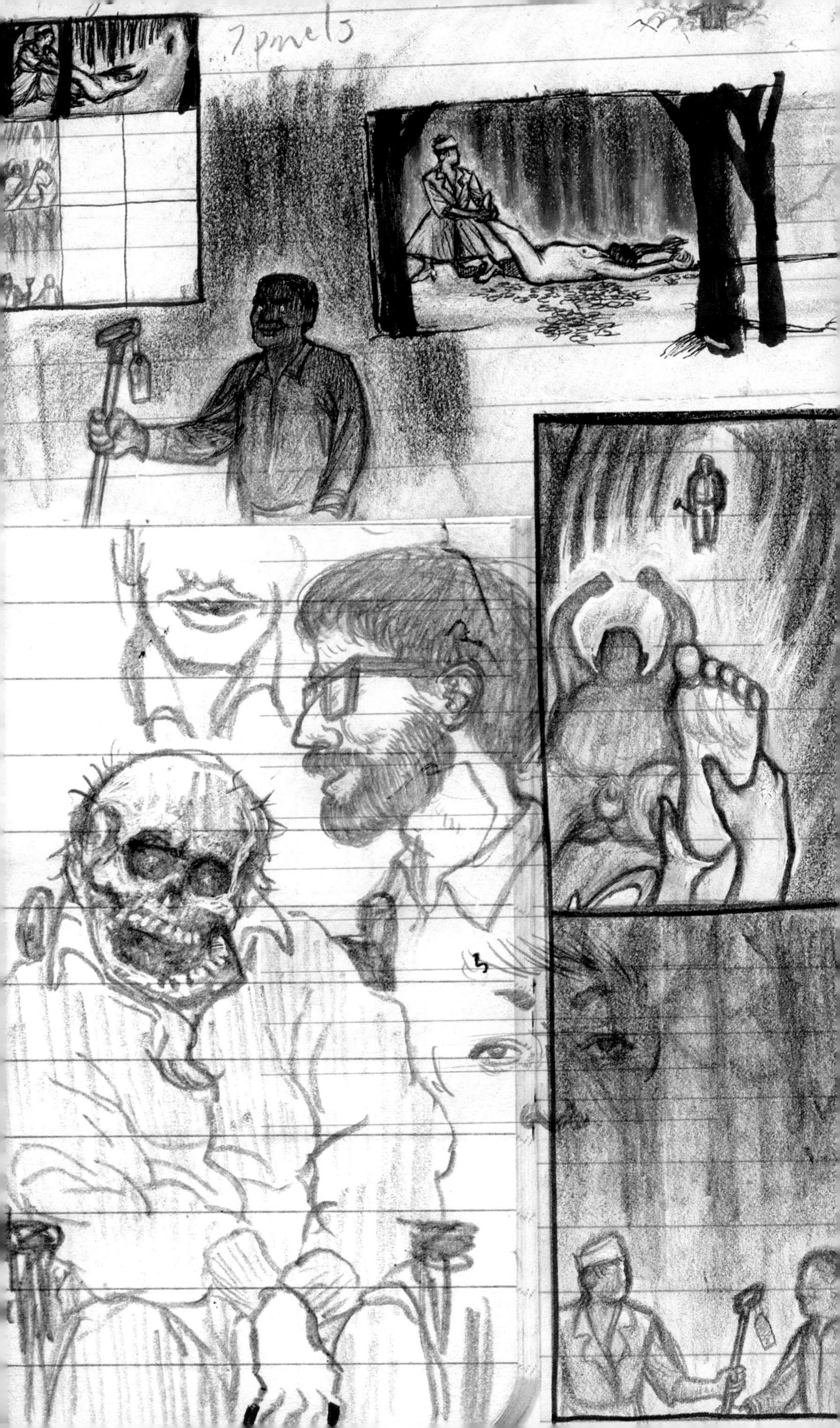
7 panels

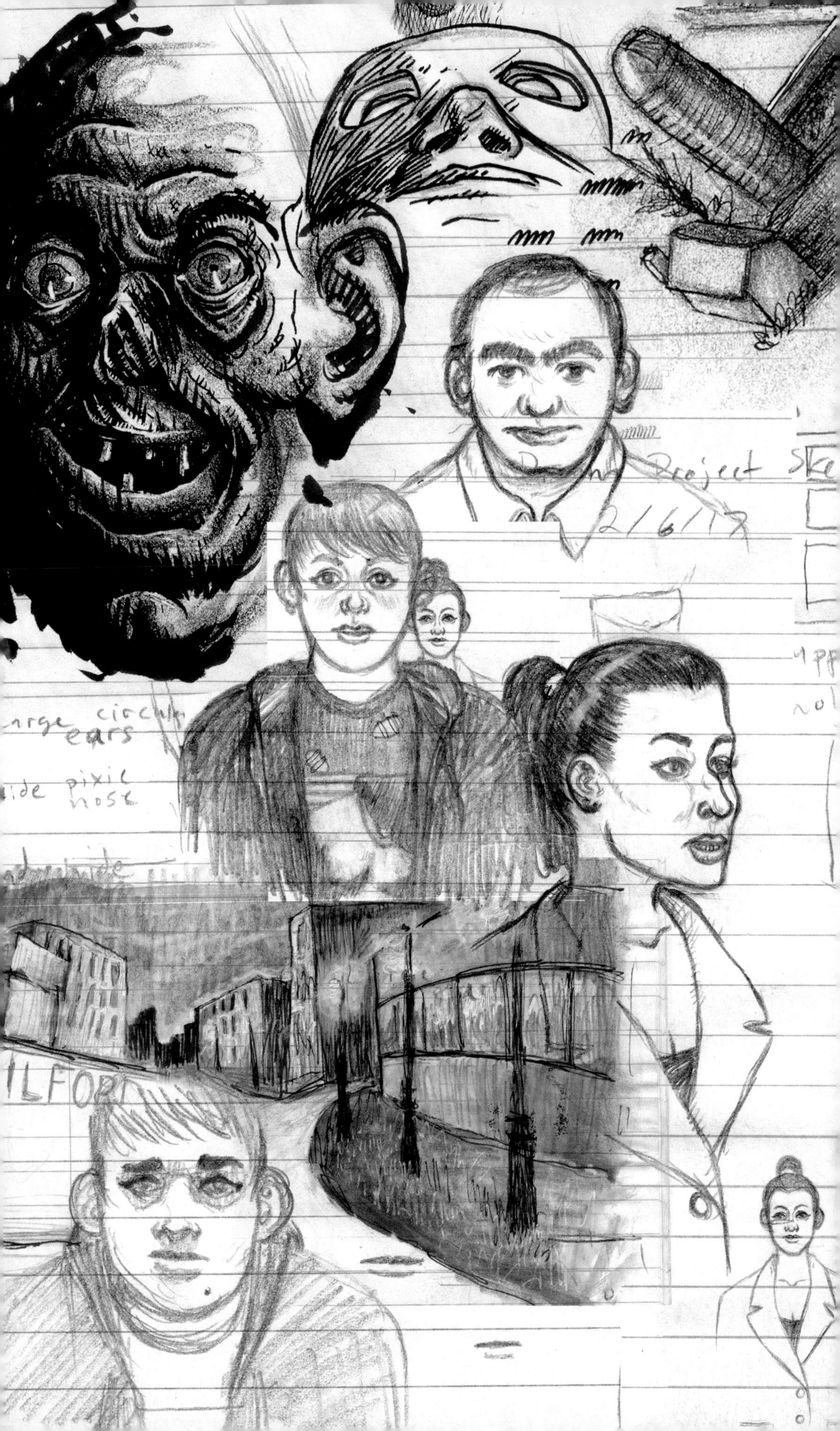
Project
ears
pixie
nose

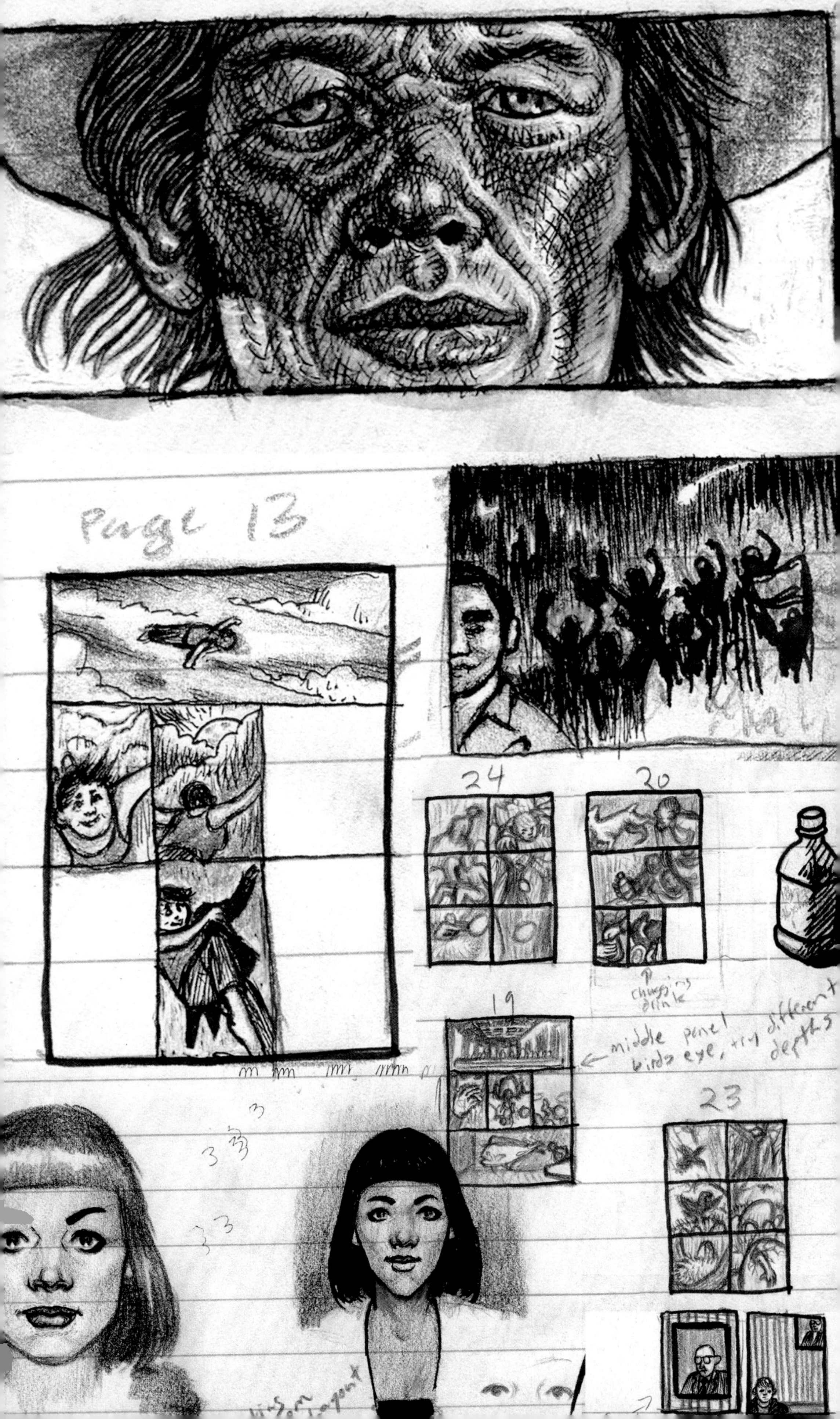
Page 13
24
20
chugging drink
19
middle panel birds eye, try different depths
23

TD11 Thumbnails

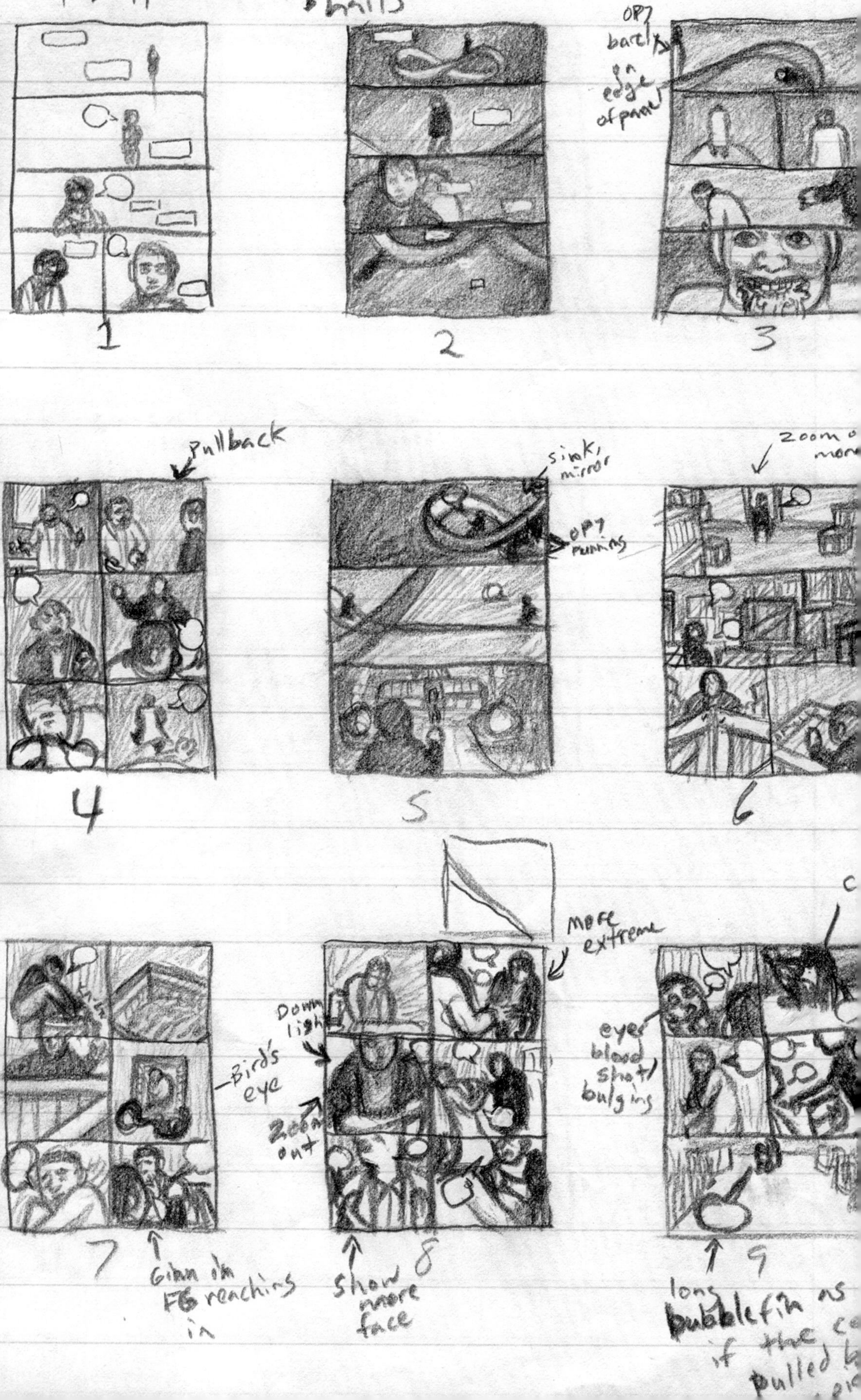

1
2
OP7 barely on edge of panel
3
Pullback
4
sink, mirror
OP7 running
5
6
More extreme
Down light
Zoom out
Bird's eye
eyes blood shot/bulging
7
Gina in FG reaching in
8
Show more face
9
long bubblefin as if the
pulled

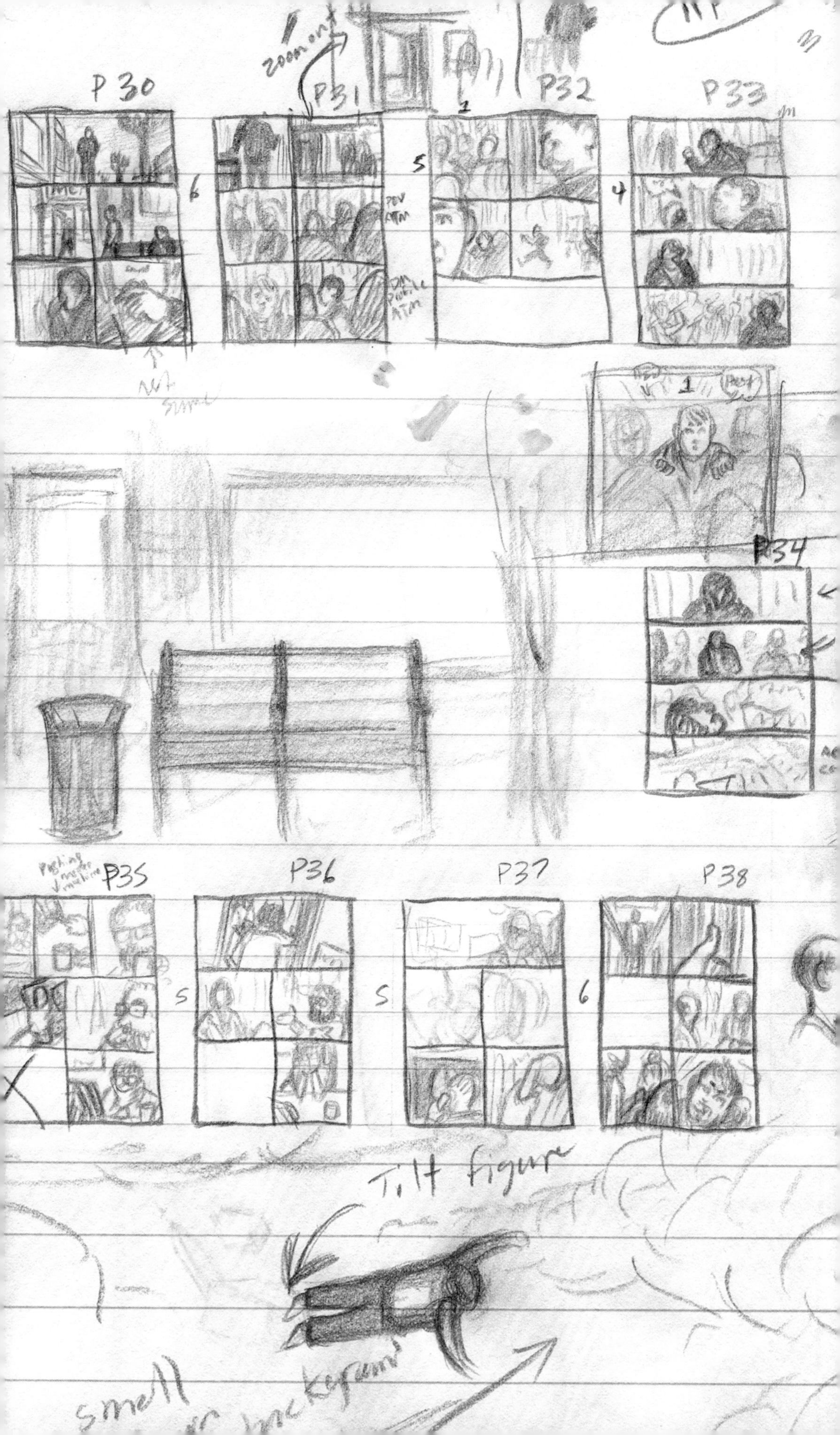
zoom out
P 30
6
P31
POV ATM
P32
5
P33
4
P34
P35
P36
S
P37
S
P38
6
Tilt figure
small

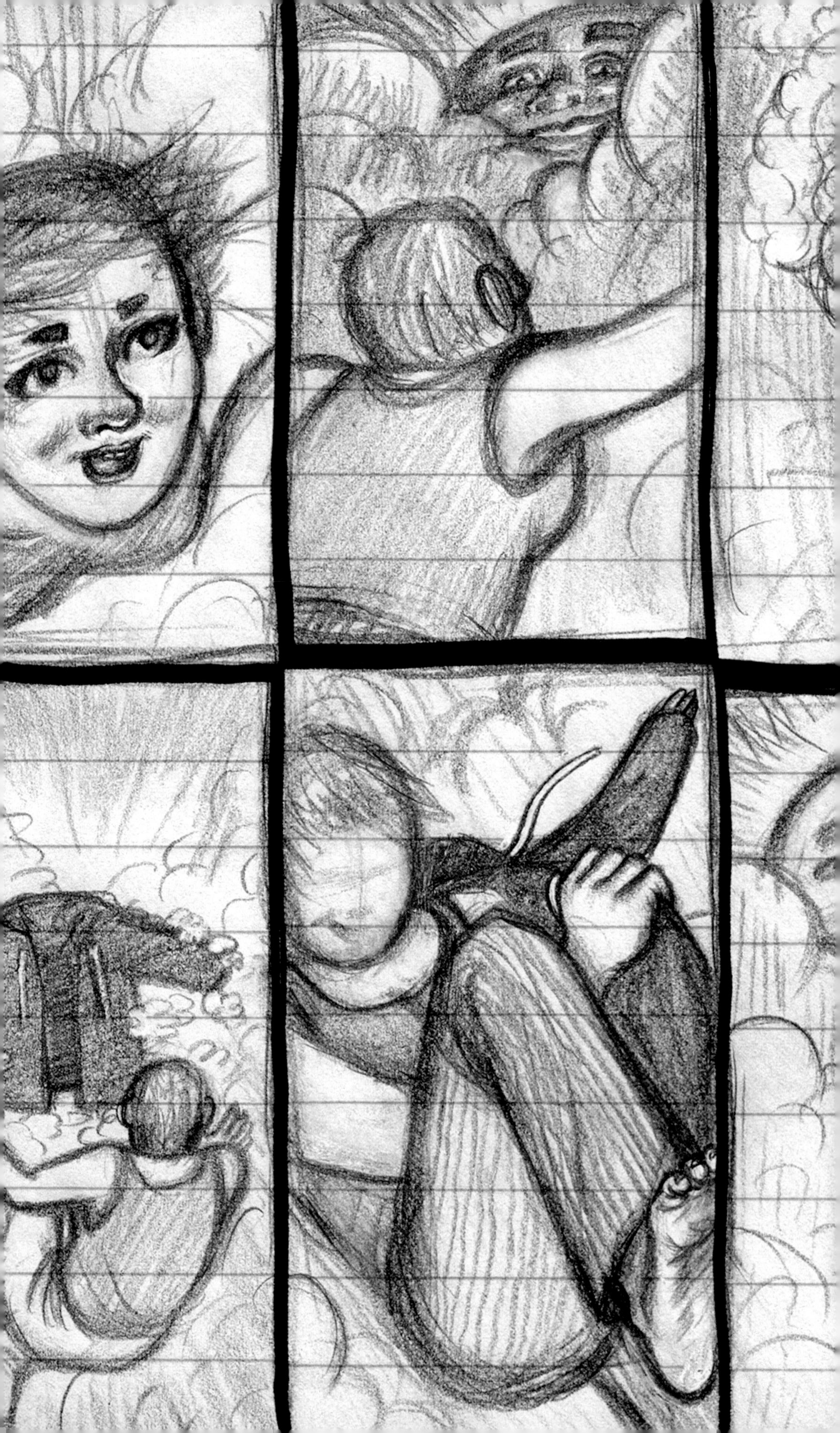

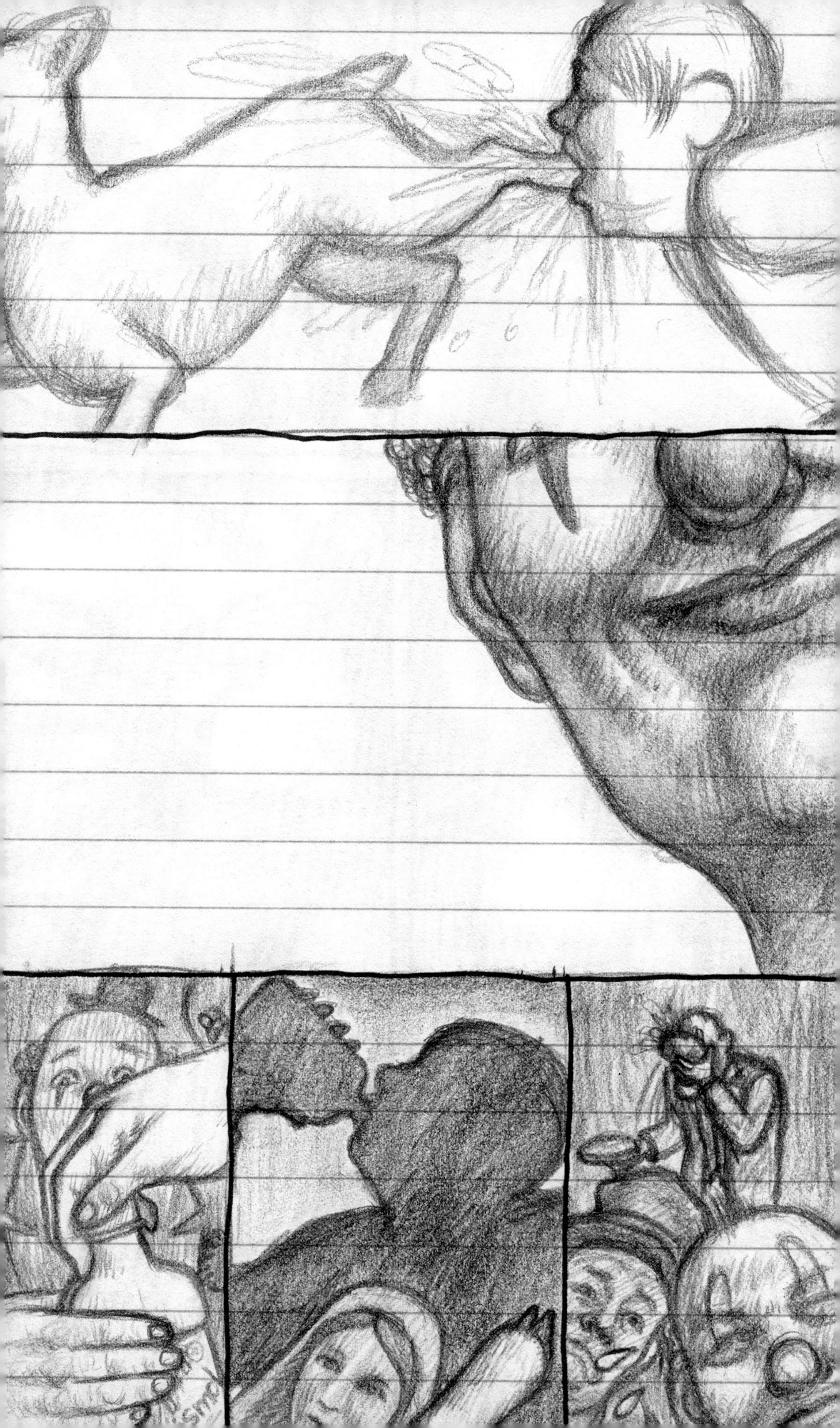

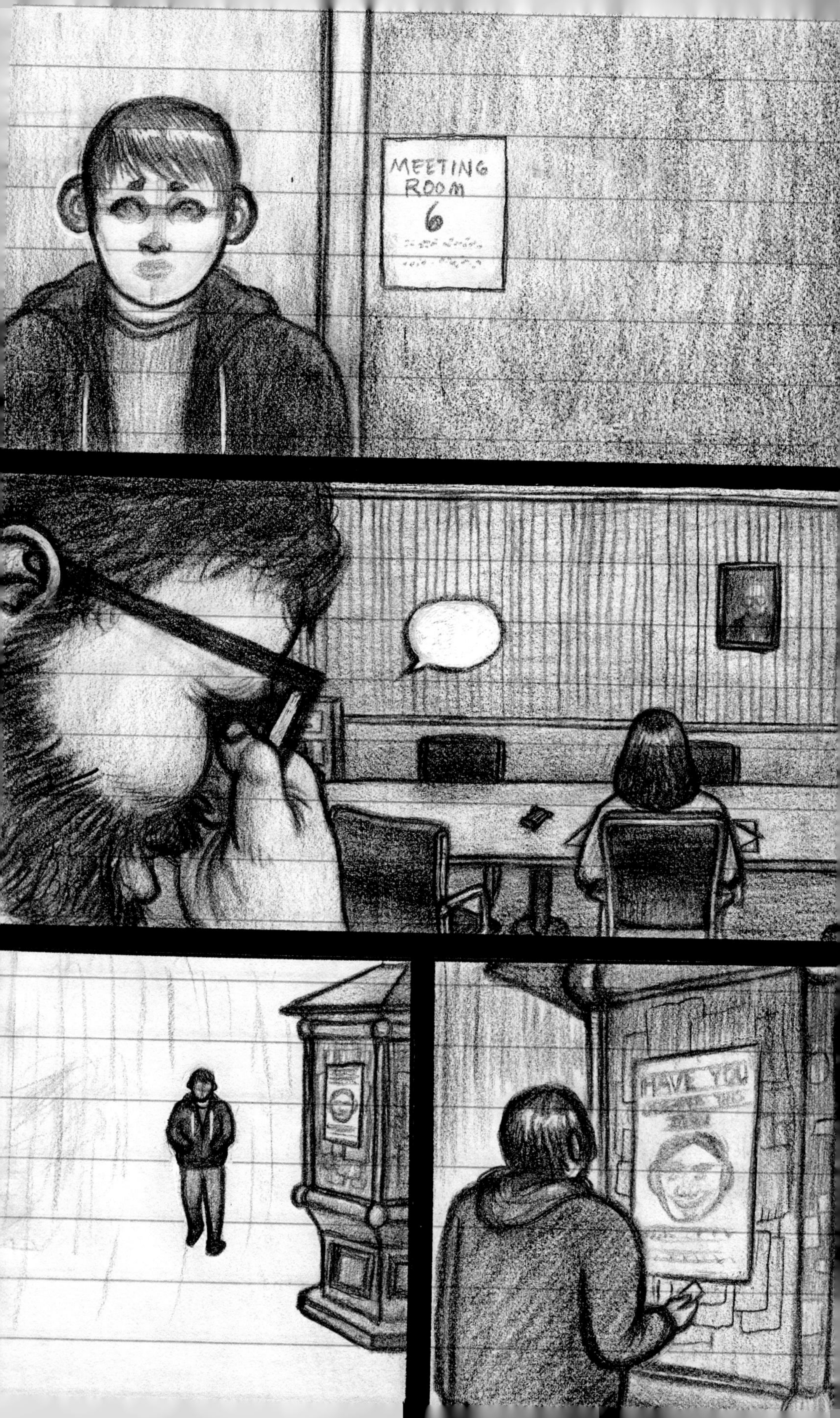
MEETING ROOM 6
HAVE YOU

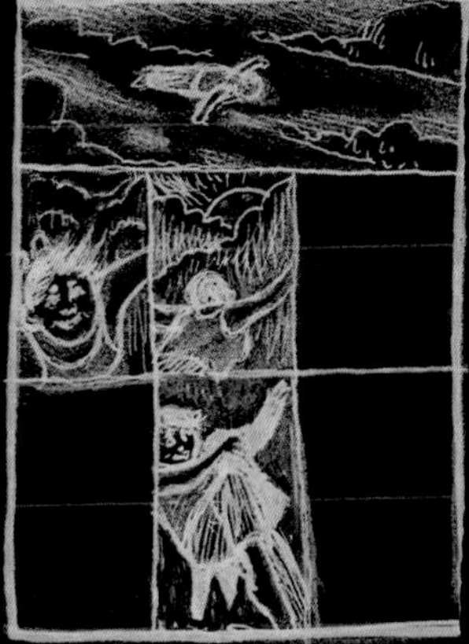

# PROCESS

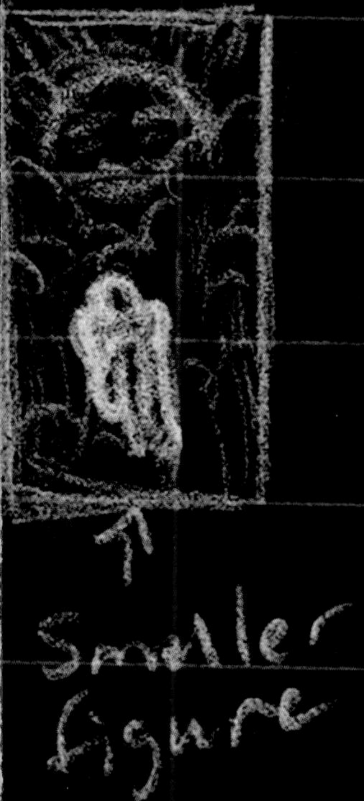
Smaller figure

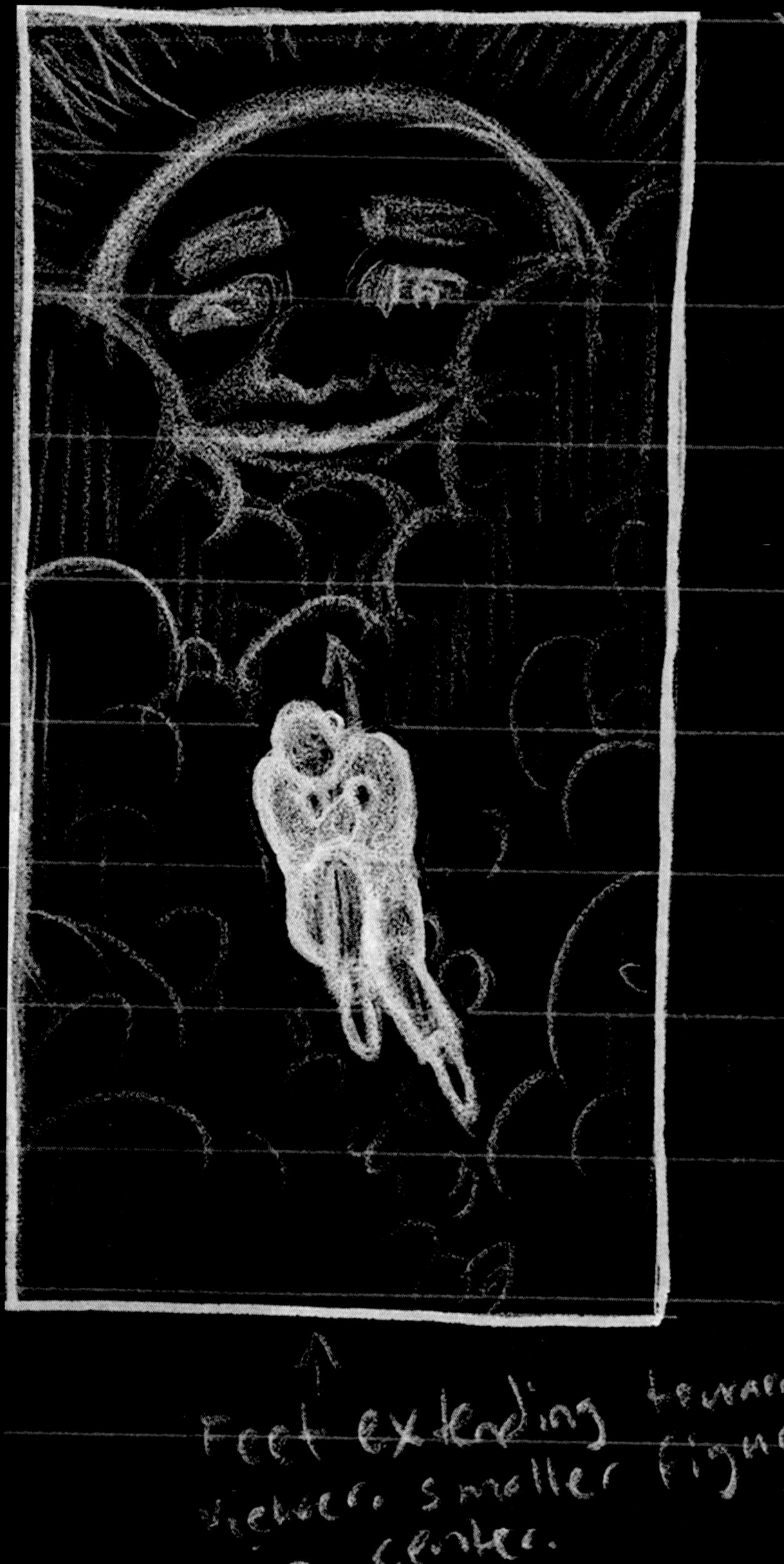
Feet extending
viewer. Smaller
center.

DURING THE CREATION OF *TREMOR DOSE* NOAH AND I DEVELOPED A SHORTHAND IN COMMUNICATION. BELOW IS A MORE TYPICAL PAGE OF THE SCRIPTS THAT HE WAS DEALING WITH. IN REFLECTION, I'M FRANKLY AMAZED AT HOW WELL HE WAS ABLE TO CAPTURE AND TRANSLATE THESE IDEAS.

TREMOR DOSE PART II ← *when in reality all are the same, no differential required*
PAGE 4   *6 panels* *on this or further examinations.*

P1-
The shot has backed off, 7 has turned now, holding a toothbrush in one hand and toothpaste in the other, presented so we can see the label, a bathroom sink on the Mobius Strip behind him with a bathroom mirror floating above it. He label on the tooth brush says "CoolGate"

7- Now that's a CoolGate smile! ← *no more* *oral* *but not on touch*   *do we look like we know what we are? no. what we doing here? no.*   *the waters no longer potable w/o advice*

P2-
Pregnant pause, shot from the side. 7 and GINN face one and other a couple yards apart. He's still smiling and presenting the toothpaste like a game show hostess. His eyebrows turned up as if scared or ashamed, she has her hands on her hips and a scowl on her face.   *or a mouth so...*  ↑ *I I*

P3-
Mid Shot of GINN, gesticulating, pointing at 7 as she speaks almost from the corner of her mouth, her eyebrow cocked in a judgemental fashion.   *note to self + other*

GINN- Now that's an asshole! You scared me with that!   *Regarde!!! → which one always lies + which one tells the truth!*

P4-
Mid Shot again, now GINN has closed the distance and is in the personal space of 7 still waving her arms as she scolds him, his head turned away as if he is afraid she will strike him.

GINN- You can't run away now, can you? I saw you today, who the hell are you? How are you doing this?   *(question)*   *remember the "coyote"*

P5-
7 shot close, looking pathetic wiping the toothpaste from his face with the cuff of his robe. He looks legitimately sad.

7- I... I... you... you...   *make sure this one is no disjointed prior @HFC*   *balanced W+B*

P6-
7 shot from behind, he has taken off running and has already cleared some distance, his robe flapping behind him, his feet both off the ground like a cartoon character.
7- You can't catch me! HAHAHA   *NOTE*

*make sure to envision the manifold curiosity w/ now*   *XXIII*

*"do you think it's "too much" to include our notes here?"*

*Michael's scripts are usually broken down into panels, but this scene (a favorite of ours) was written in a looser form to try and highlight the dream-reality of the sequence.*

*Noah, I will be adding text to these pages. I have not defined much of the panel layout as I want this dream sequence to be commanded by the images. Thanks bud... hope you've been getting enough sleep.

**PAGE 23**

A cuckoo bird flies through a sunny sky.

There is a tree, almost free of leaves, main trunk broken with a nest in the crook of the trunk and the main limb.

The cuckoo lands in the nest already full of small eggs.

ECU of the nest, there is now a much larger egg among the other smaller eggs, the cuckoo is seen flapping away from the nest in the distance.

The large egg begins to crack.

The crack has continued along the egg, a hand now emerging, some slime dripping off. The hand clutching the side of the egg intensely (think someone with their arm out of a window, scratching the door).

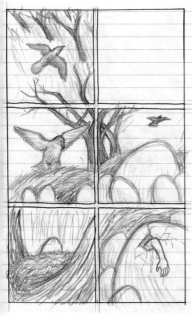

Noah's roughs are done in pencil on lined paper . . .

*"Composition notebooks are great for sketching and thumbnails. The paper can surprisingly take almost any medium I throw at it. And if the drawing sucks, I don't feel bad about it."*

The final pages are done on watercolor paper, using a combination of graphite, ink, watercolor, and acrylic paint.

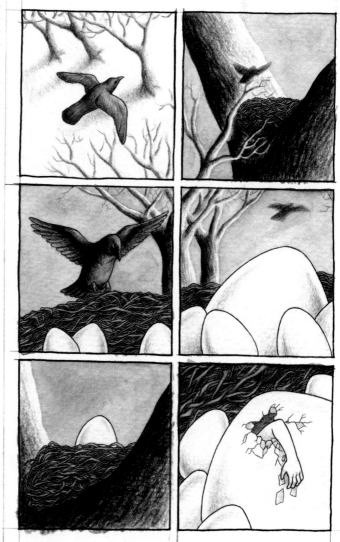

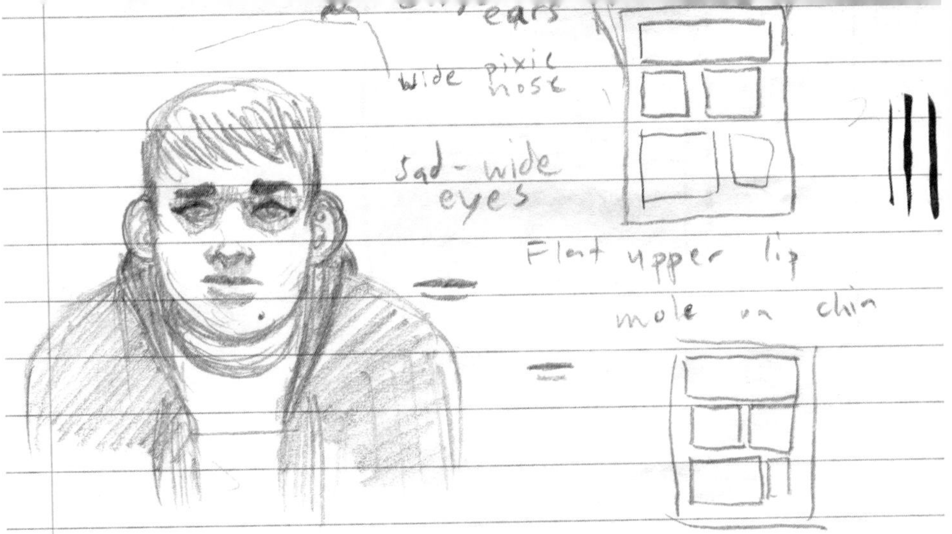
ears
wide pixie nose
sad - wide eyes
Flat upper lip
mole on chin

**PAGE 24**

Half of GINN's body has emerged from the egg, her eyes wild, her back arching upward toward the sky, gasping, rage on her face.

Now fully broken from the egg, naked and wet limbs stretching tensely, fingers curling like talons, she stares at the other eggs.

She struggles to roll one of the eggs from the nest, the egg is roughly half her size, and appears very heavy

Shot from low an egg is seen falling from the nest.

From the side another egg being rolled from the nest.

A blank panel with an egg falling.

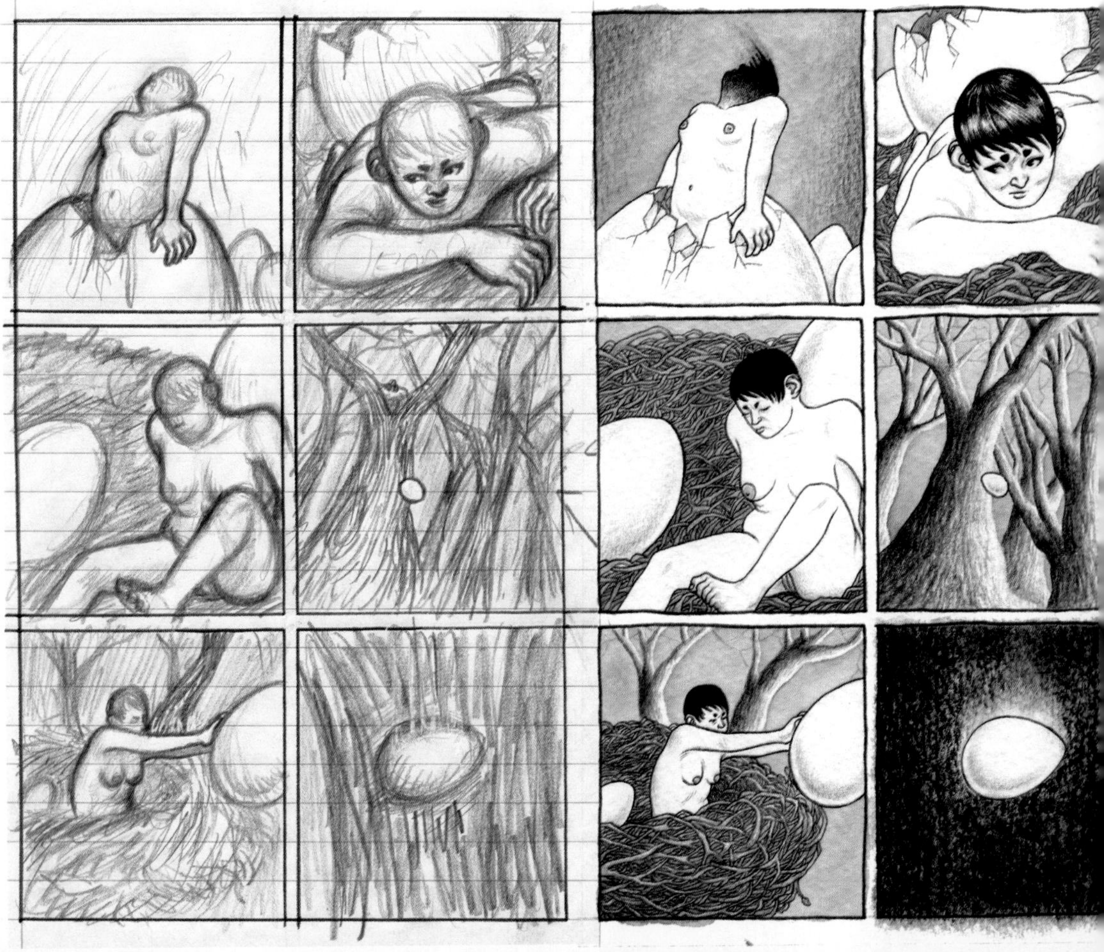

**PAGE 25**

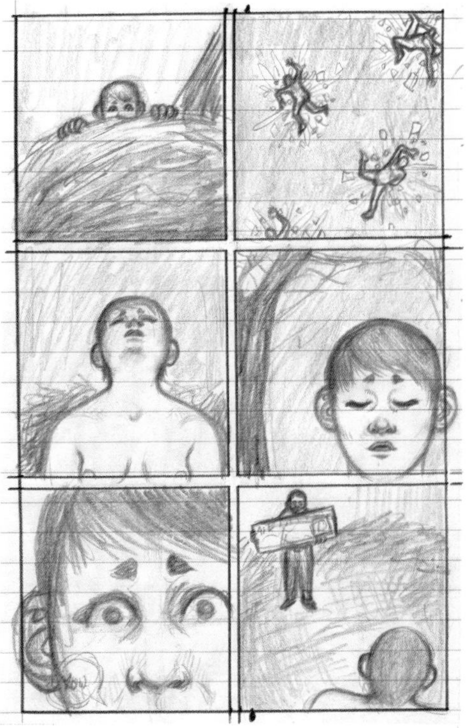

Underside shot, GINN looks down from the edge of the nest.

From GINN's POV, all the eggs are broken on the dry arid ground, fully grown dead humans are seen among the egg shells.

Mid shot directly at GINN, she is slumped against the edge of the nest, exhausted, head angled up, eyes closed.

The shot draws close to her face, head forward now, eyes still closed.

ECU of her face, eyes open wide, fear in her eyes.
GINN: YOU.

From GINN's POV, the DREAM MAN stands on the other side of the nest. He holds a sign, like a roadside sign spinner. The sign says ALL AMERICAN REALTY: THE NEST YOU DESERVE along with a photo of a realtor that looks really similar to Christopher Columbus

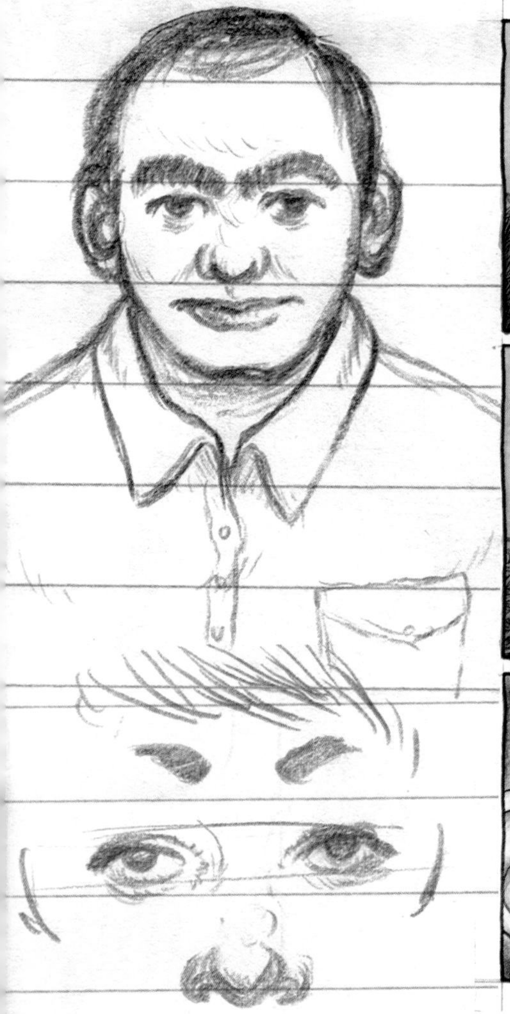

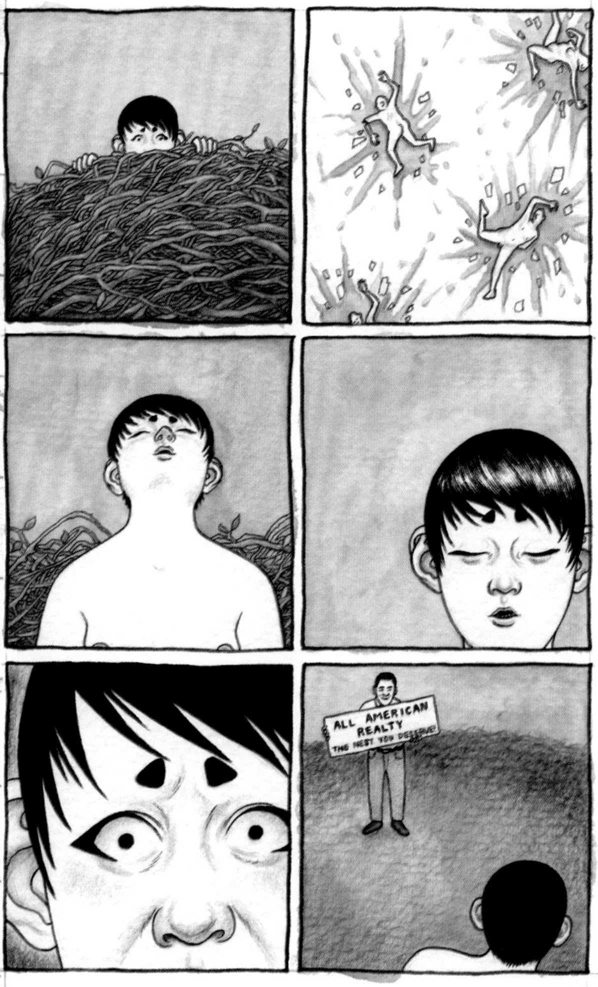
ALL AMERICAN
REALTY
THE NEST YOU DESERVE!

**PAGE 26**

Mid shot of GINN's face, she looks confused.
GINN: WHO-

THE DREAM MAN shot wide, climbs the edge of the nest.

GINN shot from low leaning over the edge of the nest with terror in her eyes.

The shot of GINN in the same position has pulled wayyy back, wide rather than looking over the edge she now appears to be popping out of a hole, along the ground leading up to her are piles of bodies, not dissimilar to the piles we have seen in the death camps of Nazi Germany. Toxic gases hover ominously, this aspect of the dream is dimly lit.

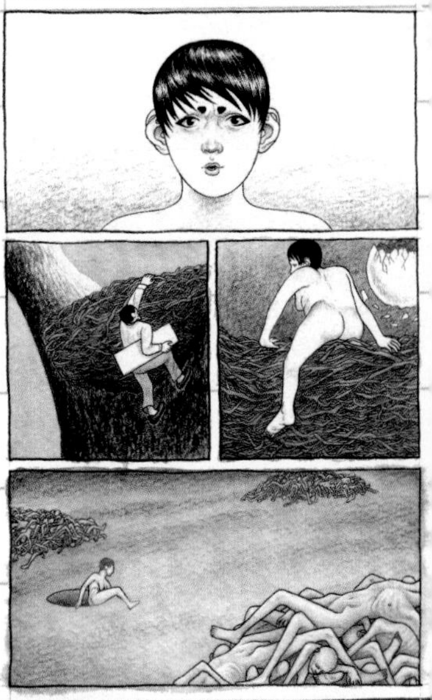

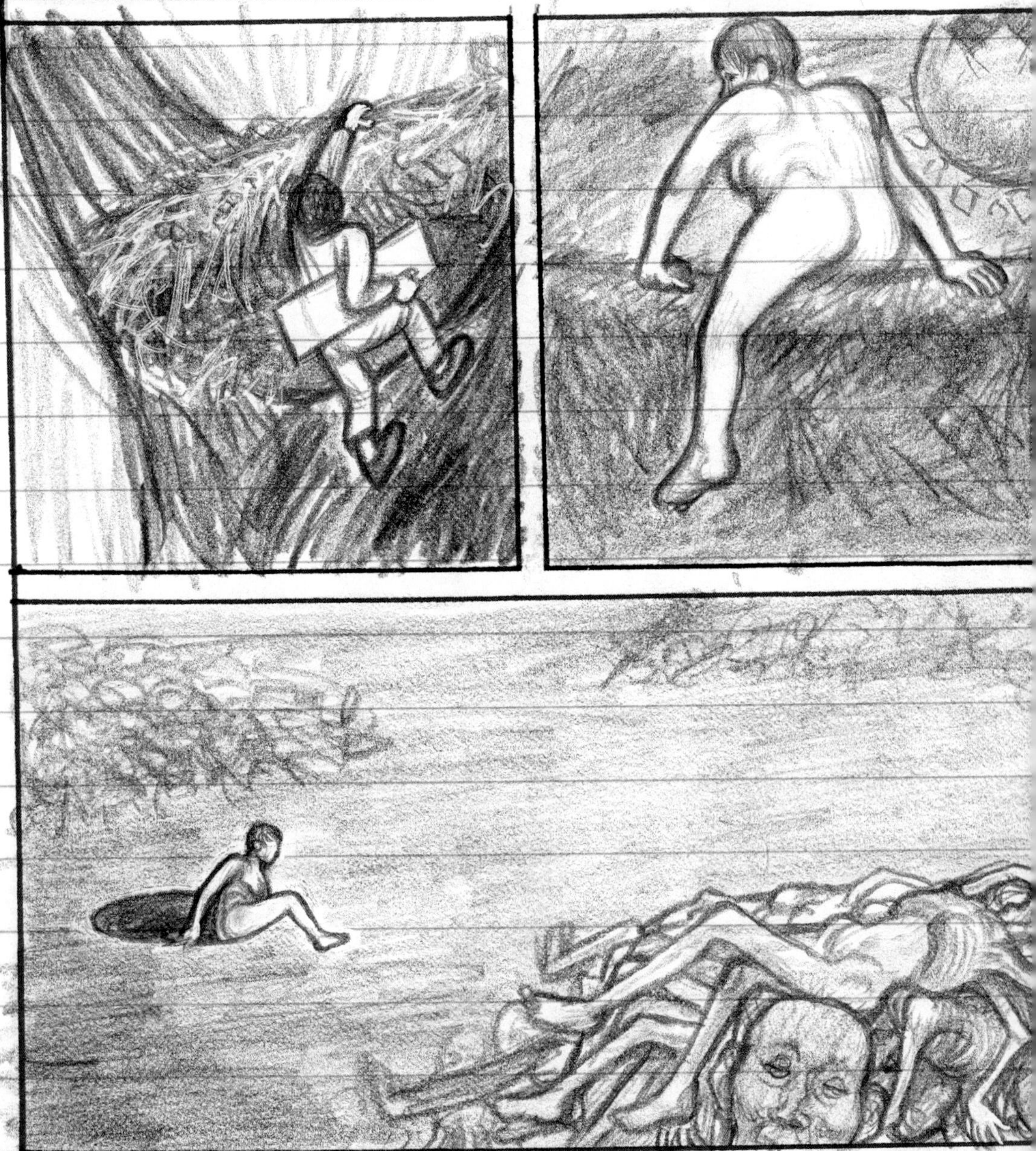

**PAGE 27**

Front shot from elevation of GINN pushing herself from the nest hole, this looks to take great effort.

Full body shot, still naked, she looks at her hands, she is now wearing cartoonish Mickey Mouse style gloves.

The shot pulls around behind her, the bodies are now a variety of analogs for famous cartoon characters, mainly from classic Disney and Warner Brothers cartoons, all dead and piled among one another.

In the distance, glowing, providing the light source for the whole scene is a variation of the McDonald's arches, along with a small sign saying McMOON'S OVER 666 BILLION SERVED, the DREAM MAN is barely visible by the sign waving in a friendly manner, as you would to get someone's attention from afar.

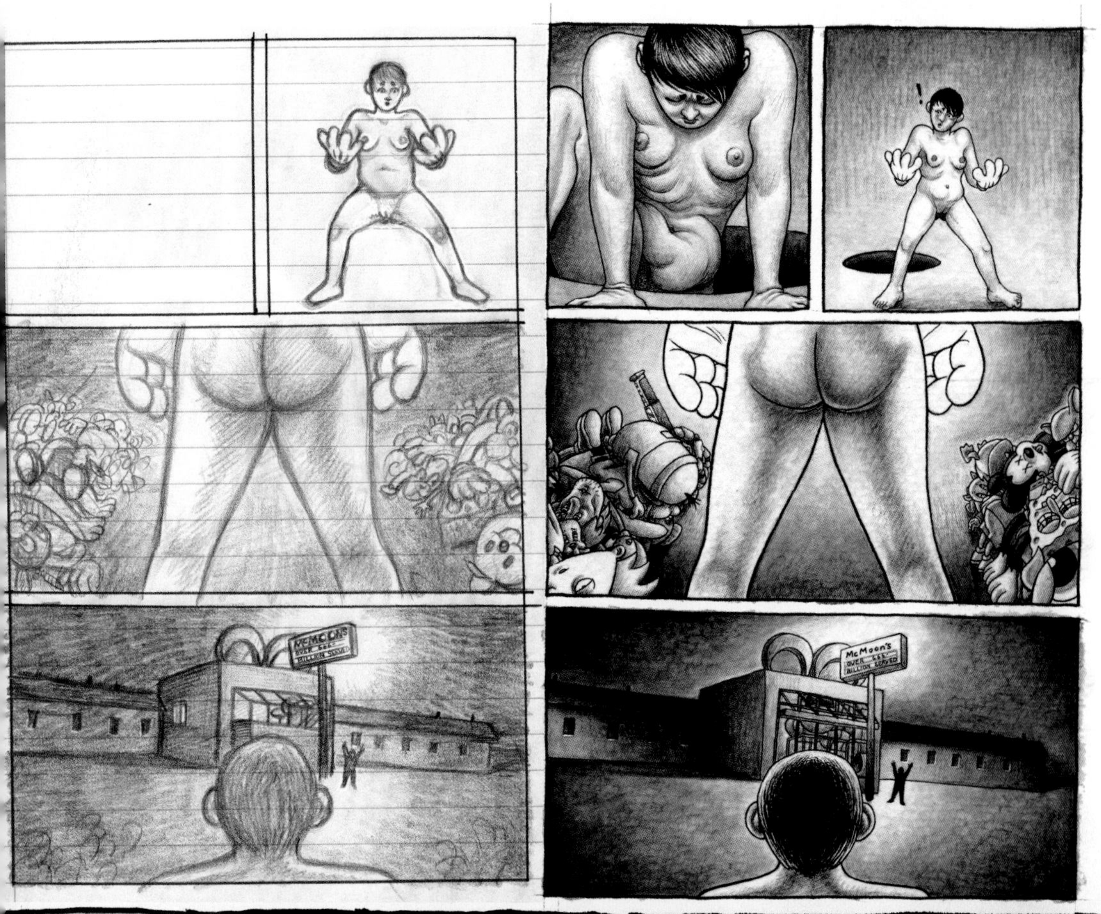
McMoon's
OVER 666
BILLION SERVED

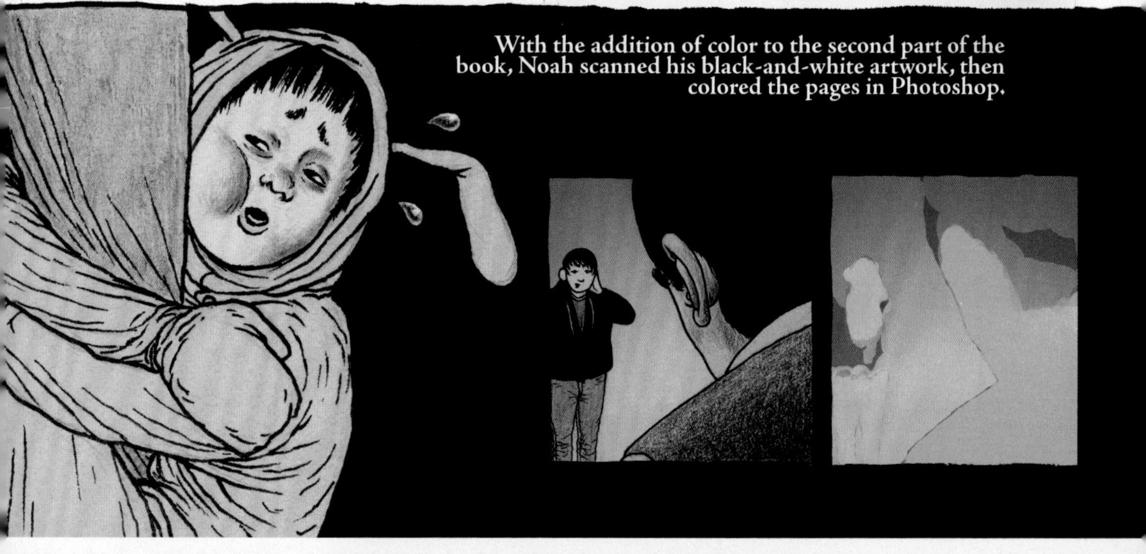

With the addition of color to the second part of the book, Noah scanned his black-and-white artwork, then colored the pages in Photoshop.

# HAVE YOU DREAMED THESE MEN?

## ABOUT THE WRITER:

*Michael Conrad lives in Austin, Texas. Born in a small town in southern New Hampshire, Michael spent his youth dreaming of one day writing stories like this, now he does. Michael has worked on books for Marvel, DC, and Black Crown Publishing.*

*With that formality out of the way, Michael would like to recommend that each of you take a moment to consider your impossible dream. Is it truly impossible, or is it just very hard? Have you really given it the time it deserves? Has fear prevented you from taking your shot?*

*Michael Conrad is no better than you.*

## ABOUT THE ARTIST:

*Noah Bailey is an illustrator and cartoonist from the Midwest.*

# THANK YOU

Michael would like to thank his partner Becky Cloonan for all of her support, but more importantly for her love.

Michael would like to thank Noah for his visionary approach to the medium, and his hours spent at the board making his stories come to life.

Michael would like to thank David, Chip, and Ivan.

Finally Michael would like to thank you for your attention and time, the greatest commodities in the world.

Noah gives thanks to:

My support team—my dad, and the rest of my family, I suppose. Kyle, my brother. My dogs. My man, Tim. And the love of my life, Maggie.

The idea machine, comix guru, and overall awesome dude and collaborator, Michael Conrad.

Fyodor Dostoevsky, Fritz Lang, and Kathe Kollwitz (and thousands of other artists that have inspired me).

And anyone and everyone that has ever encouraged me to create things. I owe you my eternal gratitude.

# COMIXOLOGY COMES TO DARK HORSE BOOKS

JASON LOO
CHIP ZDARSKY

**AFTERLIFT**

ISBN 978-1-50672-440-9 / $19.99

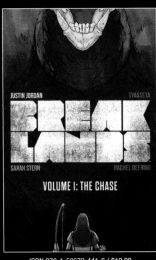

JUSTIN JORDAN          TYASSETA

**BREAK LANDS**

SARAH STERN          RACHEL DEERING

VOLUME 1: THE CHASE

ISBN 978-1-50672-441-6 / $19.99

curt pires
alex diotto
dee cunniffe
micah myers

**Youth**

Named one of "10 Comics to Celebrate Pride" by the New York Times

"Bold, genre-defying and heartfelt. Youth hits a reader like the meteor in its own pages; an angry, wondrous and transformative force." —Scott Snyder (Batman, Justice League)

ISBN 978-1-50672-461-4 / $19.99

Named one of the "8 New Comic Book Series for the End of Summer" by the New York Times

**THE BLACK GHOST: HARD REVOLUTION**

ALEX SEGURA     MONICA GALLAGHER
GEORGE KAMBADAIS   ELLIE WRIGHT   TAYLOR ESPOSITO

ISBN 978-1-50672-446-1 / $19.99

**THE PRIDE OMNIBUS**

ISBN 978-1-50672-447-8 / $29.99

JIM ZUB • MAX DUNBAR

**STONE STAR**

VOLUME 1: FIGHT OR FLIGHT

ISBN 978-1-50672-458-4 / $19.99

## AFTERLIFT
*Written by Chip Zdarsky, art by Jason Loo*

This Eisner Award–winning series from Chip Zdarsky (*Sex Crimina[l]*, Daredevil) and Jason Loo (*The Pitiful Human-Lizard*) features [ ] chases, demon bounty hunters, and figuring out your place in t[his] world and the next.

## BREAKLANDS
*Written by Justin Jordan, art by Tyasseta and Sarah Stern*

Generations after the end of the civilization, everyone has powe[r] you need them just to survive in the new age. Everyone exc[ept] Kasa Fain. Unfortunately, her little brother, who has the potentia[l] reshape the world, is kidnapped by people who intend to do just th[at] *Mad Max* meets *Akira* in a genre-mashing, expectation-smash[ing] new hit series from Justin Jordan, creator of *Luther Strode, Spre[ad]* and *Reaver*!

## YOUTH
*Written by Curt Pires, art by Alex Diotto and Dee Cunniffe*

A coming of age story of two queer teenagers who run away f[rom] their lives in a bigoted small town, and attempt to make their wa[y to] California. Along the way their car breaks down, and they join a gr[oup] of fellow misfits on the road. travelling the country together in a v[an] they party and attempt to find themselves. And then . . . someth[ing] happens. The story combines the violence of coming of age with [the] violence of the superhero narrative—as well as the beauty.

## THE BLACK GHOST SEASON ONE: HARD REVOLUTI[ON]
*Written by Alex Segura and Monica Gallagher, art by George Kamab[adais]*

Meet Lara Dominguez—a troubled Creighton cops reporter obses[sed] with the city's debonair vigilante the Black Ghost. With the hel[p of] a mysterious cyberinformant named LONE, Lara's inched close[r to] uncovering the Ghost's identity. But as she searches for the breakthr[ough] story she desperately needs, Lara will have to navigate the corrupti[on of] her city, the uncertainties of virtues, and her own personal demons. [Does] she have the strength to be part of the solution—or will she bec[ome] the problem?

## THE PRIDE OMNIBUS
*Joseph Glass, Gavin Mitchell and Cem Iroz*

FabMan is sick of being seen as a joke. Tired of the LGBTQ+ commu[nity] being seen as inferior to straight heroes, he thinks it's about d[ue] time he did something about it. Bringing together some of the wo[rld's] greatest LGBTQ+ superheroes, the Pride is born to protect the w[orld] and fight prejudice, misrepresentation and injustice—not to menti[on a] pesky supervillain or two.

## STONE STAR
*Jim Zub and Max Zunbar*

The brand-new space-fantasy saga that takes flight on comiX[ology] Originals from fan-favorite creators Jim Zub (*Avengers, Samurai J[ack]*) and Max Dunbar (*Champions, Dungeons & Dragons*)! The nom[adic] space station called Stone Star brings gladiatorial entertainme[nt to] ports across the galaxy. Inside this gargantuan vessel of tournam[ent] and temptations, foragers and fighters struggle to survive. A y[oung] thief named Dail discovers a dark secret in the depths of Stone [Star] and must decide his destiny—staying hidden in the shadow[s or] standing tall in the searing spotlight of the arena. Either way, his [life] and the cosmos itself, will never be the same!

**AVAILABLE AT YOUR LOCAL COMICS SHOP OR BOOKSTORE** / To find a comics shop near you, visit comicshoplocator.com / For more information or to order direct, visit darkhorse.com

DARK HORSE BOOKS

COMIXOLOGY ORIGINALS